To David, for your love I thank you, for your support I thank you, for your kindness and patience I thank you. For your calm, gentle spirit I am grateful. And for the daily fits of laughter I thank you a million times over. I appreciate who you are. My heart overflows.

CONTENTS

CHAPTER ONE

Grace Farm

My mum would often tell me a story when I was growing up about how she first became aware that her baby daughter loved animals. Apparently she had left me in my pram outside a shop while she went inside to buy something, back then it was perfectly safe to leave a baby in a pram in the middle of a street and no harm would come to them. The "Good old days" is what they call them and of course you couldn't do that kind of thing today. I had just learnt to sit up so I guess I must have been about nine months old at the time. Mum said she was keeping an eye on me through the big glass window and looked away for a few moments to place her order over the counter top and when she glanced back there was this huge black dog with its massive head inside my pram. The hood was all the way up so she couldn't see me so didn't know if the dog was attacking me or not. Mum raced out of the shop screaming with a few other shoppers not far behind her. And there I was with my chubby little arms wrapped around this big dog's neck. I was screaming too, not the same kind of scream Mum was doing as she ran from the shop, I was screaming with delight. She said I had this look of total rapture on my face and was screaming my little head off with happiness.

When Mum tried to pull the dog away I wasn't for letting go, she said I gripped onto its neck so hard that she lifted me out of the pram with the dog and I still wasn't for letting go. And when the dog and I were finally parted I screamed so loudly and cried so much that I couldn't be pacified. I suppose from my point of view I had finally gotten my hands on a dog and I reckon my little heart would have been close to bursting with joy in that particular moment. I would have been able to feel the fur and smell his scent and feel his tongue giving me kisses and to a person such as me that would have been total ecstasy, but then just as fast as I'd gotten my hands on him he was taken away from me and I was no doubt as upset as all hell about it. Mum said even ice-cream couldn't soothe me, yes I took the ice-cream, I mean come on I'm not an idiot, but she said I was doing hiccup sobs as I ate it.

The people who followed Mum out of the shop were laughing at me not wanting to let go of the dog, but Mum was a bit shaken up, and I have to give it to my mum for being brave. She no doubt would have been scared of a dog of that size but she was like a lioness when protecting her children. I suppose I must have seen that dog in the street and somehow gotten it to come over to me. And to be honest I am pretty proud of myself for being such a young age and still being able to manage that. I would have loved to know how I did it, and I would also love to have known what was going through my mind when that dog came into view. The dog was huge and yet I had no fear, just love, just joy and just wanting to be as close to it as I possibly could.

Years later out of curiosity I asked Mum what breed the dog was but she wasn't good on dog breeds so didn't have a clue, and even if she was well up on them I doubt she would have paused to identify the breed before pulling that dog off me. Still I sure would have loved to know what kind of breed the first dog I ever wrapped my arms around was. All Mum said was that it was big and black, in still trying to identify the breed I asked if the dog had long fur or short but she couldn't remember. In my mind it was a Newfoundland, but I don't think it has anything to do with the dog I met in the street that day because it couldn't possibly have, I was only nine months old at the time. I wouldn't have been able to remember that dog. I think it's more of an image I made up in my head from hearing the story told throughout the years and desperately wanting an image to put to a story I dearly loved hearing. Then again it could well have been a Newfoundland I mean what child wouldn't want to hug a dog as big and fluffy and as beautiful as they are.

I guess it'd be fair to say that from the time I landed on earth I had the greatest love in my heart for animals. I was instantly drawn to them, just couldn't get enough of them really, it didn't matter to me what the animal was, I loved all of them. And as soon as I could crawl I started crawling towards them and I've not stopped wanting to be near them since. Mum said she really had to keep an eye on me when I learnt to walk because I'd set off towards a dog and they didn't always want to be hugged as much as I wanted to hug them. And it didn't take very long at all for my heart to turn towards elderly animals either. I guess I was lucky because it became clear to me very quickly what I was put on this earth for. I didn't have to stumble around in the darkness searching for something to do with my life. My path was well lit from a very young age. And it was a real blessing to have that awareness early on because I believe it saved me a lot of time. If this wasn't what I was meant to be doing then I wouldn't have had this deep love embedded. I've heard it said that by the time we reach the age of five our personality, who we truly are, has already been formed. I'm not sure if this is true or not but I'd say it was pretty much accurate in my case. I know it was right because I remember an incident when we were still living in England, it's still quite vivid in my head and I know I was around five years old at the time because it was just before my family immigrated to Australia.

It was at my mum's hairdresser, she lived in a little flat behind her salon and one day while visiting she told Mum that her dog had just had puppies. Well my little ears pricked up at that, back then I didn't even have a dog, I desperately wanted one and had been begging for one for years but had always been told "No". I wasn't allowed to have one because Mum and Dad knew we were going to immigrate to Australia soon and that my little heart would be broken when having to get on that ship and leave my dog behind. And they were wise in doing that because it really would have been, in fact I didn't even want to move to Australia. I wanted to stay in England because my grandparents where there and I adored my grandparents. The only reason I agreed to go, like I had any choice in it really, was because Mum and Dad promised me that as soon as we got there I could finally have a dog of my own. And that was the only reason I marched up the ships gangway of my own accord instead of being carried up kicking and screaming.

Well the hairdresser let me go and visit the dogs while she set Mum's hair, looking back it wasn't the wisest thing do have done really, I mean I was ok, but new doggy Mum's and small children should never be left alone together. But this dog didn't bother me and I didn't bother her. I didn't even pat her, I wanted to but didn't because she seemed to have enough to deal with as it was. She seemed to be super busy and looked totally worn out. So I just sat to one side and watched her feeding all these squirming puppies and felt so very sorry for her. Mum said I had always been a deep thinker, she said I would hold my hands a certain way when I was thinking, even as a baby I did it. Well, all the way home I didn't say anything, I just sat and did my deep thinking pose and she knew the best thing to do was leave me alone with my thoughts. It was a long bus ride home but I just sat thinking about what I'd just seen. I really wish I had have said something to Mum though because it would have been interesting to know exactly how my little five year old self would have summed the entire situation up.

The hairdresser's dog was a Silky Terrier, I didn't know it back then but the image of that dog stayed with me for a very long time and years later when seeing a photo in a book I got to know what breed she was. I can still remember her now, I don't recall the puppies, don't remember how many of them there were or anything about them really, I guess they were not who I was interested in. My heart went out to the old dog, my heart always goes out to the old dog. I guess even back then I wanted to help her, but couldn't quite work out how. Maybe that was what I was thinking about on the bus ride home.

Mum said that I was never afraid of any animal of any size. Cow, sheep, horse, even animals at the zoo, no fear ever, just wanting to get as close to them as I possibly could and not much has changed for me in that area. When I was little I loved the zoo. I think I would have lived there if I could. Mum lost me there once, took her eyes off me for a moment to tend to one of my sisters and I was gone when she turned back around. I was lost for quite a while, two female staff members found me and took me back to Mum, when they found me I was sitting on a bench opposite one of the cages watching what was going on in there. Mum was panicked, I was happy. I don't remember the incident at all but I bet I was in my element just sitting there watching what the animals were doing. I've always found animals going about their business so interesting. Mum said due to my fascination she always had to keep a close eye on me so I didn't get bitten. But of course I was going to get bitten at some point wasn't I but it still didn't make me afraid. Even as a kid I tried looking at things from an animal's point of view. Two dog bites stand out clearly in my mind. Both bites happened after we had migrated to Australia. The first time I got bitten it was by a Doberman and the second one was an Afghan hound, it seemed that big dogs liked biting me for some reason. But again I wasn't scared and I didn't think it was their fault. They had been startled and dogs are always going to bite a person under those circumstances aren't they.

With the first one I had been sent to the milk bar on an errand for Mum, I was riding my bike home and went whizzing past this house that I had whizzed past on my bike many times before. I knew there was a dog living there because I was aware of all the dogs in our neighbourhood and knew all their breeds as well. I'd walk past all these houses on my way to and from school and listen for their different sounding barks, they used to make me happy. I'd walk past the houses with dogs really slow so I could hear them talking for as long as I possibly could. The other houses, the non dog houses, or as I used to call them, the boring houses, well I'd just quicken my step when I walked past those because they held no interest for me.

So I was coming past this house and I knew a really stunning looking chocolate Doberman lived there but there was a high brick fence on that house, high wooden gates too that were almost the same colour as the dog who lived there, but in the middle of the brick fence there was a row of fancy patterned white cement bricks, and the patterns had holes in them, not big enough for a kid to fit their heads through but you could definitely put your whole hand in there, and if you had been born an idiot you would more than likely have done that. I know this is the truth because I went to school with a few of those idiots. They used to peep through the holes, see the Doberman sleeping on the driveway or up by the house on a mat and they'd torment him by putting their hands in, waving them around and pulling them out fast before he got there. I never heard of any incidents of anybody being bitten so I'm assuming that these tormenting kids were either very fast or just incredibly lucky.

I gave most of the dogs I passed on my way to school names, I didn't know any of their real names but it amused me to give them each one so that's what I did. I wasn't every imaginative back then though because I named the Doberman "The Chocolate Dog". So I'm coming home from the shop, head down, pedalling like mad to get back to Mum. I came up to the chocolate dog's house real fast and this time the gate was open, it was a weekend and the man who lived there was going out somewhere and was about to back his car out. But that poor Doberman saw me whizzing by and a kid is a kid, he had no idea that I wasn't one of the kids who'd been tormenting him. He just lunged at me and sunk his big teeth into my leg. I saw it, I felt it, but I didn't stop pedalling until I was a fair way up the street. I didn't even look back to see if he was after me, just got a bit of distance between me and his house then pulled over to have a look at my leg.

I remember I had this green knitted pantsuit on, not the nice green either and it was not in any shape or form flattering, come to think of it maybe I was peddling fast so none of my school friends saw me wearing that thing. I was watching an episode of The Simpson's some years ago and all over sudden Bart Simpson walked in wearing my green knitted pantsuit, only it wouldn't have been knitted because it was his pyjamas and of course he's a cartoon character so his pantsuit wasn't real but mine certainly was, and a little bit itchy too from memory. I think one of Mum's friends made it for me, Mum wasn't a knitter so I knew it wouldn't have been her and if my nana had knitted it and sent it from

England then I would have worn it with pride because it was made by her loving hands. I didn't love the thing and I didn't hate it either, just knew I didn't look particularly good in it, maybe it was because it was a bit too small. I looked like Kermit the Frog and Miss Piggy's love child being that I was the colour of him and the size of her. A seriously scary sight as you can imagine, to be honest if I was that Doberman I would have bitten me too. The only reason I know I was wearing that pantsuit on that particular day was because even now all these years later I can still remember the thick rich blood soaking through my pant leg.

I looked down saw the blood and thought "Oh well whatever he's done Mum will fix it for me when I get home". And fix it for me she did, she wiped away all the blood so she could see the bite properly, then put me in an antiseptic bath to soak and bandaged up my leg when I got out. When Dad got home from work he had an absolute fit and wanted me to tell him where the dog lived. But I didn't want the dog getting in trouble so I told him I didn't know and that was only a half lie because I had no idea what the address was, I only knew the house. Street signs and house numbers meant nothing to me I was only interested in the dogs. But he didn't ask me if I knew the house, only if I knew the address so I lucked out with that really and come to think of it so did the Doberman. Dad let it go because he assumed I was traumatized by the event and too afraid to remember, I wasn't. I just didn't want that poor dog getting into trouble for something I didn't think was his fault. I thought his owner would hit him if he found out he'd run out of the yard and bitten a little girl and I didn't want that to happen. I figured he had enough misery in his life with those idiot kids and their tormenting games. It was a good bite though as far as dog bites go. I've still got a scar from his biggest tooth, I think it looks kind of cool actually having a scar like that, it looks a bit like a bullet hole and not too many people can say they have such a scar on their leg can they.

My second dog bite came two house moves later. I was a bit older this time and was door knocking to raise money for new play equipment for my school. All the kids in my class were given a book of raffle tickets to sell. I was only allowed to go in my street, Mum said I could go up and down then home again, but that was it, I wasn't allowed to go round the block on my own. So I did every house on the same side we lived on then crossed the road and started working my way up and back home again. Well that was the plan anyway but it didn't play out that way because the first door I knocked on on the other side of the street a big black Afghan hound came flying past the old lady who answered the door and bit my hand. Only a little bite this time, not much blood, no scar, nothing more than a scrape really. But the old lady was terrified more harm had been done so she took me inside and I sat at her kitchen table eating cake while she wiped the blood away and put a band aid on.

She put her dog outside which was a pity really because I'd not had many Afghan hounds cross my path and I would have liked to have spent some time with this dog of hers. Well it wasn't actually her dog she explained to me as she was fixing me up, it belonged to her son who was living with her for a while. I didn't blame this dog for biting me either. I had rang the doorbell and the old lady was not able to see me too well, cataracts I think or maybe it was the dark fly screen, anyway she only opened the door a crack to try and see what I was going on about but it was enough for the dog to strike, he flung the door fully open with his weight and there was nothing the old lady could have done to stop him, he was just too big and too fast for her. After he bit me he went and stood behind the lady, he was a well behaved dog because he returned to her side on first call. And he was a beautiful looking dog too, I didn't see much of him but what I did see had me in awe, such a beautiful long coat, well-groomed too, by her son she told me. "He does the grooming I do the feeding" was how she put it. The dog was not black all over either the ends of his fur had lovely brownish tones. He could well have given me a nastier bite then he did, all he really did was hold my hand in his mouth for a second or two, didn't sink his teeth in or anything like that even though he had the chance to. I don't even think he meant to draw blood. This dog was just doing what it thought was best, protecting an old lady from harm. I was only a kid but what if I had been somebody trying to scam or rob an old lady in her house on her own. That dog would have been a hero to everyone if it had saved the old lady from an intruder. I thought he'd done his job as a dog really, and there was no reason to make a big deal out of it. He was new too because if he'd been there a while I would have definitely known about him. I didn't bother knocking on any other doors after I left the old lady's house because I was a bit over it by that time. I'd had a nice chat, a bit of cake and some lemonade so I thought I'd just go home so that's what I did. When Mum saw my hand she wanted to have a look at it so half took the band aide off, had a peep, then put it back on again, no big deal, and I went on my way. But the band aide wouldn't stick properly after that, they never do, so I took it off and that was the end of that. I don't think

Dad was even told about it when he got home from work. Mum was a sensible Mother, she knew what was and wasn't worth bothering Dad with, she just kept me up to date with my shots and let me get on with living my life. And I thank her for that. To restrain me, to be one of those mothers who over thought and over worried about everything and kept me on a tight leash, well that would have made for a much lesser childhood for me that's for sure. My older sister sat inside and read books or played with dolls all day long and that certainly wouldn't have been the right life for me and totally boring for a kid who was as adventurous as I was. But god bless Mum because she let me be me, she just let me get on with living the life I wanted to live and was always there to patch me up and send me on my way again with a hug and a kiss and a suggestion of being more careful next time.

But even two bites couldn't put me off dogs, I simply adore them, they are by far my favourite animal. I've always felt a special connection to dogs, both mine and other peoples and I've always wanted to make their lives better. I always knew that I was going to take care of elderly animals at some point in my life. As a kid I didn't quite know how I was going to achieve such a dream but I knew in my heart that one day I was going to get there. I soon became aware of the way farm animals were treated in this world and that consciousness made me want to create a place like Grace Farm, a place where animals could come and live out their natural lifespan with respect and dignity and the only hands to ever touch them would be those of love and kindness. I wanted to create a place of safety, harmony and peace, a heaven on earth as it were, a place where animals could wake up in the morning and go to sleep at night and know that no harm was ever going to come to them. It was important to me to have the animals on my farm feeling loved, wanted, contented and happy, because I believe we all have the right to live our lives this way whether we've been born with two legs or four.

Although knowing what you want to do with your life and actually getting there are two different things entirely. Getting to this farm took a bit of doing. I started planning for it a long time before I met my husband. Back then it was just me and I thought it was always going to be just me on my own making a home for all these animals. But I would never have been able to do this on such a scale without David, at the time I didn't know this wonderful man was going to one day enter my life so I kept planning it on my own until he came along and started planning with me. Although at the start David wasn't on board with what I wanted to do, it took a while for him to come round to my way of thinking. I never hid the desires of my heart from him because he needed to know exactly what he was getting himself into by taking me on. But I do think my future plans overwhelmed him a little bit at the start. One because he didn't think the way I did and two because I believe he thought I was a little bit mad.

I was always planning and scheming about this and that and planning and scheming some more. Quiet people can have the loudest minds, I can be sitting there saying nothing and all the while my mind will be going a hundred miles an hour, never still, always thinking, thinking, thinking, always making plans. Never judge a quiet individual because while people all around them are talking, talking, talking there's a quiet person sitting in a corner planning their next move. You can't think properly if your mouth is going ten to the dozen. It doesn't hurt to be still and to let your thoughts come, let your idea's boil to the surface.

And I'd suggest something to David and his first response would always be a huge "No". In fact his favourite word back then was "No". And my answer would always be "Don't try and clip my wings" I said it over and over again to the point of becoming annoying to him I'm sure. Him saying no didn't deter me at all so I'd go off and think some more, get another idea and be all starry eyed and giddy with excitement, enthusiasm plinging off me like electricity and David would once again shoot my idea down and I'd tell him that he couldn't dull my sparkle no matter how hard he tried and he'd look at me like I'd completely lost my marbles. I think at times he wondered who on earth he'd married. Luckily he was madly in love with me or I don't think we'd be where we are today. I believe he thought my farm plan may have been one of those things people spend their entire lives talking about doing but never actually do it, but I was much more determined than that. I guess back then some of my plans may have been a little bit wild. I was constantly thinking of ways to help animals in need and if the first plan failed I had many back up plans. Even today on long drives I will be making plans. I'll be sitting there quietly gazing out the window and again my mind will be roaring and I think at times David is too afraid to ask me what I'm thinking about. But in the end he generally does so a long conversation will be had about my new ideas. I think until the day I draw my last breath I will always be planning and thinking of ways to make the lives of the animals of this world better.

I'd be working at jobs I didn't really like and all the while thinking about the farm I was going to one day have, it's what kept me going when bosses with big ego's became too much or the hours on my feet too long. It was like the menial jobs, the bosses and the hours didn't matter, they were not what was important. I just kept my head down, did my job, then headed to the bank at the end of the week knowing every dollar deposited was a dollar closer to getting to that place where I knew I would be able to do some good in this world. I was always the first one with my hand up in the air for overtime too. And as I was working those long hours I'd have so many visions of my farm running through my mind. But nothing compared to seeing it for real. It's a surreal feeling. Like you are actually walking through one of your own dreams and the bedside alarm will go off soon and awaken you from it. Only it's not a dream, it's real and you don't wake up from it instead you wake up to it over and over and over again, every single morning and it's brilliant to be able to do that.

When I first arrived at Grace Farm I set up a routine of walking the pugs morning and night, two walks a day to keep their little bodies and minds active, it's a routine I still do today and so too will I be doing it in ten and god willing twenty years time. Some of my most joyous moments are spent watching the pugs ambling about the place. Seeing them all walking off in a little group like that, well my heart just swells. They are constantly stopping for a sniff and having group wee's and then off they go again until something else begs to be sniffed and wee'd on. These old pugs had come from all over Australia but they were here now living together like one big happy family, it was the most beautiful sight to see. And I'd see them all lined up sleeping in their beds after the morning walk and feel blessed, same feeling when they were out on the deck in the sun. I just got so much pleasure out of watching them enjoying themselves. Even watching them sleeping was a joy, and still is very much a joy. One of my most favourite sights actually. I'd watch the rise and fall of those little old chests and feel lucky to have them in my life. They may well have been somebody else's throwaway trash, but they are my little treasures and I've always treated them that way. And today it's exactly the same, it's just that now I'm sharing my life with a different set of little treasures.

I'd smile watching them and be proud too because David and I had a little part to play in their happiness. We created a peaceful loving environment for them to thrive in, and you see them doing exactly that after living lesser lives and that's a very special thing to be a part of. We've had some real little battlers here over the years. Came here on their last legs then refused to give in. They keep holding strongly on and we are blessed to get a few more years out of them and that can really warm your heart, especially when you think they've got no more than a few months at best. But whatever they have in them they give to us, we've played witness to this time and time again. To have an old dog come in and look at you with mistrust then fall madly in love with you and give you every little bit of life they have in them, well that's just the most amazing gift to be given, the most precious gift in the world actually. We get to be rewarded by these little miracles happening all around us every day. You can't help but feel happy when you are living your life like that.

Then when I started taking in special needs pugs, well that just took my happiness to an entirely new level, because I got to be the lucky one looking after them, while I was daydreaming in those tedious jobs I'd not given any thought to having special needs animals here. No thought to the blind, the deaf and the paraplegic dogs who would one day enter my life and I think that was due to the fact that I'd not come across any of them in my life so far. I never once saw a paraplegic dog growing up. I know this for certain because I've got a great memory as far as dogs are concerned and if I'd seen one I would have definitely lodged that. The reason I never saw any was because years ago they would have been put down because that's just what people thought needed to be done back then. Thank goodness minds have been broadened. Once I started taking special needs dogs in I realised that caring for them was what I truly loved doing. Although I don't really think of them as "Special needs" I just think of them as "Special", because that's exactly what they are. And they contribute to your life and end up making it pretty special too.

I can clearly remember how good it felt to be living in the country. After all the years of planning I was finally here and the feeling was magnificent. It was like I had arrived in the place I was meant to be. The place I had been walking towards from the moment I was born. I'd stand and look at the green hills and my heart was the fullest it's ever been. I felt a connection to this way of life that I've never felt living anywhere else. I felt such peacefulness here, everything felt right. That's how living in the country made me feel, like everything was going to be alright from now on. Oh I knew I would face hardships here and I knew I'd suffer losses, because that's how life is and no matter where you live you can't escape from it, but I also knew deep down in my heart that I would be able to handle all those things better because I was living in the country.

One of the first things we did when we got here was set about planting fruit trees. Me, Dave, Sarah, Harper, Ruby and Grace, the six of us all out working in the paddock together as a family was a real treat, well we worked but after a while the pugs, being old, went and sat in the shade of the veranda and watched us. And I'd look up and smile at them all laying there together in a row. I liked that they were looking after themselves. They would wander over when a new tree got put in the ground and sniff at the fresh dirt and being little girls each one squatted down and christened it. It was like we all had a job to do and they were doing theirs. I loved watching the tree's take root and start growing. Of a night when David got home from work we'd walk round the farm looking for growth. I'd already been out looking first thing in the morning but it was a nice thing to do together of an evening so I didn't mind checking again. The pugs all bobbed about at our feet, they enjoyed going out for an extra bit of sniffing. Of course there was very little difference growth wise, but we checked them daily all the same because they were our very own trees on our very own farm and everything that happened here was thrilling. It was just a tiny shoot of green foliage our eyes went searching for, but there was much excitement when they started appearing because to us it was a sign of life and a promise for the future, our future, the one we had planned long before coming here. We'd talk about how great the trees were going to look when they were fully grown, the shade they'd cast and the beauty of their leaves. There's something special about planting something yourself and watching it grow. Trees, flowers, vegetables, herbs, it doesn't matter what you plant the level of joy is pretty much the same if it's been done by your own hand.

I'd walk around the farm and I was so grateful for being here. We were all so happy. It felt like we were living in a blissful little bubble. While the pugs were off sniffing I'd be glancing over the empty back paddock picturing it full of elderly farm animals and I couldn't wait for them to start arriving. And arrive they did and they've not stopped arriving since. But we are real country people now, we've learnt to take it all in our stride. Something happens, you deal with it, end of story. One of my husband's favourite sayings is "It is what it is". For a city fella he's summed it up pretty well really. But I do think David has always been a city bloke with a country boys heart. And he's right in what he says, because it is what it is and we will handle it no matter what. We've done things we would never have imagined doing, we've helped with operations on our sheep and loved being able to do that, I am really fascinated with this type of thing, always have been but more so when it's happening to one of my own. I'm not the type to watch ER shows on television or even be thrilled about going to the doctors and when visiting people in hospital I can't wait to leave because I don't like the atmosphere in there. But when something is going on with one of my dogs, sheep or horses I'm right there on the frontline getting as close as I can get to the action because I want to know they are alright and also because I know I will learn something. Some vets have wanted us around because we can be a calming influence over their patients and I'm all for that, I like being there when our animals need us the most. And a calm ram being operated on is so much better than a stressed out ram being operated on isn't it because it makes it all the easier on them. You have to be careful with knocking sheep out, you can't give them too little or they'll be thrashing about all over the place and you can't have that when they need stitching up. Nor can you give them too much because they could die, donkeys are the same as sheep I've been told. You have to be equally aware with both of them, get the dose spot on. An old farrier was telling me a story once about helping his neighbour with a job, it was at a donkey farm, his neighbour was a vet and he went along to help out because of his horsey knowledge and also because it was a big job. All the vets from the practice were on hand, the owners and stable boys too, everyone had a job and everyone knew what they had to do. It was all well organised and yet it made no difference on the day. He told me how donkey after donkey kept dying and how they all tried their hardest to revive them, but nothing helped, they were gone. Three donkeys died that day. It was a hard day for all who witnessed it and I could well imagine it would have been, hearing about it was sad enough. That story was told to me many years ago but it has never left my mind, it comes back to me every time one of our paddock children needs operating on.

When the sheep and horses arrived they made a meal out of most of the trees, the sheep mainly because they will eat almost anything, and they will especially eat that which you do not want them eating. I'd spot them from the window and think to myself "Oh no not our precious slow growing fruit trees" and I'd go racing out there shooing them away. They weren't meant to be in that paddock anyway so off I'd go checking out where they'd gotten through and I couldn't find anywhere that they had. So I'd put them back where they were meant to be then go and hide in the hay shed and be watching them through the small window until they escaped again. And low and behold I saw them one by one getting down on their knees and actually crawling underneath the fence. Up until then I didn't even know sheep could crawl, but the lead sheep went under and the rest were soon to follow. Everything was a learning curve for us at the start. I'd expected them to go over the fence or through it but never underneath it, but as soon as I saw what they were doing we fixed the problem quick smart.

The man we bought the farm off planted a lot of conifers and they are huge now, they are great wind blocks and very much needed around these parts, we also have some old gumtrees but I try and steer the pugs away from them on our walks because they can drop a branch at any time, not just when it's windy, and I don't want anybody getting hurt. Every now and then I'll see a branch resting on a fence, some take out the top strand of wire, others take out the whole five and I come out in the mornings and glance across the paddocks and am so thankful the pugs weren't sniffing around there at the time. Nobody has ever gotten hurt by a tree falling here, not the pugs, not us and not the sheep or horses, the closest we've come was a few years back when we'd had our morning walk and were all back up on the veranda, the pugs were sleeping and I was having a quiet cup of tea. Out of nowhere I heard an almighty crack and a tree branch took out part of the front fence. We'd only walked by that area not more than half an hour before. They only look small those branches when they are up there. Look like nothing more than twigs because they are so high up. On the ground it's a different story though and you'll need a large chainsaw to cut them up. Once cut they are carted up to the shed so they can dry out ready for winter and those branches keep our fire roaring on cold rainy days. The pugs all trot along beside us as we're carting the branches up, they look where we've stacked them and sometimes wander over and cock their legs, because well, there's something new in the shed now and everything new has to be christened. They'll follow us back down to get more wood and sniff around the area until they see us walk off again then scurry to catch up. Horses have very keen ears and rocket propelled reactions, they'll hear a crack and take off, they'll have moved out of harm's way before the branch has even hit the ground. I've witnessed that a few times here and in the neighbouring properties.

When we are out walking around the farm together David and I talk about so many different things, many good conversations get started but very few are ever finished because one of the animals will distract us, we'll be drawn to whatever it is they are doing and loose our train of thought. Of course our conversations are important but not nearly as important as our animals are. They can be so comical when wandering around the farm, it's always nice watching what they are getting up to, what interests them on that particular day. Will it be the horses that are talked to first or will it be straight down the driveway to run along the front fence or is today going to be all about barking at the sheep. Will they stay close to Mum and Dad on this walk or will everybody's focus be on racing ahead because an interesting scent has been caught on the breeze and they all want to be the first one to get to it. And old pugs run too when the mood takes them, and yes our blind pugs run as well, people don't think blind pugs run, but they can run very fast without bumping into anything once they have the area mapped out in their minds.

It's nice to see an animal having a mad hour and we always stop and watch because nobody wants to miss seeing that. The mad hours are normally done in the evening. If you've got new lambs they seem to love having a good thrash about before nightfall, it's like they are exerting all their energy so they can sleep. They run and jump and head-butt their cousins and chase one another in circles until they run out of steam. The horses are beautiful when racing around their paddock, even the sheep stop what they are doing and look up. The sound of galloping hoofs, strong heads held high, manes and tails flowing as they run. We stand watching this breathtaking scene and so do the pugs, some will run closer to the fence to get a better look and stand woofing at the goings on. The blind pugs can sense what's happening and it sets them off barking. Especially if the horses start calling out to one another, our blind pugs love that. It's like they can sense there is excitement in the air. The atmosphere changes and blind pugs have heightened senses, they pick up on these things. They'll stand near our feet, little grey faces tilted up inhaling the air and woofing. That to me is just as beautiful as the show the horses are putting on. And it's not just our own animals that get talked to and barked at, the pugs often stand at the fence seeing what's going on next door. They'll be the first to notice when one of the neighbours has a new animal. Some of our walks can take the longest time because the pugs like to spend a lot of time sniffing and we never rush them when they are doing this. A dog's life is all about sniffing. It's so important to them, and if they are blind it's even more so. I would see people walking, or should I say rushing, their dogs when I lived in suburbia, pulling on their leads because they were too impatient to stand there and let their dogs have a sniff. Walking a dog should be all about the dog, not the person or how much time they have, if you are not going to let a dog do its thing then it can be a pretty miserable walk for the dog can't it.

We don't use leads or harnesses at all here, we never have, because there is simply no need to use them. Some of the pugs have arthritic necks so I only put them on when we are going to the vet. On the farm the pugs get to wander around freely because that's what I envisioned them doing all those years ago. And because I wanted this for them the first job we did on arrival was mesh the lower part of the fences. It was a big job but a must and well worth it because I have peace of mind that everybody is safe. When I see that shuffling old body with its uncurled tail step out onto the deck and waddle down the ramp I don't have to worry about them because I know nobody can get off the property and onto the road. I know they are in a safe little haven and can sniff and explore at their will.

The horses and sheep are kept in a separate paddock and that too is well meshed. I can't have my little blessings getting trampled under food. There is too much of a size difference. A lot of my pugs are blind and some of them are deaf, they need to be protected, they need special looking after. As much as I love my horses and sheep I can't allow them to be near the pugs without a secure fence in between. Sure I'd love to have all the animals roaming around freely together in peace and harmony but I think that's what heaven is for, here on earth we have to use our common sense and protect those that need protecting. The safety of the pugs is top priority here because it has to be, they are the smallest beings living here on the farm. It would simply break my heart if I let one of them come to harm because I had a childlike view of the place. It would be 100% my fault if something happened to one of them because of my own stupidity so I try as best I can not to be stupid for all our sakes. I'm here to take care of them, that's my role and I take that role very seriously.

I was walking the pugs around the farm one summer afternoon when the thought entered my head that this little place of ours should have a name so I set about trying to think of one. And I say "I" because David probably didn't care if the farm had a name or not. I can clearly remember the day I informed David of my idea. David wasn't well that day, had one of his bad migraines and was lying in the dark trying to get the pain in his head to stop. I crept into our bedroom to see how he was getting on and whether or not he needed me to bring him something. Once the usual "Food, water, more tablets? questions had been asked I turned and was ready to walk out of the room to give him some peace and quiet but then I stopped and came back in, which caused the old pugs that were creeping from the room behind me to do a quick turn around and follow me back in. I didn't go all the way in, just got close enough so David could hear without me having to raise my voice. Because, well, he had a migraine didn't he and the last thing he needed was me screeching at the top of my lungs. "I've decided our farm should have a name" I said and stood waiting in the darkness for him to answer. "Ok" pause, "Whatever" pause, "Name it what you want" I waited for about half a second then said "Ok, I will" Then the pugs and I fled the room before he changed his mind and wanted in on the farm naming experience. I was pretty happy with his answer to be honest. It didn't bother me one little bit having to think of a name for our farm on my own.

In the dictionary grace means elegance, loveliness and beauty and I really like that. And a friend sent me a quote recently that said Grace is the most beautiful word in the language of God. It means love given freely and without expectation of return. And to be honest I can't think of a better way of describing how we live our lives here on the farm.

I had a few names I liked but they just didn't seem to fit us as perfectly as this one, sure they fit but just weren't quite right. Then one day I was sitting at my computer and Grace was one of those pugs who always wanted to sit up with you, not contented to being on the floor in a dog bed, but liked to be closer to you then that. So I'd pull David's office chair over, put a blanket on it and Grace would contently go to sleep on that. She'd paw at my leg, I'd bring her up, she'd grunt and turn around a few times and I'd hold my hand in front of her so she didn't fall off the chair, she'd paw at the blanket once or twice then when she felt it was comfortable for her she'd flop down and go to sleep. I never had the blanket flat, Grace didn't like that, she more liked it ruffled so I'd hold the blanket in the air and let it fall at will, all uneven, but that's what Grace liked best. Anyway one day while on the computer I glanced down to check that Grace was ok, she'd made a noise and I thought she may have needed something, she didn't, she was just lying there dreaming and as I glanced down I thought she looked so beautiful, so very serine and in that instant it hit me that her name would be the most wonderful name for our little farm. I couldn't believe I hadn't thought of it sooner. I loved the definition of the word grace and I loved the pug, it couldn't have been more right really. My friend Janie summed it up nicely when she said that our little old Gracie reflected the beauty of the farm and the "grace" we extend to all the animals. And she was 100% right, I think the word "grace" rings true of everything we do here.

I painted our farm sign as soon as I'd decided on the name, I'm not one to procrastinate so it was done the same day. It's old and rickety now and the letters have been touched up a few times over the years but even in its heyday it was never a professional looking sign but I love it all the same because when I look at it I remember the day it was created and there are some happy memories there. Grace has been gone quite a few years now but she was right there beside me the day I dragged the wood and paint out of the shed. I couldn't wait for special timber and paint to be bought so I just used what we had hanging around at the time, perhaps that's why it looks so unprofessional. But that's ok, the day created memories that will last a lifetime and to me that's the most important thing of all.

Grace and the other pugs followed me out to the shed and sat in the entrance sunning themselves while I toiled away. Every now and then they'd move into the shade then back into the sun again as soon as they cooled down. It took a bit of doing getting that old paint tin lid off, I dug around in David's toolbox and found a screwdriver so I used that to pry it open, I hurt my hand doing it but I was determined so I pressed on. When I peeped inside I wasn't sure if the paint would have still been good to use or not. Lord knows how long it had been sitting in the shed. It was meant to be cream but a clear yellowish fluid floated on top. The pugs looked happy and I didn't want to disturb them so I grabbed an old tree branch that was on the floor in the shed, broke a bit off and used that to stir the paint with. We had some offcuts of dowel in the house that David had been using on a wardrobe but if I ran inside to get one of those it would have woken up the pugs and they looked so contented sleeping. Besides I figured the way this paint looked it wouldn't matter if it got a bit of dirt in it or not. But to my surprise once the paint had been stirred around it looked brand new, so off I went creating the very first farm sign I'd ever made in my life. And because it was for my very own farm it was a pretty exciting thing to be doing I can tell you. So I'm standing in the shed with the paint brush in my hand looking down at the sign and I began to read the words out loud. "Grace Farm", "Grace Farm", "Grace Farm". The pugs all looked up at me as I spoke and it sounded alright to them and it sounded alright to me so I dragged the sign out into the sun so the paint would dry faster and when it was touch dry I put the second coat on and had it waiting for David to hang on the front gate when he got home from work. Although I did hold my breath when I turned the sign around for him to look at and only fully relaxed once he smiled and nodded his head.

I've often wondered what the animals have thought of our farm sign when they've been driven through the gate. If they knew how much we loved them and wanted them living here I think they'd be standing up and cheering as soon as the sign came into view. But they don't know that do they so they arrive with nervous tummies and panic stricken hearts. But David and I know it and we stand together at the top of the hill with welcoming smiles and help them from the truck as quietly and peacefully as we possibly can because once they've crossed our threshold their life changes for the better and I want that change to be made instantly. I won't have an irritable driver rushing my livestock from his truck because he wants to be on his way. And there have been some who've tried and some who've been told to "Go stand over there mate and let us do what we want to do". Then David and I set about unloading our precious cargo with gentle movements and kind softly spoken words of love. It's like we make a promise to them when they file through the gate, to give them the very best life we possibly can, regardless of the time, the money and the work required. It's lovely to be able to look a frightened animal in the eye and vow them that. That's why it's so important to me that the respectful treatment starts the very second they arrive here and nobody is going to do otherwise while they are standing on my land. One particular driver got forceful, tried to boss me around and I just looked him in the eye and said "If you want to get paid we are going to do this my way ok". He must have realised I was serious because he went and stood quietly by the fence and never said a word after that. The funny thing was it was a bit hard to look at him without smirking and I knew if I smirked it would only make him think I wasn't serious so I kept my face straight. But he had one of those faces that looked like it'd just smelt something really putrid then the wind changed leaving him like that permanently, of course it was the face he'd been born with and he couldn't help that but every time I looked at him I had the wind change thought going through my head. My Grandmother told me stories about wind changing while I was growing up, she'd threaten me with it a couple of times too. I'd be there pulling my little face for lord only knows what reason and Nana would say "Best not keep your face like that for long because the wind will change and you'll be left like that for life" I didn't believe her until I saw this guy's face and it had me wondering if there was perhaps some truth to that old wives tale after all.

It's brilliant to be able to watch an animal go from being jumpy and scared to calm and content. We let them all settle in in their own time, we never ever push them because you can't. Such things cannot be rushed, that just makes everything worse and it takes them longer to achieve that which we set out to achieve with all of our animals whether they live inside the house or outside, and that is for them to feel they are finally home. I'm a real homebody myself so it's very important to me that all our animals eventually feel that. And farm animals that have lived their entire lives as merely farm animals can take a long time to settle down. They come here and have no idea what we are going to do with them. Are we going to eat them, no, but the sheep don't know that. They seem a little shell shocked that we want nothing more than for them to be happy. But I am very happy here and I want them to feel that way too. I know firsthand what it's like to live in a place where you don't feel happy or the slightest bit content, it's an awful way to live. I want to erase their past lives quickly but their hearts heal when their hearts heal. And we just treat them with love and kindness each day until they are ready to let us in. When that happens there is such a difference about them, of course you cannot physically see that their hearts have mended, but you feel it instantly the very second things change, it's like a soul connection between you and them, you can feel that the mistrust and uncertainty has left and been replaced by something new. There's something in the air around them and you become aware of it as soon as you step into their paddock. You look into their eyes and you know, you just know.

I have always tried to keep everything here as calm and peaceful as possible because the animals deserve it. Whenever we are moving the sheep we do it slowly and gently so as not to cause any stress, it takes twice as long but I don't care because I hate seeing animals running around confused because people are rushing them and they don't know which way to go. I normally do it on my own because they are more used to me, I pat them and talk to them and we then move off together to the paddock I want them to go in. I've seen farm animals running into fences and cutting themselves open due to ignorant people with no consideration and no time to spare. I won't allow anything like that to take place here. It just wouldn't sit right with my heart.

When we were coming out here to live on the farm some people said we were making a huge mistake and I said "Maybe" but it would be "My" mistake, an experience in "My" life and that I'd rather have a failed adventure then not had the adventure at all. And it sure beat getting to the end of my days with regrets, with a pile of "What if's" hanging over my head. I didn't want that for me. I don't want to be an old lady sitting in a room in a nursing home tearful with regret. If I'm in that room at all and don't die here on the farm like I believe I'm going to, then I want that room to be filled with images of an amazing life. And if my body is twisted with arthritis and knotted like an old tree trunk because a horse pulled too hard or a sheep knocked me flying because I didn't get out of the way in time, well that's perfectly fine by me. Let my body be a map, let it be a record of how well I lived, yes it'll ache and may look a sight from the outside but I'll be smiling big time on the inside because I'll have lived the life I wanted to live. If I got to the end of my days and I hadn't done this, hadn't lived this way, I would be terribly disappointed in myself. I'd feel like I had wasted my life. The way it is now, I reckon I'll be able to look back with peace and happiness at a worthwhile life and that's a really good thing to be able to do. Sure the life I lead can be heartbreaking at times but I still want to do it, I wouldn't want to be living anywhere else doing anything else.

People often ask me what it's like running a senior pug sanctuary and I say well it's always busy, busy, busy, it's a continuous commitment, a twenty four hour a day seven day a week job. It's repetitive, it's consistent. It's exhausting but I feel the emotional exhaustion is far worse than the physical. It's beautiful, its happy, its lovely, it is so rewarding. Its heartbreak and sorrow and worry, its joy and laughter, it's exhilarating and its' devastating. It'll drain your bank account but fill your heart to overflowing. It's full of the most incredibly precious wonderful moments that take your breath away. And it's full of the saddest most painful moments that leave you doubled over, in a nutshell it's just like life really only sped up and magnified. Regardless it is worth it, even on your saddest hardest days it is most definitely worth it.

I am a mother, a nurturer, a teacher, a cleaner, a chef, a nurse, a detective, a mind reader, a diplomat, a negotiator. Most of the time I'm like Ellie May Clampett just bobbing about the farm with my critters, loving them, looking after them and being happy in their company. They bring me an enormous amount of joy. I am responsible for a lot of animals and the bulk of care rests solely on me. I have to always be here for them and that's just fine by me. I'm a real homebody, always have been so this lifestyle suits me pretty well. My days are always the same, same amount of chores, same routine, same set up, same path to be followed, unless a drama has taken place each day begins and ends in pretty much the same way as the previous one did and the one before that and the one before that. It's a full time job, I don't really think of it as a job as such because I truly love what I'm doing. It's incredibly enjoyable. But it's work all the same there's no denying that, work with no days off, ever. No weekends and no holidays and Christmas day is just the same as every other day because my animals don't know it's Christmas, they are there waiting to be fed and taken care of and you have to get up and do all that. It's a commitment, a vast commitment. You always have to be "On" "Always need to be there for them". If a pug gets sick during the night you have to get up and help them, there's nobody else to call and sometimes there can be rows of sleepless nights until they come good and again you have to be there helping them through it every step of the way. Occasionally I will have what I call an "Old lady who lived in a shoe" day. But those days I'm pleased to say are very few and far between. Maybe I'll have two a year. Mainly in the middle of winter when it's been raining for days on end and the house is full of wet washing that's taking forever to dry and the pugs can't go for their regular walks, just quick dashes outside to do their business then back inside again before the rain hits. And such things do not please them so they are looking pretty miserable and the sheep are looking pretty miserable and the horses faces look longer then they normally do.

Our home is like any other retirement home around the country. There is a heck of a lot of laundry to be done, meals to prepare, beds to change, cleaning, bathing, grooming. If I get away with doing only one load of laundry per day then that day is magical but it rarely happens, normally there are three or four loads of laundry to be done, some days more. I seem to be always doing laundry, always washing and drying something and thinking that the house resembles a laundromat. But then I start thinking "So what if it does", what does it matter what the house looks like, sure you'll never see our home on the cover of a home beautiful magazine but it's functional, it's achieving a purpose, it's a busy family home and you see the little old pugs weaving their way in and out of the clothes horses trying to find me and you think to yourself, yeah it's no show home but oh the love and adoration that is held within these small walls. A whole lot of happiness and acceptance too. I guess you could say that our house is "Us" it's an honest representation of who we are and I like that. You step one foot inside our home and you can clearly see what brings us joy, what is important to us, and what is very important to us are old pugs and their needs, well that their needs are being taken care of and you can clearly see that when you walk into our house. Our home is full of all our characters, both the pugs and our own, and I think all real homes should be like that, should have our marks stamped all over them. They should be our special places. Our homes should make us feel warm, comforted and at ease. There are so few places in the world that you can truly feel at ease in, that's why it's important to be able to feel it in your own home, it has to be your sanctuary, your happy place, if it's not then it's just a place, no connection, no emotions, nothing, and the world has enough places in it already doesn't it.

I like taking care of my pugs. Looking after elderly animals is all I ever wanted to do with my life. Of course laundry is relentless and I have other jobs I favour more, I could sweep until the cows come home and never tire of doing it, but the laundry needs to be done so you just get on with it and that's that really. And it's not so bad because I get to hang out my washing with a flock of old sheep watching every move I make. I like how the ewes interact with one another. They remind me of a group of gossiping ladies gathered in the main street of any country town on a Monday morning filling each other in on the goings on around town. My rams don't tend to get involved in this, like most men they think nattering is overrated. They go off and graze and wait for the ladyfolk to finish up and it can take the longest time. I watch the ewe's watching me watching them, their heads tilt and nod as they bend down to eat or rub their faces against their legs, then it's heads straight back up again in case they've missed something significant. Then they stand chewing and watching until they drop their heads again to get another mouthful. Pegging washing out can be a pretty boring task but not when you have a pile of animals around you while you're doing it, sometimes I can't wait for the spin cycle to finish so I can go see what my sheep and horses are up to. As I peg I amuse myself with different thoughts. I often picture how my ewes would look if I lashed out and bought frilly bonnets for all of them. As yet I've not done it, but every so often I go back to thinking about how beautiful their little old thin faces would look surrounded by frills, with lovely satin bows tied underneath their chins. It'd be a bit of work getting them on and we'd all be hot and bothered after the event but it'd make for a great photo so I've not totally dismissed the idea as yet.

And all my little pug blessings are with me when I'm going about my chores and I like that too. I'll be side stepping them with a loaded laundry basket in my arms and they'll see me walking out the door and come scurrying after me, then they'll lay in the sun while I hang the washing out, same when I'm bringing it in when it's dry, those little old legs come shuffling after me and I feel total contentment in having them there. Same with the chores inside the house, there is always a cloud of elderly pugs following on behind me as I complete each task. And because of this I try and do as many jobs as I can in the one area before moving on. You can't be dashing around all over the place when you have blind pugs as that will only confuse them, they'll have just located you and be settled only to have you take off again leaving them behind, making them come find you once more and I don't think that's fair on them. While I'm doing what I have to do I like to have them all sleeping around me. And when they sense you are close they tend to settle down pretty fast and sleep peacefully and they are old so having a little snooze does them good. But then you have to move on at some point don't you and when I do they all rise up and they follow and once they realise I am going to be staying in that location for a while they will once again lower their little bodies down and start snoring. Or not snore at all but quietly be watching me going about my business or laying down chewing a toy. Whatever makes them happiest. I have a mental list of chores in my head and keep chipping away until everything gets done and sometimes it does and sometimes it doesn't because a hiccup has occurred but you just have to be ok with that and say to yourself there is always tomorrow. And as long as you've done what's most important for that day that's all that really matters. You learn to prioritize.

But there are a lot of nights when the clock strikes ten and I'm still folding laundry, trying to get a jump on the chores for the next day. I'm always trying to be ahead of schedule. And the pugs are with me while I'm doing that but it's not only the pugs who are with me, more often than not right there beside me is my husband. Sure he's tired and sure he could easily say he was going to bed and leave me to it and he would have every right in the world to do that after working hard all day. But he doesn't, he sits and he folds and we talk and have a bit of a laugh until the job is done. It's the same with any job around the farm, if it needs doing and I haven't finished doing it by the time David gets home from work then we'll do it together. We are always together when he's home because that's how we like to live our lives.

And then there are the rarest of the rare days when all the jobs have been done, you've finally caught up on everything and you sit there a little dumbfounded. You are a bit in shock actually and you're thinking to yourself "This can't be right, surely there's something I've forgotten to do". And you are straining your brain trying to think of what it is that needs doing. But after a considerable amount of time you realise that every job actually has been done, for once you are on top of it all so can sit back and relax, grab a cup of tea and sit on the deck enjoying the view. These golden afternoons of nothingness normally come in the middle of summer when the washing is dry in no time and can be brought in and folded pretty fast. And for all the time I spend doing laundry I have to admit as tedious as it can be at times, I do kind of love seeing the pugs items out there blowing in the breeze. The colourful little rainbow coats, the pretty pink and blue blankets, the bedding, the hand towels and face washers that wipe up the drool from the wrinkly little faces. All those items hung up drying are some of my favourite sights to see, it's a heart-warming vision, colourful washing blowing on a line with a pile of old pugs sleeping beneath it. They use the washing as shade in summer, it can be a good place for them to have a lay down because they don't get too hot. It's like one moment they are in full sun the next they are in the shade, then the wind will take up once more and its full sun again but never long enough for them to overheat.

I've had people ask if I ever feel so completely overwhelmed by what I do that I feel like stopping. And the honest answer to that would be yes sometimes I do. But those days are so rare that I can't even put a number on them for you. These are the days when a lot of the pugs are unwell. I mean some people can't even imagine how it is to have six pugs let alone six pugs with gastro and you are desperately trying to not let it spread to the other pugs in the house. And you are dishing out multiple medications and somebody keeps spitting there's out no matter how hard you try to fool them into taking it. Most of the pugs take their medication well but you'll always have one in the bunch who fools you, and that pugs name in our house is Arthur. He'll either hide it on the side of his mouth or he'll do something that I find so incredibly talented that I am in awe. You see Arthur has this most amazing gift that he can separate the tablet from the food no matter what type of food you put his tablet in. I'll stand there and watch him working his tongue around and around, his mouth looks like a little washing machine, well a little tumble dryer actually, the way that food is being spun round and round. Then all of a sudden he stops and spits the tablet out. It's like he's washed it thoroughly and now has no use for it so spits it out at lightning speed and I go scurrying across the kitchen floor after it before one of the other pugs sees it. I always put it in the food he likes best but it makes no difference at all to Arthur, I even melt a bit of cheese in the microwave, wrap the tablet in that while it's still soft enough to mould then give it to him when it's cooled down, this has worked time and time again over the years for even the most fussy pug. But it does not work on Arthur. He still manages to eat all the food around it and the tablet remains intact, cleaned, but intact and spat out when he's done with it. These days I find I just have to put the tablet carefully down his throat then gently massage under his chin until it goes down. He loathes me for it I know he does but that's the only way of ensuring his meds are being taken. I can't have him remaining sick just because he's cunning.

And the pugs are not all on the same medications either so you have to concentrate fully on what you are doing so the meds aren't given to the wrong pug. I have a bit of paper with the pugs name written on it and I put the medication next to their names and once the dose is given I stop, cross out the name, then move on to the next pug and the pug after that and the pug after that, you just do whatever works to get it right and this method works best for me. I have a thick note pad sitting on the kitchen counter top and rip out the page and rewrite it again the next day or even for the night time feed depending if the medication needs taking twice daily. So the meds are sorted and then you turn around and there are puddles and more all over the floor and you are trying to clean them up but they keep reappearing and being walked all over the house. But pugs that are not feeling well don't think to go outside to do their business like they normally would do and it's not their fault, you can't blame them for feeling ill. And you are trying to get all your other normal jobs done too and you are exhausted because you've been up with sick pugs for three or four nights in a row and you are weary but you are still running around doing your best to try and get on top of things. There's only one of you and so many of them, so you keep going and going, racing along trying to get it all done.

And you'll be rushing past a window with a pile of wet bedding in your arms and glance out and spot somebody in the front paddock eating horse poo that you haven't gotten round to moving from the previous day, and because you are way behind with breakfast the pugs are getting rather testy. Testy with you and testy with each other, because we all know from our own experience that you can get a little bit grumpy when you don't feel well and you are hungry on top of that. So there'll be pugs standing in the kitchen screaming at me every time I dash past because they want to be fed and you rush out onto the veranda to try and call the poo eating pug in, but they take not one bit of notice of you, in fact they don't even look up and acknowledge you are calling their name, they are not one of the deaf ones but they play deaf because it suits them to. And a pile of pugs have followed you out onto the veranda and stood beside you while you called and now they refuse to come inside again and you know its windy and they shouldn't be left out there, but they are old and stubborn and want things their own way. So you leave the veranda door open so they can come in when the will takes them and once you are inside it can take them pretty fast because they don't want to be on the veranda alone, they want to be where you are. So you watch them filing in and race over and close the door behind them then rush over to the washing machine dump the wet bedding in and switch it on, then race out the back door to go get the horse poo eating pug in before they eat too much and vomit. And you are just hoping you get out there fast enough before they start rolling in it too because that'll mean giving them a bath, and you are watching them eating the horse poo as you cross the paddock and they look up, see you approaching, then quickly flop on their sides and start to roll. It's like they know they only have precious seconds before you take them inside so seize the opportunity while it's there and their little legs are up in the air kicking away happily by the time you reach their sides. So you stand over them smiling saying "Well you are covered in it now aren't you, what's a few more seconds of rolling going to hurt" and because they are so happy doing it you let those extra few seconds turn into minutes. But now you have to give somebody a bath as well as doing all the other extra chores. And it's a cool day so it's not just a bath but a full blow-dry as well.

And this goes on hour after hour, only slowing down a bit when they all fall asleep early afternoon and as much as you desperately want to crawl into the dog bed next to them and curl up in a ball you don't because you figure while they are resting you can catch up on all the jobs you've missed. So you try and do that but hours fly by like minutes and there is still so much to do. Then all over sudden one of the pugs will open their eyes, yawn, stretch, rise up and stagger from their bed followed closely by another one and then another and another and before you know it the fussing snorting weeing pooing demanding little blessings are all fully awake and you are once again at their mercy. The puddles start reappearing because they still don't feel well enough to walk out the door, they just squat where they stand and bark because they are telling you it's there and needs cleaning up or because they've relieved themselves now and want you to feed them. And everything that happened this morning starts all over again. The walking, the feeding, the meds, the spitting out, the coughing, the spluttering, the faking death, and once again you are late with their meal and the hungry tummies are causing screaming and they are bickering at you to go faster and you try and tell them that they have to take their medication before eating and you try and tell them to be reasonable but nobody wants to be reasoned with and it's four o'clock in the afternoon and you only just realised you still haven't showered yet. So you walk and you feed and when they settle back into their beds again you fly out the door to go feed and water the sheep and horses and you are sitting there with a furrowed face thinking that you really don't think you can do this anymore because you just don't have the energy to and you glance at the clock again and it's gone six and you beg your husband to take the helm before he's even stepped one foot inside the door. And he smiles and nods and before he realises exactly what he's in for you grab your cold cup of tea off the kitchen bench and run off to take a shower, but before you fly through the bedroom door you pause and glance back and see him standing there surrounded by all our children and he's talking to them and patting them and some are being hauled into the air for snuggles and they are all squealing with delight and that scene warms your heart. So you shower and change your clothes and peep at your tousled hair in the mirror and tell your dark roots that they'll have to wait until next week for a touch up when things finally settle down. Then you re-join your family, you sit down to dinner and start chatting to your husband and sneaking bits of food to the pugs and you realise that today wasn't so bad after all and that tomorrow is going to be better because it always is. And that night you fall into bed exhausted, just like you did the night before and the one before that but you keep going because you know what you are doing is important. And besides in a few days the illnesses have passed and the natural flow of the household has been restored. Ok you are still super busy, you are still playing catch up and will be for another day or so yet, but a much more harmonious state has been restored.

Over the years people have written to me and said they wished they too had such a privileged life and an unlimited income. I don't know where they got this idea from but it's far from the truth because we are not rich people, no sorry that's a lie, we are incredibly rich people but our riches lay solely in one another and the pugs we take in. And yes I do feel very privileged to be living here with all these animals. I feel richly blessed having them in my life. But when they talk about being privileged I think they are more thinking that we were born with silver spoons in our mouths, well they must do mustn't they if they keep talking about unlimited incomes. But we are not wealthy people, not according to our bank accounts we aren't anyway. Our farm is only small and our house is a humble dwelling, but we do the best we can with what we have. To be honest I wish we did have an unlimited income or even better be able to win the lotto because we'd definitely use it to help more animals. The more money we had the more the animals of this world would benefit because that's just who we are. But the truth of the matter is that David and I are just two average people on an average income who devote their lives to looking after elderly animals. And there is much juggling going on behind the scenes.

All my life I have had a reoccurring dream. Again my first memory of ever having it was when I lived in England. In the dream I am walking through a lush forest, and it feels to me like that forest is actually in England, it's a lovely rich green beautiful peaceful forest and I have a big pot of warm stew tucked under one arm and a ladle in my other hand. I come to a clearing in the forest and there are all these animals waiting for me. Only dogs and cats, no other animals like I have now, just dogs and cats, well mainly dogs but there are a few cats there too and they are all getting along together really well. And they are all hungry, not starving or thin like they have been living on the street or anything like that, so I suppose I must have been feeding them for a while and they all know me and start walking towards me when they see me appear and the ones that were sitting on tree stumps jump down and start coming towards me. They are not wild animals either, not mangy or tatty looking, all seem well groomed and well taken care of. To be honest I don't know why they are there or even if they are my animals, I'd say they wouldn't be because I'd never leave any of my animals in the forest on their own, I'd have them living in the house with me. I don't have any animals walking with me through the forest either so I guess I must have left all of mine at home. There are all these bowls on the ground and on the tree stumps, which by the way is really convenient because otherwise these poor animals would have to eat off the ground and their food would be gritty with dirt. I guess even in my dreams I want animals to be eating out of bowls, like my subconscious mind is looking out for them. And the bowls are clean too, not like they've been sitting out in the forest for years, even though that's exactly what they have been doing. I start dipping the ladle into the stew and serving it up. Walking from bowl to bowl to bowl and the dogs and cats that were on the tree stumps jump back up again and have their meals up there. It's a healthy stew too because as I'm serving it up I can see carrots and spinach and a few other green vegies in there. And the pot of stew never runs out until every bowl is filled. And I stand watching them all eating in harmony together, then that's it, the dream ends, just fades out. I never go past that point, never see myself turn and walk back through the forest, for all the years I have been having it, the dream is always the same, starts the same, I'm always doing the same thing and feeling really happy doing it and then it always ends once the bowls have been filled and I'm just pausing to watch them eat. I like that no animal misses out, that all the tummies get filled, nobody goes hungry. The breeds of dogs and the colours of cats are all different. Big dogs, small dogs, shaggy dogs, smooth coated dogs. And they all eat nicely together. Huge giant breeds eat right beside tiny dogs, and cats and dogs eat side by side without anybody being aggressive. Nobody's food gets pinched. And I stand back and watch them for a little while, not as long as I'd like to because that's a scene I could watch for ages, but then the dream ends just as fast as it began and I guess it's because I've come and done what I was supposed to do. Over the years I've had this same dream over and over and over again, every few months or so, in England, in Australia, in primary school, in high school, and in every job I have ever worked in. But since I got this farm and started doing what I do I've only had the dream a couple of times and in the past year never, so I think when you are living your heart's desire there's simply no reason to keep dreaming about it is there.

So let me now take you on a beautiful journey, for the remainder of this book please allow me to tell you all about the lovely elderly pugs I have had the joy of sharing my life with.

CHAPTER TWO

Sarah

S arah came into my life at a time when I desperately needed an injection of happiness, it had been a difficult few years for me personally. A time of changes and adjustments, a time of realising what was and wasn't going to be and coming to terms with it all. Life never stands still, it's all about changes. New chapters are always opening while others are coming to an end. It's also about hills and valleys and I had been in a valley for what seemed like the longest time, as all our time in the valley does. I don't know what caused something to change in me but I woke up one morning and knew I didn't want to be in the valley any more. I was way overdue for a shot of happiness. What I most wanted to do now was go and stand on the highest hilltop and be happy and I felt that if I had a little pug standing on that hilltop beside me, I would be exactly that. Happy, truly happy.

Pugs have always symbolized joy to me, pure happiness, instant elation and I longed for some of that. It had been some time since I had a pug to love and I really missed sharing my life with them. But I didn't just want any pug, I wanted a black one, I'd had fawns all my life and I loved every single one of them, to me the fawn is the real pug because that's all I'd even known, back then black pugs were very hard to come by. I had wanted one for years and had been on a few waiting lists, but the demand was huge and there were not too many people breeding black pugs in our state and in those days the thought of putting a dog on a plane, well it just never crossed my mind. Naturally I wouldn't think twice about doing that now, in fact we fly pugs in all the time, but things were different back then. I had no idea of what was going on with dogs interstate, of course it's a lot easier these days to contact somebody in another part of Australia, well any other part of the world really, but back then it wasn't so easy. I figured somebody would more than likely take our hard earned money and I'd never even see the dog I'd paid them for. So what I knew for sure was that I needed my new black pug to be available here in Melbourne.

For as long as I can remember I've always gotten giddy at the sight of a pug. I saw my first one in a book and knew from that day on this unusual looking toy breed had my heart, they were the one for me. I thought they were perfect and then some. The flat face, the expressive eyes, the curl of the tail and circling dance, they were enchanting to me and when I finally got to hear the noises they made, well it was music to my ears, a blissful contented sound that made them even more perfect to me. I've heard the pug snort compared to a broken vacuum cleaner, but I don't think that's the case at all, to me it's a melody that can lull one to sleep. I find it very comforting. My happiest times have always been when I've had a pug sharing my life. So I knew it was definitely time for me to get another one and I was filled with excitement.

That night David was barely inside the front door before I blurted out my intentions, he looked at me but didn't say much. I don't think I gave him time to, my mind and mouth were going a hundred miles an hour. He knew I'd had pugs before we met but we had big dogs now didn't we. Two Great Danes in fact. David had never had a toy breed in his life, he's a tall man, 6' 2" and big men like big dogs. David may have eventually muttered something about the size difference between pugs and our Danes but I wasn't listening. My mind was made up. After a few weeks of none stop chatter about pugs he must have realised I was serious because he began looking at the ads with me. But the ads were few and far between, no black pugs for sale after months of looking and for the last few months no pugs advertised for sale at all. We were getting desperate when an ad finally showed up in the newspaper.

FOR SALE: Pug, fawn, female. I couldn't dial the number fast enough, of course I would have liked a black pug but at this point it didn't matter to me anymore, I had been waiting long enough, black or fawn, the colour was irrelevant I was about to share my life with a pug once again and I was ecstatic.

We arranged to go and meet the pug on Sunday afternoon as it was the only time the guy was free. The house sat in the middle of a green treed street, all the houses where pretty, well cared for and huge, the house my new pug lived in had a high brick fence and a sturdy wooden gate. It took us forever to actually open the thing, David managed it in the end because I couldn't make the gate budge no matter how hard I tried, and I was trying pretty hard such was my desire to get inside. It was like the hinges were rusted and I wondered why somebody who lived in such a large house couldn't afford to get his gate hinges replaced. As I walked up the path I started wondering if he was lazy or just very busy then I thought what on earth am I wasting my time thinking about him for, it's the pug I'm here to see. The man I'd spoken to on the phone answered the door and told us to go wait in the garden and he'd bring the pug out to us, maybe he'd looked us over and decided we were the type of folks who couldn't be trusted inside his posh house. Maybe he thought we'd come to case the joint, but I had no interest in his silver candlesticks the only thing that I wanted of his was his pug.

There was a stone bench to one side of the garden so we both sat down. I glanced up at the double story house, lace curtains hung at every window and a climbing vine clung to the brickwork like its life depended on it. After an eternity the door finally opened and the man came out holding a small dog, from a distance it looked like a long haired Chihuahua crossed with something else but I didn't pay too much attention. I thought it was nice of him to bring his other dog out to meet us but that wasn't the dog I was here to see so I glanced behind him waiting for my pug to come racing through the open door. The man came closer and started talking, I smiled then quickly turned back towards the house, this time my eye lay solely on the door, my heart was beating so fast, in seconds my new daughter was going to come running through that door and I couldn't wait to see her face. They all have slightly different faces but that's another story and you have to be a true pug lover to be able to tell the difference. But the doorway remained empty. I looked up at the top windows, she must be up there, that's what was taking so long for her to come running out, her owner had left the room without his pug noticing. The pug had to have been asleep for this to happen though because pugs like to follow their people everywhere. You'd think this guy would have made sure she was behind him before coming downstairs considering we were down there waiting to meet her. Once the pug woke up she'd start searching for her owner I was sure of it, they always do and so I waited for the curtains to move and a little black mask to push its way through the lacy haze, but nothing moved, nothing happened, the curtains stayed still and the doorway remained empty.

The man put his dog on the ground in front of us. I could see it more clearly now, it was a Chihuahua crossed with some sort of terrier. I still wasn't paying that much attention so the man got on the ground with the dog and began playing with it, tickling its tummy, trying I began to realize, to make this dog appear more interesting to David and myself. It took a few seconds of listening to him talk before it sunk in that the guy actually thought this dog of his was a pug. How could anybody not know the difference between a Chihuahua and a pug or a pug and any other breed of dog in the world for that matter. I stared at the guy like he was an idiot. The look of the pug is unique, the tail, the face, the noise, unless they're crossed with a similar breed they are distinctive. Pugaliers, jugs and shrugs can throw people if they are not familiar with the pug but back then pugaleirs, jugs and shrugs weren't as popular as they are today. If his dog had been a Griffon or even a Pekingese I could have understood the mistake, but a Chihuahua, well I just thought he was a real twit, fancy house no brains was how I described him to my friends when relating the story.

I looked at the dog then back at the guy again. Was it a joke or was he just truly that stupid. Perhaps was he trying to scam us or worse was he some sort of amateur film maker and there was a camera hidden somewhere recording the entire thing, had one of my friends somehow put the guy up to playing a prank on us. Had they rung him after I'd told them about the newspaper ad and arranged the whole thing. Were my friends about to come and join us in the garden laughing their heads off. I glanced all around me, the door, the windows, even the bushes in the garden expecting to catch the glimmering reflection of a camera lens. But there was nothing, no camera, no hoaxing friends and no real pug either, my heart began to sink, we had waited all week, come all this way, I'd gotten excited beyond belief and the dog wasn't even a pug.

I stared at the man again then stared even closer at the dog, no defiantly a Chihuahua crossed with a terrier there wasn't even a hint of pug in it and it was white not fawn, it may not have even been a female, I wasn't sure, I didn't look, my heart wasn't in it so I didn't bother to check. I looked at the man then looked at David, they were both smiling and talking about something, guy stuff, cars from memory I think. Was David merely being polite or did he actually not know what a pug looked like? I watched them talking some more, observing the guy more than David. The guy really did seem genuine to me, either that or he was a very good actor, but you get a feel for people and I honestly believe he thought this dog he was trying to sell was a pure bred pug. Perhaps he himself had been conned, who knows but let somebody else tell him. I'd just had my dreams shattered I wasn't about to shatter his. I hid my disappointment told him I'd have a think about it and got out of there as fast as I could. David caught up to me halfway down the street. He said he didn't think pugs looked like that but had kept his mouth shut because what did he know, he was a big dog person after all. He said he thought it may have been a variation of the breed, I said it was no more of a pug then I was and quickly got into the car. The drive home was a quiet one, far quieter than the ride up, David concentrated on the road and I looked out the window at nothing in particular, on the back seat lay an empty harness and a blanket I'd brought with me in case my new pug was cold.

And so the search continued. Every Saturday the first person to rise walked down to the milk bar, got the morning newspaper and started searching through the ads. Back then the For Sale ads came out twice a week but the Wednesday's newspaper never had much in there so we stopped buying it. Weeks and weeks went by and there were still no ads for pugs. I was almost giving up hope then one beautiful Saturday morning while I was making breakfast David burst through the front door and started waving the newspaper in the air. "Oh you are going to be so happy baby" he shouted and started reading an ad to me. He had been reading the ads on the way home and started running when he saw the small one line ad at the bottom of the page.

FOR SALE: Female pug, black, 6 months old. Good home only.

My heart skipped a beat, a black pug. I'd never seen one in the flesh not even at the Royal Melbourne Show. I'd only seen a photo of a black pug in a book and although they were definitely a pug they looked kind of weird to me, I've always loved the black mask of the pug against the fawn head, that's what a real pug looked like in my eyes, because for so many years that's the only colour I'd ever seen and to be honest I think it's stayed with me. Even now when somebody asks if I'll take in a needy pug, in my mind they are always fawn until I'm told otherwise. I read the ad over and over a few times to make sure I'd got it right. It was like after waiting so long I just couldn't believe my eyes. I wanted this little black pug so badly that I wanted to go get her right away. But as per usual people are always busy on Saturdays so once again I had to wait, and Sunday afternoon could not come fast enough for me.

On the way there I wondered if this was going to be another wild goose chase, I hoped not, I didn't think my heart could take another disappointment. I thought about the last time we'd set out to buy a pug and wondered if anybody had told the guy his dog was a Chihuahua cross, somebody would have had to set him straight by now, probably the people who came to have a look right after us. He wouldn't have been left in his ignorance for very long that was for sure. I doubted the next set of people would have been as polite to him as we had been.

After driving for hours we finally arrived at our destination. This house was very different to the house that the non-pug had lived in, totally opposite part of town, a new house on a new estate, ugly grey bricks that looked like they'd been bought on a sale, reduced because nobody else wanted them, no front fence either. Pugs need fences because they have no road sense I thought to myself as I got out of the car. They had a big lawn area but no grass, just pegs, string and homemade flags to keep the birds away from the seeds. No trees in the street either, all telephone wires underground, the whole estate looked bare blank and boring, and a little bit sad to me.

A path hadn't yet been laid so we walked up the planks of wood and pressed the doorbell. I heard a small child crying and a small dog barking, they took forever to come to the door. I have found in life that the doors that take the longest to open are generally the ones my new pugs are waiting behind. Footsteps came close, the child stopped crying, but the small dogs bark went on and on. I strained my ears trying to hear if it was the low throaty bark of a pug, I wasn't sure, it had been awhile since I'd heard one. Hopefully it was because I didn't think I could be as polite this time if a different breed came racing through that door. A young girl, well woman actually, she was a mother after all, opened the door, supermodel thin but not supermodel pretty. Impish face, short bleach blonde hair, skinny jeans and an oversized shirt that looked like it belonged to her husband. I saw something black on the ground behind her moving about and glanced down. And there she was, a gorgeous bouncy black pug that was so shinny and glossy that she reminded me of a baby otter shimmering through the water. The woman said the pugs name was "Tegan" after a character in her favourite tv show. And I thought to myself "Yes but not for very long"

I stared at the pug for a few moments. I was so overcome with emotion that I simply couldn't talk, the lump in my throat was so huge. I've always been like that when I see a thing of beauty, a Clydesdale galloping through an open field chokes me up every single time. I'm also like this with sounds, church bells, a lovely singing voice or beautiful music. I get so overwhelmed that I have to take a few moments before I can speak. When I finally came good I just said "Oh thank God it's a pug", David said I kept repeating it over and over again to the point of becoming embarrassing, he said the woman was giving me a strange look, but I don't remember, I was too excited. The pug was overcome with excitement too, the soon-to-be-no-longer-named Tegan pug just couldn't keep still, if I was a dog I would have joined her but we humans we stay composed don't we, dogs act exactly the way they are feeling on the inside and don't care what people think. I've always thought we could take a page out of their book, it would be so freeing being able to do that, I've thought of trying it many a time but today wasn't the day.

We moved into the lounge and the woman began biting her nails which drew my attention to her face again, she was pale, looked like she could have slept for a month if you let her. She was talking but her mind wasn't on what she was saying, her eyes looked blank, like she'd been screaming on the inside for so long without anybody noticing that she'd finally given up. I knew that look and I knew that feeling, obviously a pug wasn't the answer for this lady or she wouldn't be getting rid of hers. The husband was in the kitchen feeding the little girl a snack to keep her quiet. One of them mentioned they were having another baby, early stages I guess because she wasn't showing, none of them seemed happy about it. I didn't know what to say. My eyes went back to the pug, she was doing the two steps forward three steps back thing dogs do, the talk-to-me-play-with-me- shuffle. She was so engaging, that little pug had more personality in that little body of hers then the three human beings in the house all put together. I desperately wanted to hold her but her body couldn't stay still, the little black face was so appealing and her eyes followed you everywhere you went, if somebody in the room took their eyes off her for a moment she'd give a little bark then do the stiletto shoe pose, back legs straight front legs level with the floor, once the room's attention fell back on her again she was off dancing. This little pug sure loved attention and I was the best kind of audience because I couldn't look away if I tried. I was mesmerized, obsessed, I thought she was the best thing ever. I've never understood birdwatchers but at this moment I could relate to them, that shot of electricity they must feel when coming across something they've spent years looking for, a lifetime waiting to see. This black pug was like a rare species to me. She was everything I thought she would be and then some. Finally she settled long enough for me to pick her up, I wanted to hold her to my heart and snuggle her but she wasn't having any of that, she just couldn't stay still and wriggled about so much I thought I may drop her so I put her down. As soon as those little black paws made contact with the ground she shot off into the kitchen. Typical pug I thought she's gone to see if there's any food for her. But in seconds she was coming down the hall and into the lounge again, then into the kitchen and back down the hall, round and round she went, she was fit I'll give her that because she was hardly panting. She'd slow down to turn into the kitchen then run on the spot for a few seconds every time she came into contact with the lino and be off again once she found her footing. Every time she slowed she'd look at you out of the corner of her eye, give you that "Can't-stop-now-too-excited" look. And she certainly was excited and she certainly was full of life.

Eventually she did run out of steam or got bored with the game, either way she came and jumped up on the chair next to me and allowed me to pick her up, this time she stayed still and we looked at each other for the first time. I thought I saw something in her eye so I carried their Tegan, my Sarah, into the kitchen where there was better light. I stood with my back to the window and held my new daughter up, I started slowly moving her from side to side to try and catch a glimpse of what I thought I'd seen in the lounge. There was a dot on her eye, they knew what I was looking at and both husband and wife started talking at the same time. A child had poked her in the eye with a stick they said, I must have looked horrified "When she was a few months old" they added. "What child" I asked wondering how a child could be so cruel. 'Not mine" the mother said quickly which made me think that perhaps it was. I looked at their daughter who was now peeping at me from behind her father's legs wondering if she looked evil enough to have done such a thing. She had her mother's impish face which made her look a little spiteful but I couldn't hold that against her. And aside from being a clone of her mother, she was just a normal shy little girl. I think they assumed due to the eye that I wasn't going to take the pug, the last person had backed out they said. I had no intention of leaving there without my Sarah but they didn't know that so quickly dropped the price by $200 dollars. There were many overdue bills covering the front of the fridge and I felt really sorry for this young couple but we weren't in a great financial position ourselves and I'd seen enough pug eyes in my time to know that Sarah's eye would need seeing to sooner rather than later so David paid them the money and me and the first black pug I had ever owned walked down the planks and got into the car together.

The lady didn't show any emotion when we left, no tears, no last hugs, no prying her Tegan, my Sarah, from my arms, no feelings at all really. I think she was past it, she had more problems to deal with and I think that Sarah was just one less thing she had to worry about now. Before we left she thrust a pair of show ribbons into my hand. "She's won ribbons" I asked. "Yes before the accident" "Before the eye accident" I repeated looking at Sarah and wondering if such a small flaw could make a difference in the show ring, it may have done, to be completely honest I didn't know anything at all about showing dogs, I don't have anything against it, it's just that such things have never interested me in the slightest. Some people get a kick out of being able to say their dog is a show winner. But I've never been impressed by that, to me a dog is no better because it's won ribbons and no lesser because it has no trophies to show. It's still the same dog on the inside isn't it, and in my eyes that's all that counts.

Cross breed or pure, show champion or not, they still have the same mind, same heart, same soul, and that's what is truly important, well it is to me anyway. And every grey faced, blind, deaf, wobbly legged old soul that has shuffled through my door has always been a little champion in my eyes. And far, far braver then a dog who's been lucky enough to be loved and pampered all their lives, the little old champions I take in are the ones who deserve ribbons, trophies and medals. They are the ones who've had their tiny hearts broken and carried on regardless, they are the ones who more often than not have suffered years of neglect and become sick, they are the survivors, the little unsung heroes. But no trophies are ever awarded to dogs such as these, and I think they should be because they've earned them. I guess that's why show ribbons don't impress me all that much. I said thank you for Sarah's ribbons, folded them over a few times and shoved them in my pocket.

The ride home was slow bumper-to-bumper traffic. A football match had just finished and the cars that surrounded us showed either miserable or deliriously happy faces depending on what colour scarf they wore. David grumbled about the hold up, if we'd left half an hour earlier we wouldn't be sitting still like this. I on the other hand didn't care how long it took to get home. I had my black pug, I was happy, I used the time to get to know Sarah. Being all black her face looked kind of funny to me, the wrinkles the folds everything looks slightly different when it's on a black pug. I stroked her head and talked to her, her fur was like velvet. I wanted to reassure her that she was going to be alright. I had no idea what was going through that little mind of hers, she was in a car with strangers and although her old family may not have been missing her she probably didn't share the same feelings. Her mind was more than likely going over what had just happened, why she'd left with us and not stayed with them, she was probably trying to process what had taken place. I just wanted her to know she was loved and that everything was going to be ok.

Sarah gazed out the window taking in every sight and her ears pricked up at every new sound, her eyes darted about all over the place, at me, at David, at the people in the cars next to us. If a horn honked, and believe me footy fans honk their horns a lot, Sarah pushed her face up against the window to see what was going on. David complained that she was snoting on his nice clean car and messing up the windows, I said "Get used to it you have a pug in your life now". He compared her to a sea iguana, said he couldn't believe how much of a spray was coming out of such a small thing, "Is she ever going to stop" he asked looking concerned-more for his car then for our pug "No" I said and kissed Sarah's head. In all fairness I guess I should have warned him about things like this, and if I'd thought about it I probably would have, non pug people have no idea that such things are all part of life with a pug.

Half way home Sarah fell asleep in my arms and I studied her more closely. Her eyes disappeared into the folds of her face as she snored away happily, her whiskers twitched, she was in a deeper sleep now. David couldn't believe the noise she was making. "Don't you ever complain about my snoring again" he said then his eyes went back to concentrating on the road. The volume didn't seem to match the size of the dog in his eyes, he looked stunned. Even I had to admit she was loud, louder than most pugs but there was no way I was going to admit that to

David. I kept it to myself, mine and Sarah's little secret, but she was probably one of the loudest snorers we've ever had in all our years with pugs. Horton came pretty close to her though but we would not find that out for quite a few years yet, both Horton and Sarah sounded like scrap metal being put through a woodchipper. Sarah's paws began jerking around and I wondered what she was dreaming about. Whatever it was I hoped it was happy. If she had fallen asleep in a car with two strangers she must have felt she was safe. She must have been able to feel my love and although David wasn't fully on board yet she must have sensed he was a nice guy. As we pulled into our driveway Sarah woke up and licked the side of my face. The Danes barked excitedly from the back garden and ran from one side of the house to the other trying to see what we'd brought home. I put Sarah down on the grass in the front garden so she could have a sniff. The Danes where watching her every move but Sarah didn't notice, there was too much else to see, she had a quick wee then we took her inside the house and showed her every room. Every nook and every cranny was explored with a wiggling tail, then it was back to the kitchen, pugs I have found always seem to remember exactly where the kitchen is situated in any house they go in. It doesn't even have to be their own house. When we go visiting my pugs are always quick to discover where the kitchen is, and they remember it even if it's been months since we were last there. People think that pugs aren't smart but I think it's more that they remember only what they want to, only what's most important to them.

Sarah did her backwards forwards shuffling dancing thing until we followed her into the kitchen. I didn't know when she'd last been fed so we gave her a small meal. She gobbled that up quickly and looked around for more. The thing I love about pugs is that they'll always eat on the first day of arrival, other breeds I've owned have been put off their food for a day or so on entering a new home but I'm yet to have a pug do that. After Sarah ate she seemed to settle down and followed me around while I cooked tea and folded the washing.

We thought it best to introduce Sarah and the Danes slowly, even though the Danes were getting on in years they were still big and boisterous and may have been intimidating to a toy breed. We were also very aware of giving the Danes plenty of attention so there was no need for jealousy, a lot of problems that occur with new family members is because the original kids feel left out or worse still, that you no longer love them. If you do it right from day one you find you have very few problems with jealousy, everybody feels loved, and the bonding time can be a joyous one for all of you. We were very protective of Sarah though, being so small, we never left her alone with the Danes when we were not at home to supervise. She simply wouldn't have been able to protect herself against them if for some reason they turned on her. Sarah after all was barely the size of a great Danes head and there were two of them and only one of her, she needed us looking out for her. One thing we have never done is leave dogs of different sizes alone together. It's just something I've never felt right doing. I feel accidents can only happen if you let them and you are responsible. You can't blame dogs for doing something that is natural for them, they see things differently to how we see things and we need to always remember that, it's up to us to be sensible and do the right thing. Dogs do behave differently when they are on their own together and that's just a simple fact. When you, the pack leader, are no long there being in control, the dynamics shift, the rules change and things can and do happen.

I put a bit of thought into how we would first introduce Sarah to the Danes. We took Kronos and Neelix for a long walk and brought them home exhausted with all their energy spent. So when they came into the lounge all they wanted to do was lay down. Both Danes were used to coming into the house and when inside they had been taught to have their best manners on. You can't have dogs that size running amuck, they can do a lot of damage, things will get broken. Ok in the early training days we did have the occasional ornament fly through the air, smash into the wall and die due to a fast wagging tail but that was accidental, you can't get mad at a dog for that, you just either glue it back together or sweep it onto a dustpan and move on. It's one of those things that happen when living with a giant breed. And great Danes are a magnificent regal breed of a dog with fantastic personalities you can't get annoyed at them for just being who they were born to be. I loved my Danes and I loved my pug I wanted to introduce them as quickly as possible so we could all begin being a family together. Some of my happiest times were watching the Danes sprawled out in front of the heater while David and I watched TV, I'd study the size of their paws, watch the rise and fall of their huge chests, they were so beautiful. And you'd say their name in conversation, we weren't even talking to them we were talking about them, but their ears pricked up anyway. They'd hear their name said and thud, thud, thud would go their lovely long tails. And we'd stop talking about them and go back to watching tv and their tails stayed flat to the floor. It was like they knew we hadn't called them, because if we did they were on their feet in no time coming over and laying their great big heads in your lap and looking up at you with those wonderfully soulful eyes, but they knew when we were talking about them and that seemed to make them happy.

With the Danes calm and contented after their long walk it was time to bring Sarah into the room. David stayed in the lounge with the Danes and I walked Sarah down the hall. Both Danes lay flat out with their heads facing the hallway. Sarah got to the end of the hall and stopped suddenly, we'd left the collars on the Danes to give us something to hold onto in case we needed to intervene. Sarah gave one little growly woof and the Danes heads both shot up at precisely the same time and thud, thud, thud, thud. Both tails began beating fast against the carpeted floor. Sarah started doing her little dance, two steps into the lounge then three steps back down the hall, this went one for a little while with both Danes sitting up watching her with great curiosity. Kronos tilted her head to one side as if trying to work out what this funny little creature in front of her was doing. Neelix stood up and slowly came closer, then Kronos joined him, everything was still, David and I stood close ready to pounce should one of them try to put Sarah in their mouth. Then there was what seemed like a hundred hours of sniffing, in reality it was no more than a few moments but when you are waiting to see what everyone thinks of each other it seemed like an eternity. After everybody was well sniffed the Danes went back and lay down ready to have a sleep. Sarah followed but instead of going to sleep she jumped all over them, pulled on their ears, jumped on their heads and ran along their huge bodies. And the Danes being so wonderfully natured let her.

Once she'd worn herself out she settled down to sleep in amongst their outstretched paws. And that was basically the way it was for the rest of their lives together. My family had grown but the harmony had stayed intact.

For the first few weeks Sarah stayed at home when I took the Danes for their long walk to the river. She hadn't been exercised at all, somewhere in the conversation her previous owners had told me that she would ride on the bottom of the little girls pram because she didn't like walking, I figured I'd be able to change that but I had to be mindful of her history and start building her strength up slowly. After walking the Danes I'd take Sarah for a walk round the block and let her stop and have a little sniff at anything she wanted to sniff at. People tend to stop and talk to you when you are walking a pug and Sarah was in her element with all the attention she was getting, it took over an hour to give her a half hour walk because she'd be doing her little shuffling dance for everyone we met. After a few weeks I was getting a little bit over it, especially when I had a lot to do that day, but Sarah wasn't, so I just let her dance, not only was she entertaining herself but all the old ladies in the street as well. It was nice seeing the amount of joy they gave to one another. Our walk took us by an old folks home and it was as if they were waiting for us to come along and would start walking towards the gate as soon as we were in sight. And I used to think that no, they couldn't possibly be sitting there on that bench just waiting to see us. But over the years I have thought about it and I believe they were. When Mum was in the nursing home she would tell me about the goings on in that place and how some of the residents didn't get any visitors. I think the ladies waiting to see Sarah and watch her dance must have been those that had nothing else to brighten their day. If I'd realised that back then I would have made more of an effort with them, would have stayed longer, talked more, maybe even had them over for dinner. Gotten to know them a whole lot better than I did, but I was younger then and you just don't think about such things, it's only when you've lived a bit yourself that you come to realise, come to see things differently. But I had a mother and a grandmother and I visited them a lot and if they were in a nursing home I would have visited them even more. I just assumed this is what would have been happening here with these ladies. I just thought they were perhaps waiting for a coach to take them on an outing or something like that, or even waiting for their families. It hurts my heart thinking back over it all now, thinking about them being so lonely because their families didn't come. I never even found out their names, they didn't know my name either, everybody knew Sarah's name though because she was the center of attention. She was what everybody was talking about. If I had found out their names I would have honoured them by naming some pugs after them. I think that would have been a nice thing to do, I love old lady names, I think they suit little granny pugs perfectly.

After about a month I began walking the three dogs together, and again I feel bad now because I no longer took Sarah by the home and those ladies would have been waiting to see her. But like I said I was young and had no idea that that was the case. My mind was on walking my little dog family together. And the Danes being so big needed more than an around the block walk. And I also wanted to give Sarah a better longer walk with more interesting things to sniff. It was lovely when we got down to the river and everyone was off their leads. Sarah never left my side, we'd walk along the top of the embankment together while the Danes ran up, down, across and sideways zigzagging all over the place. There is something quite beautiful about the sight of a large breed running flat out like that, and my Danes due to their size resembled race horses. Kronos and Neelix crisscrossed and played, chased one another around, and even other dogs of similar size got in on the act until their owners called them away because it was time to go home. Occasionally they'd come back to me for a pat before running off again, every time they'd come back Sarah chased after them with her little legs going as fast as they could but the distance between them multiplied in seconds and she'd trot back to me exhausted. I enjoyed watching all my dogs at play, the difference in the two breeds was never more apparent than when we were out walking. We'd spend hours walking by the river, looking over to the other side at the huge beautiful houses, that's where the money people lived and their wealth was reflected in their dwellings. Neat perfect rows of big beautiful double storied homes sitting along the water's edge. Grand designed homes so well thought out they looked like nature had created them to complement the water. I was on the poorer side but I was happy, I had my dogs and a neat little red brick home that I loved. It was the first home David and I bought after we got married. We moved in on our first wedding anniversary, it was a small home, a cheap home, a home that needed much improvement, but I felt contented living there, it was special to me. We'd looked at a lot of units before finding this house, units and flats were the only things we could afford but we had an English Mastiff then and those places were no good for Tessa, she needed somewhere with a garden, something big enough for her to stretch her legs. When I spotted this little red bricked house my heart skipped a beat, it was sort of in our price range, but you never know how things are going to go at auction. I thought it was the most beautiful little home, fell in love with it before we'd even seen the inside and as I walked around the place my heart felt more and more at home there. And we were very lucky because we were the only people interested in buying come auction day, the rest of the people there were just nosy neighbours curious to see how much it was going to sell for, they went away disappointed when it got passed in. But we drove off happy and went straight to the bank to see if they'd lend us the money. It was a bit of a wait before we found out if we'd been approved or not, they said we wouldn't find out until early in the New Year. But the bank manager took pity on us, he rang Christmas Eve to tell us our loan had been approved. It made that Christmas a very special one for us because it was our first one as a married couple and soon to be home owners as well. Sadly Tessa died the first year we were living there, and then we adopted the Danes.

After our daily walk we'd all go back home and the dogs would settle inside or outside depending on the day, I'd leave the back door open and if the sun was out Sarah would go and lay on the pavers with the Danes, I always kept my eye on her and listened for any disturbances. You can't one hundred percent know what is going on in a dogs mind, in the whole time we had Sarah and the Danes she was never left alone with them unsupervised, not even once. If we went out and for some reason couldn't take Sarah with us she was left inside the house with a pile of toys. I never left her in the back garden with the other two dogs. When we got home the entire family was reunited again.

The Danes had been in other homes before coming to us and you never know what has gone on in their previous lives. I firmly believe you should never leave large and small dogs alone together no matter how much you trust them and no matter how long they have been living together. You have to remember dogs are a pack animal, they settle things differently to how we do. As much as we love our dogs and I love my dogs with every ounce of my being but for the sake of what can happen in your absence it just isn't worth the risk. It wouldn't have been the Danes fault if the worst case scenario happened it would have been mine for making an unwise decision and I would have had to live with that on my conscience for the rest of my life. And how would it have been for poor Sarah, what a horrible way to die. Even if the Danes and Sarah had been bought as 12 week old pups and grown up together I still wouldn't leave them alone while I'm away. Even today I hear about small dogs being killed in their own backyard while left with larger breeds and it pains me so much because you just wonder why anybody would do it. The only dog I'd leave with a pug is a pug, or another flat faced breed, never with another dog that has the long snout, wide jaw advantage. And really it's not just attacks you have to worry about, it could simply be that they were playing and accidently hurt the smaller dog in the pack, vet bills are expensive and they can be avoided if thought is given and care is taken. And it's not even the vet bills really, nobody likes to see their dog in pain. If the Danes were playing roughly together and Sarah had tried to join in, she could have ended up getting her eye knocked or something like that and pug eyes are very important, they need special looking after. It doesn't take much for them to get injured.

Even today here at the farm I will separate some of my pugs when I go out, you get to know your dogs and who is going to sleep the entire time you are away and who is going to play with a few toys or go and bark by the window until you return. I don't leave them a lot but when I have to go out I want my time away to be a pleasant time for the pugs. It makes it nice for them and nice for me. I can run my errands with peace of mind. Most of my pugs are old and a lot of them are exactly the same age but just because they've lived the same number of years doesn't mean they are equal. The needier ones need protecting from their more agile siblings so some go into another part of the house. I can't have a seven or eight year old knocking one of the real oldies flying when playing or running around. It takes no more than a feather to send Ruby off her feet and she deserves to be left in peace. She doesn't need them to be jumping on her head while sleeping near the window if they spot something outside and start barking at it. That goes for the blind ones too, they can have a sleep on a soft bed in another part of the house with their quieter siblings. You have to get to know your dogs and know who will be happiest being left with who, it just makes for a happier life for all of them.

Well life with Sarah was a wonderful thing and that shot of happiness I was after, well I got it a hundred fold, it had been a long time between pugs and I didn't realize how much I'd missed them. I was the happiest I'd been in a long time, things didn't suddenly change because I had a pug in my life, it was more that I changed because I had a pug in my life. I think if you can look at things from a happier place it makes a whole lot of difference and that is what Sarah did for me. She was my little friend and I loved sharing my days with her, I adored her antics and how she saw the world. I couldn't believe how worried I had been at the start that Sarah may fear the Danes because she feared nothing and no one, she was completely fearless of every situation, courageous in everything. I used to joke that she was a pit-bull personality in a pug's body. She was completely in love with the Danes, didn't have a favourite she loved both of them, at times I think a little bit too much. She was a rough little bugger, jumping all over the top of them, pulling on their ears, pawing at their noses to initiate play. And the Danes were true to their outstanding natures, they didn't murder my pug puppy even though at times I think they may have desperately wanted to. Instead they put up with everything she dished out and tolerated her beautifully. To them I think Sarah was nothing more than this annoying little fly that kept coming buzzing around their heads from time to time then go off and come back again a little while later.

Kronos would lay facing the entrance of the hall, every so often she'd open her eyes and look around for Sarah and when she'd hear her coming Kronos's large heavy tail would thump the floor. I didn't even have to look up the hall I always knew when Sarah was about to enter the room because Kronos's tail would tell me. Then the two of them would play together, well Sarah would play and Kronos would play dead. She'd let Sarah run round and round circling her then up the hall and come zooming back again and start circling her again, occasionally she'd stop and start tugging on her tail or ears then she'd be shooting off up the hall again, or out the back door, do a lap of the garden then in the house again, in and out, out and in until she got tired, then the two of them would sleep soundly side by side. Looking back I miss those times, that image of the large and small breed in heavy slumber was a lovely one to see. All breeds of dogs are remarkable. I think if you've got a dog in your life regardless of its breed you are a very fortunate person.

I wasn't sure if Sarah would want to sleep with the Danes or would prefer a nice smaller bed of her own. The first week she was here I went out and bought her a lovely little plush pink girly bed. I had visions in my head of a four poster canopy bed but my local pet shop didn't cater to the elite. And I didn't think they had anything suitable for me at all then just as I was about to walk out the door I spotted a little flash of pastel pink peeping out from beneath a large stack of plain brown and navy coloured beds so dived down and dragged it out. Last year's stock was what the lady shouted over to me as she shovelled chicken feed out of a large sack and into smaller bags. "The only one we have left" she added coming closer. The thing is I didn't believe her, I mean she was probably telling the truth but when sales assistants say things like that to me in the back of my mind there is always a little teeny tiny untrusting voice that says "Sales are short today, there's plenty of those out the back, a stockroom full of them actually and as soon as your car pulls out of the parking lot she'll dash out, grab one and have it positioned right by the door with its little pink edge peeping out for when the next sucker comes along" I mean I don't know why I do this because I worked in retail for a good many years and never lied to a customer once. And besides she wasn't a used car sales man sitting in the corner of a dodgy yard or anything, she was just a plain middle aged woman in a boring half buttoned up beige cardigan, about as harmless as one could get really.

Anyway I put the voice out of my mind and bought the bed regardless because it was both pink and suitable. It was round and I thought Sarah would hop in and be able to rest her little chin on the edges. Pugs like having chin rests, I remembered that from last time, it makes for a more comfortable sleep. When I got home Sarah took to the bed pretty fast and gave it a good sniffing over, she didn't sleep in it all the time but it did give her choices. Sometimes Sarah slept with the Danes, Kronos mainly, she'd go and lay in-between her large outstretch paws, then move to her own bed so she could rest her head better and fall fast asleep in there. Then one day the Danes decided it would be fun to drag the little plush pink girly bed around the lounge room with Sarah still in it. There was so much excitement in the air when they were doing it too, at first I thought they were annoying Sarah. It wasn't that they were dragging her fast, more just clamping down and taking a few steps backwards and another few after that and a few after that. But I thought they were disturbing her sleep and could have been upsetting their little sister. But after observing them for a while I realised that Sarah was in fact absolutely loving the ride. I know this because when they stopped dragging her round she'd bounce out of the bed paw at their heads then jump back in again and bark for them to come and pull her along the floor once more. And she'd sit there totally enjoying the game, like a little princess on a float in a parade, only there were no other floats in this parade, just Sarah so she was getting all the attention and loving it. She seemed to be enjoying it more than the Danes were because after a while they would grow tired and stop. Well try and stop anyway but Sarah wasn't for letting them, she'd once more flip out of the bed, paw at their heads again then jump back in and wait to be transported, they'd drag her round the lounge room and up and down the hall. And when one got bored the other one took over and this went on for a couple of months until the little plush pink girly bed fell apart.

The more time I spent with Sarah the more her personality grew she understood so many words you just had to say something to her and she got it right away. I thought she was one of the smartest pugs I had ever come across in my life and I stand by that to this day, just so incredibly clever. Once home I was like a mother with a new baby although David at times didn't quite know how to react to this tiny little thing. If Sarah picked up on how David was feeling she wasn't fazed at all, in fact the first word she learnt was Dad. I'd say it and she'd instantly look over at David like her little mind was saying "Yeah that's right, I know who you are". I'd tell her to go get Dad when it was time for tea and she'd race down the hall do a sharp turn into the study and a few moments later come back with David not far behind. He thought she'd come to tell him she needed to go outside for a wee but I'd say no dinner is ready and I told her to go get you.

I think David was pretty impressed with how great this small breed was. He'd laugh at her silly way of doing things, she behaved differently to the Danes and I think he liked having something different to watch. He'd walk in the door of a night and ask what she'd gotten up to that day and she'd always done something worth mentioning. I think he liked the fact that she wasn't a timid shaking little thing, maybe that's what he had expected from a toy breed but pugs aren't like that at all and Sarah was especially fearless regardless of her size and he seemed impressed with that. For Sarah's part she just adored David, she'd go nuts when she heard his car come up the drive. She'd run to meet him at the door and with the Danes being so much taller and therefore so much closer to David's hand got patted first. So Sarah figured out that if she jumped up on the couch she'd be just as close to David as they were. David still patted the Danes first though, made a huge fuss of them because it was only fair, they'd been in the house longer than the pug had. We were at all time conscious of not letting the Danes feel left out.

Sarah would sand on the couch trembling with excitement waiting for David to finally acknowledge she was there, when he did at last come over to see her Sarah would jump off the couch into his arms. She would smother David with kisses and gasp for air then start kissing again, she was in love with him. She would almost stop breathing, the thrill of having him home again after such a long day was almost too much for her to bear. He had a nightly routine of chasing her round the house. Once the Danes had gone back to lay down David would put Sarah on the floor and she'd shoot up the hall as fast as she could go. Most of the time she'd be running while looking over her shoulder just to make sure he was coming after her. If he happened to start talking to me and didn't go up the hall right away she'd come flying back into the room at full speed to see what was taking him so long. She'd run from room to room doing her puppy yelp and as long as she wanted to run David would chase her. Sarah loved this nightly game. When she'd had enough she would run under the kitchen table and sit there panting until her energy returned. She thought David couldn't get her if she hid under there so we let her think that. She was a pug after all, she needed to have somewhere she could go to calm down a bit, she loved the game but got very excitable and I liked her to sit still until her breathing returned to normal. When she got her second wind she'd shoot out from under the table and fly up the hall again, she was always up for another round even if David wasn't.

I had explained to David about pugs and their eyes and with Sarah already having the mark on one eye I told him we had to be even more careful with her. On the weekend when David was home the whole family got to have a walk together. Well as together as we could get, we always started off together but the Danes wanted to make it to the river as fast as they could and Sarah wanted to stop and sniff everything. One day I was up ahead with the Danes and we were getting close to the area where I'd let them off their leads. I glanced around to see how far David and Sarah were behind us knowing that once the Danes were free there was no stopping them, they'd run full length until it was time for their leads to be put back on again. When I looked back I saw that David was carrying Sarah. Well that sight worried me so I dragged the Danes back with me to see what was wrong. The Danes weren't impressed with having gotten so close to being off the lead only to be turned round again, I pulled one way and they both pulled the other, I think they thought I was going to take them all the way back home without having had their full gallop. It was taking forever battling with them and I wanted to see if Sarah was alright, so I checked the river made sure nobody was down there with little dogs then set the two free. The Danes were great with small dogs but the owners of small dogs don't know that, they can get pretty worried when they see two huge dogs running their way at full speed. I watched the Danes galloping away together then turned my attention behind me.

I raced towards David and Sarah frantically trying to read my husband's face. If something was wrong with my pug it would be written all over his face, he knew how much she meant to me. Neither one of us has ever been very good at hiding things from each other, no poker faces in our house. I concentrated on Sarah trying to see if one of her legs was hurt. But I couldn't tell, with her being in David's arms it was hard for me to see her properly. She was giving kisses though so she must have been alright, or if she was hurt it mustn't have been too badly, then again pugs, well all dogs really, are such happy little creatures they can be in pain and still keep up a happy disposition. Me, I'm not like that at all, wish I was but I'm not. And pugs are brave too, that's what David had said he liked about them just the other night, so had my poor little pug hurt herself and was just being courageous because she didn't know what else to be. I couldn't reach them fast enough. David looked up, saw me coming and waved, then put Sarah on the ground so she could run to meet me. My eyes were scanning her as she ran trying to see if something was out of place, when she reached me I grabbed her up and checked all over to see if there was anything wrong. David caught up to us looked at me strangely and asked what I was doing. "What am I doing?" I said my voice a little bit higher and more screechy then it normally is due to being panicked. "What are you doing carrying her? I was still searching Sarah's body as I spoke. He said he didn't want her to get a stone in her eye so he carried her over the gravel part of the road. With that I stopped searching. I looked at David and I thought oh my goodness you are such a goner, it may have taken a few months but you are a goner alright, this little black pug has wound her way into your heart. I loved the fact that he was taking good care of her. I had worried that he may never take to the pug breed, may never see in them what I saw in them, may be a big dog man for the rest of his life. I didn't say anything to him, but inside I was thrilled to bits. After his initial reluctance to having a small dog it was nice for him have a change of heart.

Sarah was with us for two and a half years before that little spot on her eye ulcerated. We'd always taken precautions with it, taken good care of her and protected her eyes, but you just knew that one day something was going to go wrong with that eye. It was a feeling I had when we'd first bought her and that feeling had never completely gone away so I was kind of expecting it. Sarah had been feeling out of sorts for a few days, kept asking to be picked up and carried around, wasn't as interested in the walks, that sort of thing. I couldn't see anything physically wrong with her, just knew from the behaviour something wasn't right, you can't really take them to the vets until you know what you are going for so I kept an eye on Sarah and waited until I had something I could tell the vet. Two days later I woke up and noticed Sarah's eye was slightly opaque, we had her to the vet within the hour and came home with a fist full or drops and medication. In a week there was little improvement and she was in pain, eyes are such a sensitive area, for us and our pugs. Our local vet said he had done all he could do other than to remove Sarah's eye. It was time to see the specialist in the hope that the eye could be saved. I have always been of the opinion that if you can save a pugs eye you save the eye, regardless of the cost. Removal would have cost $150.00 to save the eye was $2500.00. We decided to try and save the eye. Sarah was only a young dog, three years old at the time, a neighbour thought I was stupid to pay all that money for a dog and I said to him if your daughter had the same problem would you be removing her eye or trying to save it. He didn't answer, he didn't have to, the look on his face said it all. Just because Sarah had been born a dog didn't mean she was less important than his Bethany was. She deserved a chance at life with vision in both eyes. So a graft was put on the eye, they took a little bit of the white of her eye and grafted it up and across to where the ulceration was to allow blood to flow and heal the eye, and it worked, she had vision. And so we began on the long slow journey towards recovery. I'd never gone through this type of surgery before so I didn't know what was involved. The surgery was complicated and the healing time consuming, but boy did they do a fantastic job on that eye. It looked very much like a normal pugs eye, you had to get up pretty close to see that it wasn't. Sarah would be sitting by my side looking up at me as I spoke to her and I used that time to get a good look at the eye. Such skill went into that graft. You know how tiny the instruments would have been that were used during that surgery and you'd just marvel at it all. I was glad we had gone to this particular surgeon because she really knew what she was doing.

But it took a real lot out of Sarah that operation, all that time with the Elizabethan collar on, the weeks and weeks of drops and medication, the follow up visits. If Sarah had been older, say over the age of ten, I don't think I would have put her though it, fixing that eye wasn't an easy thing to do and I don't feel that Sarah if given a choice would have wanted to go through it. She was never the same pug after that, it had an effect on her, changed her personality somewhat. I've known other pugs who've had the same surgery and were fine, I guess it's just an individual thing, some people don't like hospitals, don't like operations and some dogs are the same. Looking back both David and I feel we did the wrong thing by Sarah, we did the right thing by the eye but the wrong thing by the dog. But of course we had no way of knowing it would affect her the way it did, if we had known we would have acted differently. I honestly think Sarah would rather have gone through life with only one eye then to go through all that she did. We just put all our attention on that eye, wanted to save it because she was so young and because what if we'd taken the eye out and a few years later something had gone wrong with her good eye. She would have been five years old and completely blind. I know there are many blind dogs out there that live wonderful lives, I know it because I've got some of them living here at Grace Farm with me now and they are very happy little beings. The most blind pugs I've lived with at the one time is seven, and believe me those seven blind babies of mine were the happiest most contented little souls you could ever meet. But I didn't have that knowledge back then. I'd never shared my life with a blind dog before. We had a chance at getting vision back in that eye so we took it because that's what you have to do. Eyes are very important, so you do everything in your power to save not only the eye itself but also the vision in it. You try at all costs to save an eye because you just don't know what's round the corner. And it's exactly what we would still do now and in fact are doing now if one of our pugs has an ulcerated eye, we will again try and fix it, we will always,

always try and save an eye and get vision back in the eye rather than remove it. Removal is always the last option, and sometimes it's your only option and so you'll take that too because you wouldn't ever leave a dog with pain in his or her eye, that's cruelty, that's not how good parents behave. I think Sarah was just a one in a million case, I've never had a pug get so bothered by an operation before and over the years we have gone through many, many, many procedures and not one of those pugs had the same reaction Sarah did.

Sarah had vision in that eye for almost all of her life. The operation served her eye well. Over the years the graft turned blue with age, but she could still see a little bit with it. Not full vison but a little bit of vision and we were grateful for that. I suppose we could have gone back and had it looked at again when she hit double figures but we decided not to. Not after the way she'd reacted to the first operation, we couldn't do that to her, well not unless we had to due to her being in pain. But there was no pain with the eye at all just discolouration and some loss of vision. Her other eye was in good order so she managed just fine. And the good thing was she never needed an operation of any kind after the one she had on her eye and we were really glad about that. Sarah remained trouble free, just a healthy happy little girl who bobbed around the farm with that blue eye of hers not having a care in the world about what she looked like.

Sarah went on to live for 13 and a half years, she stood beside us when we put the two Great Danes into the ground. She moved with us from the little red brick house to our home by the lake and she was with us when we finally made the move to our much longed for farm. In fact she sat on David's knee while we signed on the dotted line, the transaction wasn't done in an estate agents office but right here in our lounge room while sitting around Johns old worn kitchen table. And I liked the informality of it all, signing for our farm while sitting in our soon to be farm house with all four pugs by our side made perfect sense to me and I was glad the whole family could be together while such a momentous event was taking place. It seemed right, like that's how it should be, if we had been buying a house in suburbia the pugs would not have been allowed into the agents office and therefore not able to be part of the event. But there were no formalities on that day Sarah was on David's knee, Grace was on mine and Harper and Ruby were busily sniffing underneath the kitchen table for muffin crumbs. And once the paperwork had been sorted we all went for a walk around the paddocks and admired the views. Well mine and David's eyes were up and marvelling but the pugs were all glancing down sniffing having no idea that this would soon be the place we called home.

Sarah watched old pugs come into our life and made sure she was always top dog, pack leader over all of them and regardless of their size and weight not one of them dared challenge her for the title. She kept pugs twice as big as she was in line with nothing more than a stern stare, never a growl, that wasn't needed, a stare from Sarah was enough. All packs need a top dog and Sarah was a fearless leader. I guess keeping a pile of old pugs in line was nothing to her, she'd grown up with two great Danes after all, the old pugs were easy. And I think she got a kick out of bossing them around, really liked telling everyone what to and what not to do. And she did all that with a whole lot of stomping and huffing and puffing and of course that long slow stare. She'd stomp about the place making sure her siblings were behaving themselves. She'd wake up and stomp out the back door and go down the ramp with a line of elderly pugs following her. If she rose up from her bed, most of them rose up too. They figured if Sarah was going out they may as well follow her because she always seemed to know what she was doing. I think it had a lot to do with that confident walk she had. Only a little pug but a huge amount of self-confidence dwelled within her body and the others all picked up on that. A new larger sibling would enter the house and Sarah was barely eye level with them, yet it made no difference, within a week they too were following her wherever she went. Nobody copied her walk though, they all kept their own, which was a bit of a shame really because I think it would have been pretty funny seeing a pile of old pugs in a line stomping out the back door.

Sarah walked differently on the farm to how she did when we lived in suburbia. No lack of confidence or anything like that, but she just took off on her own when we got here, seemed to settle into the place quite well which made me think that perhaps her breeder may have lived on a large property and she was used to the open spaces. When I used to walk Sarah and the Danes by the river, once her two big siblings were off and running I would take Sarah's lead off as well and she would just fall in behind me and off we'd go. I wasn't aware of how she was walking because I don't have eyes in the back of my head but one day an old man stopped me and asked if I'd trained Sarah to walk that way. I said I wasn't sure what he meant. Then he explained that Sarah was

swapping from one of my legs to the other every time I took a
step. He said it was fascinating watching her continually jumping
from one of my legs to the other. Sort of jumping from side to side
as I walked, he said he'd never seen a dog doing that before. He
also said he'd seen us out and about many times and just couldn't
hold off asking any longer. I told him that I'd not trained her to do
it, that it was all her. And to be honest I wouldn't have even begun
to know how to train a dog to do such a thing. It was just part of
Sarah's uniqueness I guess. I mentioned it to David when he got
home from work and he said "Yeah she's been doing that for ages,
doing it almost from the moment she first came" and I said to him
"Then why didn't you tell me", he said he just assumed that's how
she walked and that she was doing the same thing with him when
he was up ahead. But she wasn't, she just trotted by his side,
slightly back but still by his side not completely behind him. The
leg swapping, well that seemed to be something she just did with
me for some reason. David said that she would hop from one of
my legs to the other only coming out from behind to run after the
Danes when they came back to check on us. And of course I'd
seen her chasing after the Danes but had no idea what she went
back to doing once she fell in behind me. Near our house there
was a group of about five shops and each had big glass windows,
and I really wanted to see what Sarah was doing so I slowed down
on the way home that day and sure enough there she was
zigzagging behind me. The Danes were always in front, their leads
pulled tight as they dragged me home and there behind me with
her little thin red lead hanging slack was Sarah jumping left then
right, left then right. I really wish we had captured it on film, but
we didn't have mobile phones back then or a video camera either.

So I had to be content with slowing down as we went by the five shops and seeing our reflection in the windowpanes and after it was brought to my attention what Sarah was doing I watched our reflections every single time we went by those shops. And was always disappointed if a group of people were standing around talking, getting in the way of my view.

To date my relationship with Sarah is the longest one I've ever had with a dog. Thirteen brilliant years we were together. I watched that black shinny fur of hers turn silver. It was her paws that started turning silver first and her face and tip of her tail followed a few years later. Sarah was always by my side. She made sure to always be the pug that was right next to me no matter how many pugs we had in the house at the time. She would be beside me looking up with one blue eye and one black one. Sarah was the only one of my pugs that wasn't a rescue but she really did save me, she brought me joy and gave me so much happiness at a time in my life when I desperately needed it. Sarah was a turning point, she changed my life around and every pug that has come after her is here because of the change Sarah made and she is always going to be special to me for that. All these elderly pugs and special needs pugs came into my life because Sarah set me back on track. I carried on along the path I was born to walk down at the exact time I was meant to walk down it. At that point in my life I could have very easily turned left or right and if I had done that, well I'm not sure what would have happened. I guess I would have eventually found my way back, but who knows how long that would have taken me. Sometimes finding your way back can be the hardest thing in the world to do and if it had taken me a while then we wouldn't be where we all are today. And I would have missed out on the pugs I have been sharing my life with. Oh I know there would have been a farm at some point, but it may not have been this one, and I definitely know there would have been elderly pugs, but they wouldn't have been the same ones. If one thing had changed everything would have changed. And if it had I may never have gotten the chance of loving and looking after Horton and that would have been a true tragedy. All the pugs I've been blessed with over the years wouldn't have been if one thing had happened differently. Any small change alters the course of your life. And I wouldn't have wanted that, I am happy with the way my life has gone so far, so very happy with all the pugs I've had the opportunity and pleasure of loving. I have a real lot to be grateful to Sarah for and I am. I am deeply grateful to Sarah for all she did for me. The joyfulness she brought me just spread and spread and got us all to the point we are today. These sheep and these elderly horses too are all here because Sarah entered my life when I needed her the most.

I have a painting hanging on the wall that makes me think of Sarah whenever I have time to dreamily look at it, which I do when one of the pugs isn't well and I'm sitting there with them on my knee afraid to move because I've just gotten them settled and I want them to rest and heal. So I sit there and look up at the painting and all sorts of memories come to mind. First I admire the scenery and when I'm done doing that all those other beautiful memories start flooding back. I was walking by a picture framing shop one day after work when I first saw this painting, just minding my own business when I looked left and saw this amazing picture in the window. The framing shop sold the odd print and I'd seen them hanging there from time to time, none of the others had taken my fancy but when I saw this one I stopped dead in my tracks, knew I had to have it, knew it had to be mine, so I marched inside the shop. The only thing I didn't love so much was the price but I think it was the frame that made it more expensive, and it was a picture framing shop after all so that's how they made their money. I asked if they did laybys and was so relieved when the lady said they did so I fished around in the bottom of my handbag gathering up all the loose coins so I could give them the percentage they wanted me to put down. I'd never spent that kind of money on a painting before but what it did to my heart when looking at it was worth it. And I had been working so many long hours of late that I decided I needed a treat. When I got home and told David what the painting cost he said "Why didn't you just buy yourself a bar of chocolate instead" and we both laughed. But when he finally saw the painting he knew why I had to have it. I loved both the picture and what it was called. Both struck a chord with me. The print was of three white cockatoos, stark white, and beautiful, deep yellow crests, one is sitting on an old broken fence, the other two on old rusted wagon wheels, in the background were yellowing fields and a sky that looks like rain may be is on its way, with the colour of the paddocks it must have been summer, hay season, the cockatoos were in the forefront of the print, pulling at some long stalks of green grass. I bought the print as a form of encouragement, as a sign that I was definitely going to be getting a farm one day. There were many, many years where I started losing hope of ever being able to make my dream come true because everything seemed to be taking so long, a lot longer than I wanted it to. I needed something that signified all was not lost, that I was going to make my dream come true no matter how long it took. And did the painting encourage me, yes it really did. I'd come home from working overtime and flop down on the couch, right opposite that picture and no matter how tired I was seeing that farm scene made me smile. It was a fairly large print, filled the spot above the heater quite nicely in my little red brick home. I remember how long it took me to pay it off. Longer than a regular layby should take but the owners of the shop let me take a bit longer because they knew how much that painting meant to me. I turned up every Wednesday afternoon without fail and when they saw me parking my old white tank out the front they'd reach down and grab the layby form from underneath the counter. All the other layby forms were nice and neat but mine had added bits of paper stapled to it because they'd run out of space on the original form. When I finally picked it up I think the owners of the shop were as happy as I was, I think it had been taking up space in their back room for far too long. For me bringing that painting home was such a special occasion, so special that I took Sarah along with me to join in the celebration. I was ecstatic and because I was ecstatic Sarah was too, only she didn't know why, she was just feeding off my emotions. She stayed in the car with her little face pressed up to the window while I raced into the shop, it was a really cold day and I wanted to get the print in the car before it started raining. But I struggled to get it in the back of the car, I told Sarah to hop in the front seat while I worked out what I was going to do and she stood on her hind legs with her face peeping over the front seat watching what I was doing. Hanging there in that shop window I hadn't realised just how big this painting was. I leant the seats back and balanced the print on an angle then drove home very carefully, the last thing I wanted to do after paying it off all those months was shatter the glass. The print is by the Australian bird artist Greg Postle and is called "The Waiting Game" and that was pretty much what I was doing at the time, waiting and working and saving for the farm. I'd promised Sarah a treat after we'd got the painting, I figured if I was getting a treat then Sarah should too. She knew the word treat and was looking at the painting balancing there on the back seat no doubt thinking to herself "I can't possibly eat that". So we dropped the print off at home and then went out again to get Sarah something special to eat. I could have just stopped somewhere on the way home but I was nervous somebody was going to rear end us and smash my much longed for print to pieces. Sarah was happy to be going out in the car again and even happier that the second trip yielded a treat.

Sarah, David and I, we've carted that print along with us to a few houses and it always brought me joy. As it got hung on the wall in the next house I'd be thinking to myself one day I'm going to be looking at that image for real, those cockatoos will one day be on my farm, ok I didn't know they'd be sitting in our apple tree screeching, eating all our apples and chucking half eaten apples down on our heads. If I'd known that back then I probably would have laughed. But when you are actually living the life for real and you see your little apple tree shaking like crazy and you know why it's not nearly as funny. I thought those cockatoos were so rude, one to eat all of something and not leave some for anybody else and two because you just don't chuck things down without looking when there are old blind pugs about. It used to annoy me that they were being so wasteful too, they wouldn't even wait for the apples to be fully ripe before tucking in and they wouldn't eat the whole thing either. I would have been more alright with it if they did, I didn't mind them coming to the farm and feeding, to be honest that kind of thing makes me happy. But they'd only eat half the apple then chuck it on the ground and move onto another one and do the exact same thing with that. Eating the entire thing before moving on would have been more alright with me. Even if they handed the apple round to their mates so they could all have a go. I used to see a few of them there on the top branches as me and the pugs were approaching and veer off to keep the pugs safe. I could tell by the way the tree was shaking how many of them were in there and they outnumbered us ten to one. I didn't want them upsetting or hurting my pugs so I lead them away. Imagine being blind and having a half eaten apple landing on your head, you wouldn't know what was going on, you'd think the sky was falling in. I didn't mind sharing my apples with those birds but the wastefulness of them was what got to me. Seeing all those half eaten apples scattered on the ground around the tree didn't seem right. I'd finish walking the pugs and take them back inside the house, grab a bucket and go gather all those apples up and feed them to the sheep and horses. The cockies would see me marching down the hill with a determined look on my face and start screeching even louder, maybe they thought they could scare me off. They are quite intelligent birds. And they are inquisitive too, some would move a few trees over and sit watching and screeching. Telling me off I guess, telling me to go away so they could fly back across and continue what they were doing. I think cockatoos really like the sound of their own voices, well they must do mustn't they because sometimes they just seem to screech and squawk for the sheer joy of it. Perhaps it entertains them. Didn't entertain me, it was ok for a while but then it'd start to wear a bit thin, especially when you are down on your hands and knees picking up their wastage. I bet a few of them would have been laughing at me too. Maybe that's what all the screeching was about, telling their mates to come fly on over and get a load of this idiot cleaning up our mess. But I'd get a big bucketful and go and feed the horses and sheep and when I went back inside the house my mood was lighter because you can't help but get joy from seeing green frothy juice streaming from your horses mouths. And they won't even finish the one they're eating before they'll be nuzzling at your arm for you to give them another and if you're too busy dishing them out to somebody else they'll just help themselves to the stash. I'd walk into their paddock and was as popular as an ice-cream van that'd just pulled up outside a house where a children's party was going on. I'd walk back into the house and the pugs would all start sniffing and licking at my clothing, they too like apples and they didn't mind licking the green frothy stains. And as usual Sarah would be shouldering the others out the way so she could get the most.

Sarah was my mum's favourite pug, they had a very special relationship. Sarah just adored my mum. And it wasn't just the treats she had in her handbag for Sarah either, ok they helped make Mum's visit even more exciting but I think Mum could have walked in the house with no treats at all and Sarah wouldn't have bothered. When Mum came for lunch Sarah wouldn't leave her alone, not even for a second, she even used to follow Mum into the toilet and Mum would be calling me to come get her out and I'd tell Mum not only was it a pug thing, a thing all pugs do with those they truly love, but an honour as well. When Sarah first came we bought her a pile of new toys, toys that were more suitable for a little pug's mouth. Of course there were plenty of toys in the house when Sarah arrived, but they were all for Great Danes and most of them where the same size as Sarah was. But she wasn't deterred, she'd drag them round the house regardless and looked so funny doing it, but she really did need some toys that were especially for her. We used to call these toys of Sarah's "Her luckies". It started off with me telling her how lucky she was whenever she got a new toy. David would walk in the house of an evening and present Sarah with a new toy he'd bought her during his lunch break and I'd be saying to her when she came over to show me "Oh you lucky, lucky little girl" In the end she thought that's what toys were actually called. I'd say go get your toy and she'd look up at me like I was speaking a different language, so I'd say "Where's your lucky" and she's shoot over to the toy box, fish one out and come dancing around my feet with it. Sarah would present her luckies to visitors too, like she was bringing them her most prized possessions. Sarah would go nuts when people came to the house and be dancing round the lounge room, like skipping almost and doing that in circles until all the excitement was out of her. More or less what she was doing with me the first time I met her, only we didn't have the same house plan her previous owners did so she had to make do with our little lounge room. And round and round and round she'd go, not letting anybody pat her until she'd calmed down. Then she'd go over and greet them properly and once that was done she'd dive into her toy box and start showing people her luckies. The first lucky that ever got shown to people was "Poo" a plastic brown dog with a big orange nose. "Poo" was Sarah's favourite lucky. We weren't very inventive with names back then, the dog was brown so David called it "Poo". I really liked that dog and so did Sarah, I don't know if it was the texture of the plastic or that the dog was in a laying down position and Sarah found him easy to carry around in her mouth. She'd bring "Poo" over to you but wouldn't let you take him off her, it was like she would give him to you but never right away, you always had to wait until she'd done a few laps of the lounge room with him in her mouth first. And the amount of laps she did depended on how excited she was that day, she'd come wiggling by your chair and you'd think she was about to drop "Poo" at your feet and be about to lean down and pick him up and thank her for him, but she'd trick you, see you shifting in your seat getting ready to pick him up and she'd shoot off again doing yet another lap of the lounge. She would never give him to you until she was ready, you could have been ready to receive him a hundred times but Sarah didn't care, dropping "Poo" at your feet was always done on her terms, as it should be really because he was her lucky after all. So "Poo" would come out and be shown to all the visitors and if David was around he would laugh and tell everybody the toys name, me I never really bothered telling anybody, but David thought it was hilarious, it's a boy thing I think. Anyway once they'd acknowledged "Poo" and whatever lucky came next and the attention was off Sarah and back on other things she'd jump down from the couch and go fish another toy out. You could tell what a person meant to her by how many of her luckies she'd bring over. She was really excited when Mum came, we had this little old floral two seater couch and Mum would sit on one side and Sarah on the other, me, I'd be on the other side of the lounge room on one of the kitchen chairs I'd dragged over. But it was nice because I got to see Mum and Sarah interact. By the end of the visit Mum would be completely covered in luckies and Sarah would be sitting there next to Mum looking on proudly at all the luckies piled high on Mum's knee.

Mum used to come down on the bus and we'd walk to the bus stop to meet her and as soon as that bus turned the corner and was in view, that was it, Sarah started screaming and she screamed even louder when the bus doors opened and Mum's face appeared. One day we were running late, Mum used to come for lunch once a week and Sarah seemed to know the day. Well perhaps she saw me making a special effort with lunch and figured out why. I mean you can't just have plain old sandwiches when your Mum's coming for lunch can you. I used to make sausage rolls some days and Sarah would help, help by eating a couple of balls of the sausage mixture before I added the onions. It was like she knew when I added the onions that was it, she wouldn't be allowed any, "For your own good" I'd say "Toxic for dogs" I'd tell her as she looked up at me. She used to bark when she smelt me cutting the onions up, especially when I'd forgotten to give her any of the meat. So she'd remind me and she'd get some then sleep on the floor by my feet while I carried on with what I was doing. But I couldn't throw the sausage meat packet away until Sarah had gotten every last bit of it. I'd be there squeezing hard trying to get every bit I could possibly get out, holding it like a tube of toothpaste and Sarah would be hanging on the end of the pack waiting for more to come out. She would hold it in her mouth, wouldn't let go until I held up my hand and said "Finished". One day I was way behind schedule and we didn't make it to the bus stop, we were walking out the front door as the bus went flying by our house. Well Sarah saw that bus and she went absolutely crazy. We had a little red brick wall in the first home we bought, bricks to match the house, but not enough to build a decent height wall, it was an embarrassment of a wall to be honest, a glorified speed hump really. Like it started out wanting to be a wall then suddenly just gave up. I always felt they were just using up the bricks that were left over from building the house and sometimes wondered why they bothered. Building a BBQ out the back would have been a better use for those bricks because what we had out front wasn't really what you could call a true wall, just a half wall really, only pug height. Well pug height if your pug was standing on its hind legs, which being nosy is exactly what Sarah did with a lot of her time. Well Sarah ran to the front wall and her little head was just high enough to peep over the top of it, from the other side looking in you could only see Sarah from the eyes up. But that was fine by Sarah, she could see what was going on out there in the world beyond our fence and when she saw that bus she must have known it was Mum's bus and was so incensed that we weren't there to meet it. The bus stop was at the end of our street and Mum could hear Sarah screaming as soon as she got off the bus and when Mum came through the gate Sarah flung herself at Mum and wasn't for leaving her side.

We had a little lemon tree in the back garden, it was the only tree we had on site, and it was only waist height but pretty all the same and boy did that little tree give us a lot of lemons. It used to almost be buckling under the weight. Mum loved that little lemon tree of ours. If the weather was nice we'd sometimes go and sit out there after lunch, take our cups of tea with us and sit there chatting away happily and Sarah always sat on Mum's side of the blanket looking up at her lovingly. She used to cry when Mum went home and I'd say "Don't worry Nanny will be back to see you next week" and sure enough a week later there was Mum's face again and Sarah once again went ballistic.

Sarah died in May 2011. She was the fourth pug we lost that year. Sarah is buried here at Grace Farm next to her little brother Horton. And to this day I still carry Sarah's "Poo" lucky around with me in my handbag everywhere I go. I was at the Doctors one day and dropped my bag on the floor as I was heading off to find a seat and all these toys from pugs passed came flying out and were scattered all over the floor. I was having a panic attack almost because of what they meant to me and the waiting room was full of children and I was scared some child would pounce on one and not want to give it back and well, those toys are precious. A pile of people in the surgery on seeing my reaction jumped up and started gathering up my things, about a dozen half used lipstick were in my handbag too, as well as pens, note pads, coins and keys and they all got gathered up and given back to me, my purse was handed to me first but I didn't care about that, they could have all my money I just wanted Sarah's lucky and the rest of my pugs favourite toys. "Poo" was the last thing to be found and I was shouting out to David "Where's Poo, I can't find Poo" people were staring at me, no doubt thinking I was deranged, but I didn't care I just wanted all my meaningful little treasures back in my handbag, safe where they belonged. Anyway David spotted "Poo" sitting underneath an old man's chair and politely asked the gentleman if he could move his leg and inch so Poo could be retrieved. I guess I dragged poor David into all that, I bet we both looked like a couple of utter and complete lunatics in the Doctors surgery that day and David being a shy guy it would have been pretty hard on him and I was sorry for him for that. But what people thought of me, well I was beyond caring because it would have been a lot worse for me if even one of my treasured possessions had been left behind. But I got them all back thank goodness and so now I always do the zip up on my handbag whenever I'm going out.

CHAPTER THREE

Harper Anne

I fell in love with Harper pretty fast, smitten within seconds, besotted for life. It wasn't a hard thing to do she was so beautiful, well beautiful to me anyway. I had no idea what she looked like before I went to meet her, only that she was a fawn pug that an old lady was looking to sell at a reasonable price. But Harper was an older pug so the price had to be reasonable didn't it. I didn't know anything about the lady when I spoke to her on the phone but it became pretty evident what she was once I got to her house. I have always been a sucker for what I call "Tongue Pugs" pugs that permanently have their tongues hanging out of their mouths. Again I didn't know that this was the case until I met Harper and when I saw that face of hers I just instantly melted, I loved her so much. She had beautiful big eyes too, the most soulful eyes I'd seen on a pug, almost like cartoon eyes when the artist wants the dog to look dreamy. There was just something so special when you looked into them. And I would find out later that those beautiful eyes of hers matched her amazing personality perfectly. You had to meet Harper in person to see it, photos didn't do her justice, the lens couldn't possibly pick it up, but there was something extraordinary about her and I was drawn in at once. Harper had a presence, an aura, a light. And it was noticeable to me that very first day, stood out a mile even though Harper wasn't in good health when we bought her.

Harper came into my life after I had witnessed an act of animal cruelty. Not towards Harper herself, although her life was far from rosy, but an act of cruelty all the same. The Danes had long passed away and Sarah was more or less living as an only child and being spoilt rotten because of it. We still had our old cat "Secret Agent Beow" named because of the way she used to patrol the place and the sound she would make at dinner time. It was not a normal cat's meow, just a "Beow, beow, beow" in a very distinct manner. Sarah and Secret Agent Beow got on really well and would spend summer days laying on the warm cement path in our back garden. I used to have to step over the two of them when I went to peg the washing out. They weren't for moving, neither one bothered to even look up at me, they were too groggy from the gentle sun and their slumber so I'd step over or step round and carry on my way. Did the same thing on the way back into the house as well, and again was ignored, but I'd leave the back door open so they could wander inside and find me when they finally woke up.

Harper came from a backyard breeder, an elderly lady who said she was finishing up breeding and going to live with one of her daughters. Harper was disused stock, or should I say overused stock, stock that had once proven very productive but who was now, due to her age no longer of use to the breeder. Harper had been over bred for years, no break between litters, no resting her body, just bred and bred and bred for profit upon profit upon profit. Bad backyard breeders and puppy farms are the same in my eyes, neither is interested in the welfare of the dog, both are motivated by money and the dogs in their care suffer greatly because of this. Harper had given birth to litter after litter of puppies without rest since she had become old enough to breed with. We didn't need to be told, it was written all over her body, one look and we knew what her life had been like up until that moment. When David and I first saw her she was a mess health wise, like I said I loved her at first glance but that glance also revealed to me that she was suffering.

But as unhealthy as she was Harper was still engaging, still wanting to be stroked and doing everything in her power to make that happen. That's the kind of pug Harper was, always happy, always wanting to be near you, to be patted regardless of the pain she was in. I think she was just glad to have a visitor at the house that day. Glad to have somebody giving her some attention. She was in the kitchen when I first saw her, I came round the corner of the hall and there she was. I thought it was funny she hadn't barked when we'd rang the doorbell, normally if there's a pug in the house and the doorbell rings they go nuts. But Harper wasn't allowed into the rest of the house I found out and I think she was too unwell to bark. She sat on the golden metal strip that signified the end of the vinyl and the start of the carpeted area, that was her boundary, she wasn't allow past that point but I didn't know it at the time so I called her to me.

"Darling, darling" I called out in my happy voice. I didn't know her name. I forgot to ask it at the door so I just called her "darling" all pugs seem to respond to that. But I really think I could have called her anything at all and she still would have shot into my arms. She shook with delight and was about to come over the strip when the breeder appeared behind me and she shot back. I didn't know the rules of the house, Sarah was allowed in every room of our house and so were the Danes, I had no idea what was going on so I called her again. Chunky paws patted the floor, her body still shaking with excitement and a huge smiley face with its tongue hanging out bounced around in the entrance of the kitchen. Again I called her, she was so beautiful, I just wanted to hold her in my arms so badly but she wouldn't come. I thought it was because I hadn't used her real name so I turned to the breeder.

"What's her name" I asked and my heart sank to the floor when she gave me the answer. I moved further down the hall and called her again. "Darling girl" I said making my voice sound even happier this time, just doing all I could to get this little pug to come to me. The breeder with her disapproving face was still behind me but Harper no longer cared, she shot over the line and into my arms. And that was it, in that quick instant both of our lives changed for the better. I felt it and I know Harper did to because she never gave the breeder a second glance after that, she was too busy with me and David smothering her with attention. She was one of those pugs that as soon as you stopped stroking her paw would come up and start patting at your hand, her way of saying "More affection please" and David's and my hands instantly reached out for her to stoke her some more, although I think I was doing most of the stroking because I became covered in thick fawn fur, I had almost as much fur on me as Harper did. David would give the occasional stroke but I could tell he wasn't comfortable being in this house. His body language was speaking on high volume but it seemed I was the only one picking up on it, the breeder didn't notice and neither did Harper. But I had known David longer than they did so his uncomfortableness was pretty obvious to me.

Harper wasn't well looked after that was for sure she smelt to high heaven, the breeder knew it, made an excuse about needing her daughters help her with bathing the dogs these days because she was too old to do it. She said her daughter hadn't been down for a while. Harper hadn't been brushed in ages either and her long tongue was coated quite thickly in loose fur. Loose fur was sticking to her eyeballs and was up her nose and in her ears too. Surely the breeder could have managed to wipe her face with a damp cloth, surely that was not beyond her capabilities especially when you've got somebody coming to buy the dog. To be honest I shouldn't have had to pay this breeder for her dog, she should have been paying me to take her. Harper was in no state to be sold, certainly no state to put a price on, but the breeder wanted money, she wanted to get one last bit of cash out of her dog so we handed over the cash to just to get Harper out of there. When you find yourself in a situation like this you just want to get the dog out of there as fast as possible, want to get her home and to a vet, just want that part of her life to be over forever. And besides we weren't going to grumble about the money, the breeder was wise enough not to charge a fortune because she knew full well with the state Harper was in she couldn't possibly get it. $200 seemed like a very small price to pay for Harpers freedom.

I must pause here to say that not all breeders are bad breeders. I've known some fantastic breeders, breeders breeding from their own homes that do take good care of their dogs, there are honest breeders around you just need to look for them. So please when buying a pug, especially a puppy do your research otherwise you are only adding to the problem. And while people continue to buy without thought, they are keeping puppy farms and bad backyard breeders in operation and their pockets fully lined. Don't only think about the pup you are buying, give some thought to the mother, what her life is like? Don't be afraid to ask to see the mother and see what the breeding set up is like, don't be afraid to ask lots of questions and if you're not satisfied with the answers walk away and find a breeder who is in it for the love of the breed, one who looks after their pugs. And I'd say ask the questions when you have the breeder on the phone, it can be very hard to walk away when you are sitting there with a cute squirming puppy on your knee. Have a list of questions by the phone ready and put a tick or a cross near the questions once you hear the answer. If you are not sure how to find a good breeder call the Kennel Control Council in your state. They will be more than happy to give you a list of decent breeders. And lord knows we need good pug breeders because without them my beloved breed would die out and I wouldn't want that. You can go on a waiting list for a puppy if they don't have one at the time and believe me for peace of mind and to put an end to the cruelty that is continuing to go on with over breeding, it is well worth the wait. The only way bad breeders are going to dry up is when they have nobody buying their pugs. They'll soon lose interest once there is no money to be made.

I was thrilled to hold Harper in my arms for the very first time but there was no mistaking she was in pain, I saw it and I heard it. When I picked her up she gave a sigh, not a happy to be in your arms sigh although I'm sure she was, it was the sigh an animal gives out when there is pain in their body, we didn't know how bad she was until we got her to our vet. She had abscesses and an ear and throat infection, she had a lot of joint pain too and areas of swelling in her body. With all the money this breeder had made from selling Harper's puppies you'd have thought she would have at least put a bit back into looking after this truly lovely natured old pug.

We stayed and talked to the breeder for a while, we wanted to get going, get Harper out of that place so she could begin her new better life but the breeder was fiddling about trying to find paperwork. We weren't interested in bloodlines or if she'd won any ribbons- she hadn't, Harper was no good for the show ring due to her tongue. The house was messy and there were piles and piles of junk on every available surface and this old woman insisted on going through each pile, real slowly as old people do- to be honest I think she was stalling because she was lonely, in a normal situation I would have felt sorry for her but this wasn't a normal situation. This house wasn't a nice place to be in, not for Harper anyway and I just wanted to get going. But the lady kept talking and searching through pedigree papers. I couldn't see the point because Harper didn't even have a name-that's what she'd told me when I'd asked her in the hallway, a pug with no name was what had made my heart sink. I watched the old lady going through the papers and wondered how on earth she was going to be able to find the correct paper work for this pug. She could have given us any old pedigree papers with anybody's name on it and in the end I think that's exactly what she did.

It didn't matter that the breeder didn't give Harper a name because I already had one picked out. I wanted her to be named after my grandmother, she was a truly wonderful lady and I was very close to her, when she died I was devastated. I wanted to name this pug after her as a way of honouring her memory. My Grandmothers name was Anne Harper but everyone just called her Annie. Friends, family, people in the street, it didn't matter how you knew my Grandmother she was Annie to everyone she met. Harper was meant to be called Annie, Annie Harper, but she didn't suit it, she didn't suit Anne either, none of those names matched her face. So I was a bit stuck. I wanted to have my Nan's name in their somewhere but my Grandmother didn't have a middle name. I gave up, thought I'd save Annie or Anne for some other pug and tried to come up with another name for this wonderful new pug of mine. I thought of all sorts of names for Harper, dragged out my baby name books from the bookshelf but couldn't find anything I liked, nothing suited. I think I could have flipped through a dozen baby name books and still not been able to find one. Because I wanted the name to be that of my Grandmother nothing else was ever going to be right. But Harper needed to begin her new life with a name, not having one in her old home was bad enough. I couldn't believe it when the woman told me she didn't have a name, I mean who doesn't give their dog a name. But I don't think any of her dogs had names because they weren't treated as normal dogs. They were just profit makers, their value depended upon how many puppies were in the litters they produced. It was like at the breeder's house Harper didn't even warrant a name, she just wasn't important enough to have one. Imagine going through your first five years of life without having a name. That just broke my heart. It said a real lot about the kind of life she was living there. I know a lot of pedigree dogs have very long names so are given different names altogether or the long breeding name is shortened to make it easier when being called. But Harper never got called over, not for a hug and not acknowledged in any loving way, not even when she had puppies. I imagined the breeder peeping into the whelping box and greedily counting how many puppies had been born, then doing a mental calculation in her head before walking away and leaving Harper to it.

In my house things were going to be very different for Harper, she was going to be an important member of our family and she wasn't a lesser member because she had been born with four legs either. And her value wouldn't ever again be dependent on how many puppies she could produce. She was going to not only have a beautiful life from now on, but a beautiful name to go with it, a meaningful name, a wonderful name to make up for the fact that it would be the first name she had ever been given. And she'd waited many years to finally hear it. "Why not just call her Harper" David said a few days after Harper arrived in our home. I loved it instantly. I'd never even thought of doing that. For about half a second I thought that using my Grandmothers surname could have been disrespectful to her memory but that thought didn't last very long because I turned round and said it to Harper and she came running over to me fast, it seemed she loved her new name as much as I did. David said he was sure my Nan wouldn't mind and also it was my Mums maiden name too so how could it be wrong. And so Harper became Harper and even now it's one of my most favourite pug names. Harper's Haven was even a name I was considering for our farm. Harper's Haven and Harpers Run were both floating around in my head for a little while before Grace Farm was finally settled upon. For some reason my youngest nephew decided he was going to call Harper "Harper Anne Smith". He never just called her Harper but would walk through the door calling out "Harper Anne Smith, Harper Anne Smith" and Harper would race over to greet him as fast as her short little legs would carry her.

Eventually the breeder handed over some paperwork. I can't tell you what name was on it because I barely looked at it, I did however glance at the date of birth, but I needn't have bothered. To this day I will never fully know what age Harper was when we got her, the breeder said four the paperwork said five, she could have been much, much older who knows. We went with six because she certainly didn't look any younger. Sarah was about to turn five and because I didn't believe the paperwork we were given had anything to do with Harper we decided that she could just have the same birthday as Sarah did, that way they could share their birthdays together and we could make a big fuss of both of them on the same day, so for years that's what we did.

Once the paperwork was found we were offered a drink by the old lady, we'd come a long way she said we were probably thirsty. We weren't but I said we were because by this time I'd found out she had more pugs and I wanted to see if she'd let us take a look at them. I wanted to know if they too were in the same state of health that Harper was in. While she slowly got us a drink I took in more of my surroundings, the house was filthy, the glasses we were given hadn't been used in a while and dust balls floated on the top of the water. We fished the balls of dust off and took polite sips, well I did and nodded for David to do the same. With the old lady looking at us and smiling, we took the smallest sips we could get away with. The remaining balls of dust touched my lips, it was a really awful feeling but I persisted because I wanted to have a look at those other pugs and figured being polite was the only way of doing it. That's the reason we stayed, that's why we said we'd have a drink, just to get on her good side and hopefully she would show us these other pugs of hers. David is a neat freak and this house with its years of rubbish and old newspapers piled up everywhere was freaking him out big time, I could see it in his face. I was just hoping that he could hold it together for at least a little while longer, because the look on his face told me that what he desperately wanted to do was get the hell out of there as quickly as possible. I asked to use the bathroom, even the bath was full of rubbish, well rubbish to me anyway but more than likely precious gems to her otherwise why would she have held onto them. Most of it looked to be piles of old magazines, four piles tied up with string stacked high in the bathtub surrounded by other rubbish. For fear of ending up the same way I made a mental note of going through the six or seven magazines I had sitting on my desk. As I washed my hands I thought to myself that this lady probably started out many years ago with just a few magazines on her desk. When I got home I went straight to the study, grabbed the magazines and marched directly to the garbage bin. I knew I had kept them for a reason, no doubt an article I wanted to read again or even keep forever but the fear of becoming a hoarder made me chuck them out without bothering to go through them. David stood there with Harper in his arms watching me do it. "What on earth are you doing" he asked. "Protecting our future" I said lifting the bin lid. "You'll thank me for it one day" I added as I walked back inside house.

I picked Harper up and sat her on the kitchen table in front of me, normally I wouldn't have done such a thing but with everything in that house being in the state it was in I figured the lady wouldn't mind having a dog up on the table, she didn't and sat beside me chatting away happily. Glad to have company because she was talking about everything she could think of. It was like something would enter her mind and she'd talk about that then quickly think of something else to talk about before the conversation stopped. Knowing I wanted to see her other dogs and having an audience she was making the most of it, it was like she hadn't had a decent conversation in the longest time and I couldn't help thinking that if she was a nicer person this wouldn't have been the case. People are either drawn to you or repelled by you depending on who you are as a person. And every one of us has it in us to change if we want to. So I can only assume the old lady was happy with who she was. David couldn't bring himself to sit down, he stood on the opposite side on the room, the side nearest the hallway, no doubt planning his escape. I thought the old lady may have thought he was being rude not wanting to sit down and a few times when she wasn't looking I tried to catch David's eye to get him to come over and sit with us, but he was avoiding eye contact with me. Oh I knew full well he could see my sneaky gestures, but he knew what I wanted him to do and there was no way he was going to sit down in that house. I looked at the old lady, she didn't seem to mind that he wasn't being sociable, to be honest I think she was just relieved at not having to clear the rubbish off any other chair. When she'd cleared my chair she stood in the middle of her kitchen with a bewildered look on her face before walking off into the lounge room, when she returned she seemed pleased with herself for having found a place to put the rubbish down. I had a feeling that was how she would have spent her days, just moving rubbish round from one place to another. I did worry that she was living in a fire hazard. If one of those piles of newspapers had caught alight there was no way known she'd have made it out alive.

I sat stroking Harper and holding her on the table so she wouldn't fall off, I'd put her there so I could get a better look at her. Not that it mattered really, we were going to buy her no matter what. But I guess I just didn't want her sitting on that dirty floor anymore. After what seemed like an eternity of me trying to bring the conversation back round to the pugs and the lady constantly talking about something else entirely I found out that the other pugs were outside. That's where they all lived, and no doubt that's where Harper had been until we rang the doorbell. Maybe that was why it took so long for the old lady to answer the door, she was probably bringing Harper in from outside. Sorting her out from the rest of the pugs and carrying her up the back stairs. We must have stood at that front door for about ten minutes. David even went back to the car to check the address just to make sure we were at the right house. But I stayed put, I wasn't going anywhere in case she came to the door while we were gone. She sounded old on the phone and old people can sometimes take a while getting to the door, also older people generally have the manners to not go out when they have organised somebody coming over.

It saddened me that the pugs were outside no pug should ever live outside, they are not outside dogs, it does something to their personality let alone shortens their years, they need to be kept warm in winter and cool in summer. Also they love to be with you, do what you are doing and join in on all the family fun. Finally she agreed to show me her other pugs. The old lady told us to wait in the kitchen while she went to the garage to get them. I was about to follow her outside but she didn't want us to see where she kept the pugs and to this day it makes me wonder what filth they were living in if she didn't want us seeing it. I felt so sorry for those pugs. If the house was in this state you could only imagine what her garage looked like. While she went to get the pugs we stood in the kitchen, I was looking out the window trying to see the pugs. I watched the old lady disappear into her garage, the pugs must have been in pens or cages if they didn't all fly out as soon as she opened the door. David took the opportunity of us being alone to have a major meltdown about the house. To be honest his voice startled me, I was very lost in my thoughts, concentrating on the pugs I was about to meet and thinking about the lives they were leading. I had almost forgotten David was there. But he made his presence known in a very loud manner, which is unusual for my husband because he normally has the softest gentlest voice. He was louder than normal because he was in total freak out mode. He was going on about the smell and telling me off for telling him to drink the dust ball filled water. I told him to be quiet because I didn't want the old lady hearing him and changing her mind about showing me the pugs. It had taken a lot for her to agree to show me them in the first place and I didn't want it being ruined now. I suggested that he may like to go and wait in the car with Harper but he said there was no way in the world he was going to do that, he wasn't going to leave me in this house alone. I said "Why are you scared I won't be able to find my way out through all the rubbish" with that we both started laughing and the laughter caused David to calm down a little bit. But then Harper started coughing and that caused David to started ranting about the filthy house again. The sound of the back door opening was the only reason he quietened down.

When she opened the door six fawn pugs came running in. I couldn't help but smile, I thought it was the best sight I had ever seen in my life. I'd never seen so many pugs in the one room before and to me it was the most wonderful sight in the world. I started laughing and bending down and patting as many of them as I could, I wanted to make sure I got them all but who could tell, they were circling and jumping up and dancing about and my hands were running all over them, I no doubt patted a few of them over and over again in trying to get to them all. So many pugs made me so incredibly happy. I wanted what she had. I told the lady she was living in pug heaven, because that was my idea of heaven, living with all those pugs, looking back it was a really stupid thing to have said. Those pugs weren't living in a heavenly state, being locked up in a garage was as far away from heaven as you could get and they deserved better. But being so overwhelmed with seeing so many pugs at the one time and loving the pug breed as much as I do I was just overcome with emotion, taken to another world and wasn't really thinking straight. But I did note that these pugs were a lot younger than Harper was. As I write this I wonder if she'd only brought out the younger ones and were there perhaps more pugs like Harper sitting in that garage who needed rescuing. The thought just never crossed my mind at the time, I just figured she'd brought out all the other pugs living there on the property to show us and hopefully she had but who knows. I'm an honest person I figured she was too. Nowadays after being involved in this world for as long as I have been I would have known exactly what to do, but back then I knew nothing, I thought everybody who had dogs treated them the same way I did, it's only in getting deeper and deeper into the rescue world that you get to see how many dogs and other animals are being mistreated. Thinking back I should have told the breeder what I thought of her and those like her, but then she may not have let us leave with Harper, no money had crossed hands at this point, sometimes you just have to not say what is so desperately in your heart to say in order to get a dog to safety.

I looked at these six pugs more closely now, once they'd settled down it was easier to get a real look at the condition of them. I had expected them to be like Harper, older, sick, in bad health that's why I desperately wanted to see them, but those six pugs were perfect. All very healthy young dogs, she was reluctant to show us her other pugs at the start and I had just assumed it was because they were not in a good way, but when I looked at those pugs I knew the real reason she didn't want us to meet them. This old woman was craftier then I gave her credit for, she had no intention at all of giving up breeding, she was just getting rid of her old stock and these six young pugs where her new breeders. I reckon the only time she'd give up breeding was when they wheeled her out on a gurney, that's if a gurney could have been wheeled out of that house at all and I don't think it could have been. The undertakers would have more than likely just had to zip the body bag up, throw it over their shoulders and walk through the piles and piles of rubbish just to get her out of there. But that wouldn't have needed to happen for quite a while yet, because the cunning old bag seemed to have a bit of life left in her still. I could see it in her eyes when those six young pugs ran in.

The old lady gave us a towel to wrap Harper in on the journey home she said she didn't want her fur getting all over the car. David was happy about that because although the car wasn't brand new it was our new car we'd only had it a few weeks and David was in love with the thing. Harper sat up front on my knee, David said she'd have been ok in the back seat, I think he was thinking she'd make less mess if she was back there but I wouldn't have it. I said it wasn't Harpers fault she was in this condition, that she'd been on her own long enough. I wasn't going to have her sitting by herself one second longer. But she really did smell. We had to keep opening the windows to change the air on the way home, and her fur was blowing everywhere, I ended up with it in my mouth because I was talking so much, David was wise enough not to talk when the windows were open. It got in my eyes too and up my nose. It was all over the car, front seat, back seat, everywhere, but to David's credit he just decided to let it go. I expected him to keep having a fit about it but half way home he too must have realised that Harper wasn't to blame for this. It took weeks and weeks to get all that fur out of the car and a decade later when that car got written off in an accident I reckon when the guys at the wreckers crushed it that wafts of Harpers fur would have come floating out.

When we got her home it was a two second hello to Sarah and Harper was put into a warm soapy bath. It was the middle of winter and late afternoon when we arrived home but I couldn't leave the bath till the morning I had to wash her then and there. I just couldn't let her live in that condition for a moment longer. In half an hour I'd gotten rid of the smell, washed away her old life and had a sink full of dirt and grit to prove it. Harper sat happily in the laundry sink looking up at me as I washed her, I don't think she was happy or not happy to be having a bath, she was just one of those pugs that was contented regardless of what she was doing. As I was washing Harper I kept saying to her that once I pulled this plug that was it, no more old lady breeder, no more sleeping in a garage, no more longing for love. Within an hour Harper had eaten, had a blow dry and was laying in front of the heater with Sarah sleeping. She had a really good meal of decent food, we have always fed our dogs an excellent diet and Harper seemed to love what we gave her. I don't think she had ever eaten anything unprocessed in her life. Breeders make the most amount of money out of their dogs than any other dog owner I know yet seem to put the least amount of time into good nutrition, into food preparation. I've never understood it myself, it's not hard to give a dog a better diet, it just takes a little bit of time but the rewards are well worth the effort. Again I'm not talking about all breeders, like I've already stated there are some good ones out there, the one who bred Harper just wasn't one of them. Perhaps she was too old to do anything other than throw a handful of dry food into a bowl, if so give up the game, why should her dogs suffer because she wasn't up to doing her job properly. Then again maybe she didn't care what she fed them, breeders aren't trying to get a long life out of their dogs, they hardly want to have 14, 15, 16 and 17 year old dogs wandering around the place do they. That is my job, that's what I love to do but not what breeders love to do. They just over use their little bodies then sell them off cheap when they are too old to produce decent sized litters.

Harper settled into life with us very well considering what she had been through. She didn't like being left alone though, ever, I think she'd had enough of being on her own and now she had a real family she wanted to be with them always. She'd cry and become distressed when she wasn't by your side. Most pugs don't like you leaving them, they prefer to accompany you wherever you go but Harpers situation was a bit more than that, it was true anxiety. And so both David and I were aware of how she was feeling at all times and tried as best we could to see things from her point of view. We only ever left her on her own when there was no other choice. She did however get better in time, when she knew we were always coming back and her life would resume as normal she didn't panic quite as much when we went out.

We had to wait a while to get Harpers teeth done, she was in such bad health and so overweight she may not have come through the surgery, our vet was concerned, we were concerned, it just wasn't worth taking the risk. She got antibiotics for the infections and that helped a lot. I didn't like the fact that her teeth were still giving her trouble, but I didn't want her to die while under sedation, in the back of my mind I had a nagging feeling that she would not have pulled through. I've always listened to that inner voice when it comes to my pugs, well everything in my life really, I think we hear it for a reason and when you hear it that strongly you shouldn't ignore it. Our inner voice, our gut feeling, I believe is there to help us, we should never brush it off. It would have been really sad to have rescued Harper from those horrible conditions and rushed to get those teeth fixed up only to have her die on the operating table. She deserved a chance at life, to know how it felt to live a happier existence, to live life as a real dog for once and not just be used for breeding. She didn't have to reproduce to be valuable to us, all we wanted from Harper was for her to be happy, get well and to stay with us as long as she possibly could. That's all we ever want for any of our pugs.

So I mushed up Harpers food to make it easier to eat and once the antibiotics started to kick in I gave her a little walk each day until the weight came off. In the beginning I couldn't get much of a walk out of her. Harper would come out our front door walk to our letterbox and that was it, back inside the house we'd go. Then after a few days she'd manage to make it to the next door neighbour's letter box and collapse flat out on the footpath and there was no getting her up. Not that I tried too hard to get her moving again, if she'd done enough for that day then she'd done enough for that day, end of story, no sense pushing her. It was very important to be guided by Harper, only she knew what she could and couldn't do and to push her would have only caused more problems. I didn't want her heart giving out and I didn't want her legs to be in pain because then she wouldn't have enjoyed walking and I wanted the daily walks to be enjoyable for her. I felt she deserved that after the life she'd lead so far. And it was that very life that had made walking so hard for her, if she hadn't been trapped in that shed and allowed more freedom of movement then her mobility wouldn't be as bad as it was. I knew there was always tomorrow and if she took just one more little step on the next day's walk then she did today, well I could be happy with that, because it would be progress and progress was what I was most interested in. So I just picked her up and carried her back home and kissed her little ears and told her what a champion she was. And she'd look up at me with those lovely eyes of hers, so soulful, so beautiful, so full of love; she really did love receiving praise, well spoken to at all really because there hadn't been much of that in her previous home. Can you imagine how it would feel to a dog, to be man's best friend and to only see your owner at meal times or when you were ready to deliver your puppies. Imagine how Harper's heart would have been crying out for attention, for love, for companionship, only to have the garage door shut again without receiving any of it. I had a lump in my throat just thinking about it so I could only imagine the sadness Harper would have felt and the heartache all dogs living this way feel on a daily basis. So the next day Harper would be happily gearing up for her walk and another step would be taken and I was so excited and proud by it that I showered her with praise, in fact I praised her so loudly at times I reckon the entire street would have heard me. She loved that walk and she loved that praise and she'd be scooped up and snuggled and told how wonderful I thought she was. Her fur was so soft and she smelt like a dream, a coconut scented dream. And I'd carry her back to the house singing her praises as she caught her breath.

Harper wasn't a lazy dog she just physically didn't have another step in her, if she had one I've no doubt she would have given it to me. I never measured it but I'm guessing it was no more than about thirty or so small footsteps and she'd be down, legs trembling because they just couldn't support her weight for very long. In that first fortnight I ended up having to carry her back home every day. And I didn't mind that, I just let her walk as much as she wanted to walk and let her sniff at anything she wanted to sniff at because I knew that would encourage her to walk a bit more, but when she lay down I knew it was over so I'd pick her up and she'd have a rest in my arms as I walked back to the house. Once home I'd put her on the cool kitchen floor until she recovered, then she'd stagger over for a drink, walk into the lounge room and fall asleep on the carpet. Her last litter had probably only been taken off her the week before she was sold and her teats hung low and with her added weight they were almost scraping the ground, another half an inch and they would have been rubbed red raw. My heart really went out to her in those first few weeks in my care. She weighed just over 12kg and was only a medium sized pug. She was basically a barrel on legs, well a sick barrel on legs.

Once Harpers throat and ear infections cleared up she was a different dog and with the new diet she was on she just seemed to come more and more alive by the day. Those beautiful eyes that were once dulled with poor nutrition and pain now simply sparkled. Big glossy clear pools of love looked up at me whenever I spoke to her. Now she was feeling a bit better I'd walk her up the street in the morning and in the back garden in the late afternoon. Up and down the small path that led to the washing line as many times as she wanted to do it, up and down we'd go with Sarah leading the way or doing circles around us depending on her mood or how energetic she was feeling on the day. I built Harper up slowly we just did what she could physically handle. Up and back we'd go five or a six times a day until it became easier for her then we'd do seven, then eight. I had to put the harness on otherwise she would have sat at the bottom of the path, she wasn't used to walking on a lead either, she'd never been on one before coming to us but she took to it beautifully. That was her nature as long as you were with her talking her through it she'd do anything for you. She'd come with me when I hung the washing out and those first few days all she'd do was sit there beside the line and watch Sarah sniffing about in the garden. The garden path wasn't a very long one but it was long enough for Harper and she'd walked it with me once so now she needed a rest. Then one day she decided to follow Sarah as she sniffed and really enjoyed doing that. I don't think Harper thought she was exercising when she was sniffing but she was and I'd pause and watched the two of them walking around the garden together, yin and yang, black and fawn, wherever Sarah went Harper was always a few steps behind. When you think about it, grass and outside garden smells and long leisurely sniffing by flower beds was something that had been denied Harper her entire life. So was squatting for a wee on green grass. Sarah did it all the time so you just take it for granted and don't give it too much thought, but for Harper all this was brand new. She was used to sitting in a cage on a concrete garage floor. The delights of the garden where fabulous for her and it wasn't even a very big garden but she loved it all the same, it must have been like paradise to her. She'd walk over to our little lemon tree, have a wee and give a little kick, blades of grass would go flying through the air. I bet if felt so good to her to be able to kick up some earth, and even better to be able to feel its lushness and softness underneath her feet, a dream come true after that cold concrete floor. When Harpers weight dropped just below 10kg we got her dental work done, the nagging voice in my head had gone but you are just never 100 percent sure when it comes to pugs and operations. I didn't sit still until the vet nurse rang to say she'd pulled through. Her lungs were in better shape with the weight loss and the walking, she could go all the way round the block now, slowly and of course having a good old sniff at everything she came across but still it was an achievement which is what I'd tell Sarah when she'd stamp her little feet impatiently waiting for Harper to get a move on.

Harper took a while to come good after the operation, it took a lot out of her and she needed to rest, be pampered for a while. She loved all the extra attention she was getting I think she was way overdue for a bit of spoiling. So we did what any loving parent would do and spoilt her rotten. Not with junk food or too many treats, because we couldn't let the nutrition side of things slip. Not after how far she'd come and how well she was doing. She had been eating a bad diet all her life so every mouthful had to be benefitting her in some way. But we did splurge on half a banana a day and the price of those things was through the roof at the time but she loved them and they were good for her to have and soft too so she could easily get them down with the few teeth she had left. And of course Sarah didn't mind having the other half, and I'd hand it to her and tell her that she had to take the bad with the good and that next time she was getting impatient with Harpers leisurely sniffing she should remember how good the bananas tasted and ease up a bit on the foot stomping. Once Harper recovered we began walking, building it up slowly again, after six months I was taking Sarah and Harper along the river where I used to walk the Danes. They enjoyed it, in summer we'd go early in the morning before it got hot, same path same routine, different smells every day. Harper was sitting on 8.6kg to 8.9kg by this time. She had a lot of loose skin which swayed from side to side as she walked and swayed even faster as she ran. But she didn't pant or gasp anymore she'd trot along the riverbank sniffing at anything that caught her fancy and was just enjoying her new life. We met a lot of people on those walks, pugs always draw attention and the more you have the more attention they get. I guess to some people, those who'd not seen Harper in the early days, who'd not known how hard she struggled to get where she was today, she still looked big.

It used to really annoy me whenever anybody said Harper was fat, to pick her up she was light, lighter than a lot of other pugs. But although she had lost an incredible amount of weight her body didn't snap back into shape, it couldn't, it had been overused and abused for far too many years. Stretched beyond repair giving birth to and feeding litter after litter, and her feet were permanently splayed due to the extra weight she was forced to carry time and time again making money for that breeder. Yet she'd be there walking along the river doing a great job, her mouth would be wide open and her tongue would be hanging out and she was happy. She had one of those pug faces that always looked like they were smiling. And yet still we'd get the occasional idiot who'd call her fat and it really did ruin my day at times. I shouldn't have let it but stupidly I did. Again I was young and not confident enough to tell people that I thought they were being rude. Instead I'd start explaining about Harper's previous life and all that she'd gone through and accomplished. Nowadays I'm not so polite, I let rip when some idiot is being rude and offensive, it's the beauty of getting older and feeling more at ease in the world and in your own skin. And you know what, I kind of like it. It's probably the only thing I really like about getting older.

But the riverbank walkers didn't seem to care, to them Harper was just the fat fawn pug trotting along with the small black pug, nobody ever said anything about Sarah's weight which was funny because in the end there was only around half a kg weight difference between the two of them, it's just that with all that loose skin Harper looked a lot bigger than she was. I used to think about what their reactions would have been like if I'd bought one of Harpers many puppies instead of Harper herself, everything would have been completely different then. I'd be there with a healthy happy bouncy giddy squirmy wriggly little thing and people would flock to see that. But no thought would be given to the producer of the healthy happy bouncy giddy squirmy wriggly little thing and what her life was like. She'd be still there living in that garage on that bare concrete floor, in ill health and crying out for some love and attention. But just because she didn't look the way people thought a pug should look, and really how could she possibly look any different to how she did, she was being called names. I looked at Harper's used and abused body and saw her as a warrior, a fighter, a hero, a pug that had been subjected to horrid conditions and yet never once gave up or let it dampen her personality. She raised all those puppies even though she was in ill health and not feeling the best at the time, yet she never left them to die, she nourished them even though it took everything out of her own body doing it, left her worse for wear. In my eyes those river walkers should have been making a parting for Harper to walk through and chapping and cheering for her as she did. That was what Harper deserved in my eyes and nothing less.

In the end I learnt to ignore the comments and just enjoyed being out and about with my pugs. Life with one pug was good, life with two was fantastic, especially after Harper got well. She went from being this sick chubby poorly nutritioned badly taken care of pug who couldn't walk to this energetic bouncy happy go lucky pug that dragged me across the room as soon as her lead was clipped onto her harness. She'd leap in the air and spin around in circles every time the harness came out and would practically knock Sarah and I flying just to be the first one out the front door, nobody could beat her in those days and nobody even tried. No matter what state the weather was in Harper loved to walk. Those walks were important to Harper, she lived for walking, exploring, and meeting new people even if the miserable strangers at the river weren't always as enthusiastic about meeting her. Harper loved everybody and a discriminating face and judgmental attitude didn't bother her, she'd lived with worse during her time with the breeder. She'd lead the way to the river then run ahead sniffing before coming back to Sarah and I and running a circle around us then go bouncing off again in search of something new to smell. She was always about ten steps in front of us and always coming back to tell us where she'd been, we could clearly see her but Harper didn't know that so she'd come flying back to us with her big smiley face. Harper was actually walking twice as far as Sarah and I did because of all the backwards and forwards she was doing. I guess she was making up for all those years being locked in a small pen in the breeder's garage. But she was handling it so well, her breathing was excellent and her movement just flowed so smoothly, splayed feet or not she was running about happily, apart from the excess skin you'd never have known she had once been so big and unhealthy. I couldn't take my eyes off Harper on those walks, she was so beautiful, so full of energy and it thrilled my heart to see it. There was such a vast improvement in her health, life had been breathed into her, everything about her changed. I felt like I'd really achieved something getting Harper back on her feet again. And I was so proud of every single step she took.

Sarah didn't share my enthusiasm; she was jealous, she didn't want to share her "luckies" with Harper, didn't want to share her parents either so we got Harper some toys of her own and tried to give Sarah more of our attention. We more or less treated Sarah like we had treated the Danes when she had first arrived in the house. We made sure Sarah was patted first and her food bowl was put down first that kind of thing, we needed to let her know she was still important to us. Sarah was first in the house after all. And she decided that she would be the head dog, no matter how small a pack is all packs must have a leader, it's how dogs work. It works in the wild and it works in our homes too and you can't decide who becomes head of the pack it's all up to them it has nothing to do with us, the best thing you can do is stay out of it. Well keep an eye on it so things don't get too nasty, you are in charge after all, but you can't force them to have who you would like to have as a leader, your favourite dog may end up sitting at the bottom of the pack and you just have to leave it alone and learn to be ok with it. Just because a dog is your favourite doesn't automatically mean they have it in them to lead and forcing them to be something they aren't is just outright upsetting for everybody. And it takes things longer to settle down. At the start when all this was being worked out, and it's always worked out in the first week or so, Harper simply wasn't up to the job due to her health. And besides Harper was a lover not a fighter, her strength came with nurturing and she rose to that role superbly. That was why Horton was so drawn to her when he first arrived, he sensed that beautiful caring nature of Harpers and got a real lot of comfort from her and it was beautiful seeing the two of them together. She mothered him like he was one of her own and I loved her for it. You need all these different personalities in the pack, just as you need all these different personalities in your family. I have certain family members who I can go to for certain things that other family members are simply not capable of and it's the same with our dogs. And what does it matter who takes on what role. As long as all the needs of the pack are being met that's all that's important, leaders, nurturers, guarders, protectors, sensitive souls, you need all these different natures in the pack, it makes it work, it makes for a lovely little unit because all needs are being met.

Sarah had the stronger personality of the two, then again Sarah had the strongest personally of almost any other pug I've ever met. It just wasn't in Harper's nature to lead, she happily let Sarah have that role all to herself. She was just contented to be living in a real home environment for the first time in her life. Although it could have just as easily worked out the other way round, Harper could have come into the house and decided she was going to be boss and if Sarah had been born with a more docile nature she would have let her. And of course it would have been up to the two of them who was going to be top dog not me, naturally I am not oblivious to what's going on because I can't be. I do a lot of observing, always keeping an eye on what's going down. The stomping around puffing themselves up circling each other is harmless but if it looks like it's going to turn nasty I will intervene, because I won't have bloodshed. I'll separate the two until things have calmed down and then reintroduce them later on when they have decided to be reasonable. It's all just common sense really. Sometimes they'll have worked out their roles within a day or so, other times it'll take longer. And if you are working with different breeds it isn't always the bigger breed that'll end up being boss.

Stature has little to do with it, it's all about personality and the nature of each dog. Some dogs are like some people, kind of laid back while others have to be in charge of everyone and everything and it makes no difference on the size of the dog or the size of the person either, it's all about what they've got going on within.

Harper didn't understand the playing with toys thing because she'd never had them in her previous home, she simply didn't know what to do with them. Sarah tossed hers in the air or brought them to me or she would carry hers around wagging her little curly tail until I'd acknowledged what she had in her mouth. I called Sarah's toys her "luckies" and if she wanted your attention she'd go and grab a "lucky" and wander over wagging her tail so hard that her entire back end would be going with the flow. She'd also go and get one of her "luckies" when David got home and present it to him like a prize. But Harper was different, Harper simply grabbed a toy and scurried off to the nearest bed. She began licking it, caring for it, mothering it. The way she cared for that toy I could tell she would have been an excellent mother, no wonder the breeder kept hold of Harper for as long a she did. If Sarah came near the toy Harper became anxious, started growling, protecting the toy, she thought it was her baby. And why wouldn't she it was the only thing she had ever known how to do. We called Sarah away and let Harper be alone with her toy. She could well have been grieving for all those puppies she had lovingly raised only to have them taken away as soon as they could feed on their own and then of course she would have had to go through the entire thing again six months later. And be heartbroken again too, I figured Harper had a lot of grieving to do and she couldn't do it with Sarah constantly in her face so Sarah came and sat on the couch with me and Harper lay there caressing her baby. I felt Harpers heart needed some time to heal and if Sarah was still being a problem then I popped her outside so she could go and spend some quality time in the sun with Secret Agent Beow.

I had to introduce toys to Harper slowly and she couldn't be left with them all the time because when she had a toy to protect she became a snarling guarding defending mess. You took the toy off her and she returned to her happy normal state. I separated Sarah and Harper for a few hours every afternoon so Harper could have some time alone with her toy. It didn't feel right to take the toys off Harper altogether, I mean I could have done and it would have stopped the arguments but I didn't want to rush her or push her towards her new life if she wasn't yet fully ready to leave her old one behind. She'd been through a lot I didn't have the heart or felt I had the right to take her pretend babies away from her so she had a few hours with them every afternoon. I have read that when a human Mother loses a baby they sometimes get a doll, the dolls are called reborns and they look so much like a real baby that you almost expect them to breathe. Nursing these dolls can be beneficial to the grieving process, some even get the dolls made to look like the baby they have lost. As far as I am concerned if sitting in their unused nursery rocking a reborn helps a grieving mother's heart to heal then I am all for it, and who wouldn't be, you have to put yourself in their shoes. I am never in judgement about anything that helps somebody going through some of the most heartbreaking times of their lives. Everybody has a right to do whatever they need to do in order to cope. Life is hard at times and very unfair and if you can think of a way to make it easier for yourself during those times then you must do it. This is why I gave Harper time alone with her pretend babies. She had a right to a healing process too and could take as long as she liked to heal her damaged little heart. And it seemed to work. After a while Harper lost interest in the toys. One day she left her toy sitting in the middle of the lounge room floor and followed Sarah and I outside, she never looked at it again. Not as a toy and not as a baby. I think her heart and mind had healed and she was ready to move on, she was now ready to fully leave her old life behind.

I had hoped one day Harper would start seeing the toys as just toys and begin to play but she never did and I always felt sad about that, felt sorry for Harper that she never got to play. But she enjoyed her walks and living her life by my side, she loved being part of our family and she liked the occasional pigs ear so every so often she'd have one of those. But I had to watch her whenever she had one because she was a bit of a food aggressor. Perhaps the toy playing thing was more for me then it was for her because Harper was happy regardless. I could tell she was happy she didn't have to play with toys in order to prove it. Harper enjoyed every aspect of family living, the walking routine we did morning and night, the sitting in the kitchen watching me cook, the lying flat out in front of the heater on winter nights when David and I were watching a movie. She slept by the side of my bed in a laundry basket with a sheep skin in it. We'd take the two pugs out for their last wee of a night and Harper would wee first then dive back into the house, go bouncing up the hall and be in her bed before the rest of us were in the back door. I knew she was in bed because I'd hear the laundry basket thump against the wall as she jumped into it. We tried her with a dog bed, bought her the most beautiful bed in earth tones, but she wasn't interested. She'd walk right past it every time and go jump on top of the washing, in the end I said to David if she's happy doing that then we may as well get her a laundry basket of her own. So we bought a big pink plastic laundry basket put a fluffy cream sheepskin in it and Harper was set. If I got up in the middle of the night for anything she would bounce out of her bed fast and follow me round the house, in winter I'd tell her to go back to bed. I wanted her to stay warm, to look after herself, but she wasn't having any of it she would never leave my side, it was like "Wherever you are going I am going" kind of thing. I guess she had taken so long to find a real mother she wasn't about to let me out of her sight. In every sense of the word she was my shadow.

People commented a real lot about Harper's level of happiness. Sarah was the more serious one, the boss, the one in charge so I guess Harper's joyfulness stood out more against her sister's personality. Harper would be bouncing around acting the fool while Sarah stood alongside looking at her like "What on earth are you doing that for you big stupid idiot" a few times it looked as if Sarah was about to join in on the fun but instead she'd walk off, I think she thought one clown in the house was enough and figured Harper had that role down pat. I don't think there was a time when Harper was not smiling. While in poor health when she first arrived she was smiling, having a bath, even though she didn't want one, she'd still be smiling. Battling to walk and gasping for air she'd be panting and yet looking up at me and still smiling, just come out of an operation with many less teeth, still groggy from the anesthetic and again smiling, last thing at night- smiling, first thing in the morning- smiling, following me around the house - smiling. You just couldn't seem to wipe that big grin off her face. She was happy and it was fantastic to see. I've always thought pugs would make great human beings and I think Harper would have made the finest of the fine. Still pugs are alright just as they are, aren't they, a truly brilliant little breed.

There was a series of events that brought Harper into our lives. We were living as a one dog household at the time, the last of our two Danes had passed away a few years ago and Sarah was basically running the house the way all one dog household pugs do. They have all the attention on them at all times and they get used to it, they really like living that way. They are often spoilt rotten too because you are mad dog lovers and you have nobody else to pour all that praise, love and devotion on. They become your world, your entire focus, it's just you and your husband and this vain demanding attention loving tiny black pug. She becomes a ham, a show off, and yes I'm about to go here - A DIVA - and it's the two of you who have made her that way. You created the monster you are now living with and the thing is you have no idea what you have done. Your ignorance is as blissful as the state you are living in. And if this fact is pointed out to you by a well-meaning friend, you think they are mistaken or because they don't own a pug, have no idea what they are talking about. You may even mistake their actions as pure jealousy as you, your hubby and the long waited for little black pug all snuggle up on the couch together watching TV.

You and your husband look at each other and think this friend will soon change her tune when she gets a dog to share her life with. But she doesn't change her tune because she doesn't ever get a dog, she becomes a cat person and late at night when you are laying there alone with your thoughts you can't shake the nagging feeling in the back of your mind that perhaps it was you and your pug who made her that way. Then as quickly as that thought enters your head you shake it off, because it can't be right can it, or can it, you shake it off again convincing yourself it's pure nonsense then pull the covers up under your chin and go back to feeling the contentment you felt just a few moments ago while listening to your husband and your little black pug snoring. You watch your husband sleeping for a few moments then roll over and hang your hand over the side of the bed and stroke those velvety soft little ears and go back to trying to figure out which one of the two is snoring loudest. You stay awake a little while longer counting your blessings then fall asleep listening to the harmonious snoring of the two greatest loves of your life.

It finally hit me how bad the situation was with Sarah after we brought Harper into the house. It hits you so fast and so squarely in the face that it hurts. It stings your heart and makes your soul smart. The fog of bliss quickly clears when you see out of the corner of your eye a little flash of furry blackness come shooting down the hall and go flying across the room. It sinks in deeply that this naughty, showing off, attention seeking missile may not actually be half as cute as you once thought she was. When she was chewing on the Danes ears it was comical, when she did the same thing to Harper, not so much. No harm was ever done to the Danes due to the difference in size, they barely knew Sarah was there or if they did they weren't at all bothered by her. But when she is on top off and clinging to a poor unhealthy pug that has just staggered up your two front steps, into your lounge room and flopped, out of breath on the floor, it's easy to see the error of your ways. That's when logic kicks in and the training of not only your dog but of yourself as well truly begins. I realized the situation we were living in was not a good one for Sarah, it was an unnatural and unhealthy state for her. Dogs need structure, a leader, they are pack animals and all packs need leadership. It was time for David and I to step up and become true leaders and after living the way we had for so long it was a shock to all our systems I can tell you.

David and I once again took charge like we had done when we had the Danes. I think because the Danes were so big we concentrated more on discipline, they were obedient. They had to be, I wouldn't have been able to let them off the lead by the river if they weren't. We put a lot of training into the Danes, many hours of teaching commands, they were fantastically behaved, came at a whistle, stopped in their tracks. Even if they were running flat out at full speed and the dog approaching looked interesting they stopped turned around and galloped back towards me. With Sarah I just threw everything I knew out the window and it was a mistake. I'd wanted a black pug for so long and had been through so much before I got her that I just completely lost myself in it all and confused Sarah because of it. Now she had to go back and learn some basic rules, it was difficult for her and even more so for me, it would have been much easier on all of us if I'd just taught her properly from day one. Sarah wasn't at fault, I was, and those first few weeks of training were hard. There were many tears, and they weren't shed by Sarah, she took to being trained so well and so easily. I think it was the treats she received when she got it right, so being as intelligent as she was and being ruled, as all pugs are, by their tummies, she made sure she got it right every time. It took a little while but in time we had ourselves a well-trained pug and the entire household was so much better for it.

One Saturday night David and I were walking Sarah, it was dark, late, much later then we'd normally walk her but we'd been out all day and just gotten home but no way was Sarah missing out on her walk so we changed our shoes and popped the harness on. We didn't go to the river as there wasn't much point, way to dark down there to be able to see anything so we just walked Sarah round the streets. It was a leisurely stroll and we were happily talking about our day out. And due to nobody being in any rush Sarah was taking advantage of sniffing everything she came upon of interest. We were all just enjoying our evening walk. A few houses from home all that changed, in an instant everything was awful and the reality of the cruelness of human beings came crashing into our world. There was a party going on, from the noise, the lights and the many cars in the street we could tell. I hadn't been aware when we'd set off because we'd gone in the other direction, but we'd been walking a while and the music had got louder as the party goers got drunker. David and Sarah were ahead of me and I was behind them just sauntering along thinking about life as I so often do.

As I got to the house I sensed something wasn't right, felt the air change, I've always been sensitive and observant, especially when it comes to animals. I thought maybe it was the loudness of the music or the crowd of people standing on the front lawn that was unsettling me. I've never been good with noise or liked large gatherings. Perhaps it was just because I'd had a big day and I was looking forward to some sleep which from the sounds of things I wasn't going to be getting. As I walked by the front of the house, I noticed three young guys standing in the garden, nothing seemed out of place, they had a ridgeback with them, pure I thought but it was dark so it may have been a cross. If it was a cross it was crossed with a larger breed, they didn't speak to us and we didn't speak to them, they held the dog by its collar so it wouldn't attack Sarah but David picked her up and carried her just to be safe. I couldn't shake the uneasy feeling I'd felt coming up to that house, we were about to go in our front gate when I turned around and began walking back. There was loud hollering and hooting going on that I hadn't heard previously, the guys had flash lights and a long metal stick and were laughing and cheering. David came up behind me with Sarah still in his arms, he told me to come back, they were just being drunken idiots, I said "I can't, something isn't right here, I think they are hurting animals, I have to go and see what they are doing".

I got to the end of their driveway and saw that the three guys were knocking some possums out of a tree and their dog was ripping them to pieces and from the way they were laughing they thought it was the funniest thing it the world to be doing. One guy shone the flash light into the possum's eyes blinding it while a second guy hit it with a long metal pole knocking it to the ground. They then all stood around cheering as the dog tore that live animal to pieces. I flew into their garden and started having a fit, going berserk at these men, they were all over six feet tall but that didn't stop me. I called them every vile thing I could think of and said if they didn't stop I was going to go home and call the police. This was before mobile phones became as popular as they are today, having a mobile phone on me that night would have made things so much easier, I would have been dialing the police while I was standing in their yard. I told them that possums where protected, that what they were doing was cruel, barbaric and illegal, there were probably a few other choice words thrown in there as well, there always are when I am that upset, I tend to forget I'm a lady when I'm that angry. And I was ropeable that night.

I think to them I must have seemed like a crazy middle aged woman, I was nowhere near middle aged but young people tend to think older people are a lot older than they are. In reality I was probably only five or six years older than they were but they weren't treating me that way. They smirked and told me to go home and have a good evening. They started patronizing me, telling me they got it, that I'd had my say, telling me to go home now, to mind my own business. It was like "Yeah yeah lady whatever you say" I suppose I could have rang the police instead of confronting them myself but I just didn't think of it at the time, all I knew was that I had to stop what they were doing as quickly as possible. If I'd gone home and rang how many more possums could have died during that time, that's even if the police came right away. They may have thought possums weren't worth driving out for. I may have gone home and been in bed thinking all was well and the police hadn't even bothered to show up. I think if you've been born with a love for animals then it's your duty to stand up for them, speak out, say something and definitely without hesitation always, always, always stop abuse when you are confronted by it.

Next thing I knew David was beside me, he had taken Sarah home then come back for me once she was safely inside our front door. And I was glad he'd done that because I didn't want their dog tearing Sarah to pieces the way it was doing with the possum. As David dragged me away I was yelling at those guys telling them that if they hit one more possum I was going to call the police. I told them I knew their mother, I didn't really know the lady who lived in that house all that well because she kept to herself but I knew she lived there on her own so one of those guys had to be her son otherwise why would she have been throwing him a party. As we walked away I noticed David had an injured possum inside his jacket, he was trying to keep it warm, to keep it alive. When we got home we looked the poor little thing over to see if we could help him. He seemed to be in shock, and of course he would be, he had a bit of blood on him but we couldn't quite see where it was coming from. The poor thing was shaking like a leave. We thought the best thing to do was to rush the poor little baby to an emergency vet hospital and get an expert to help him, so we wrapped him in a blanket and set off into the night. As we backed out of our driveway I got David to stop the car while I ran back to see if the guys were still hurting the possums, they weren't, they were nowhere in sight. Maybe some enraged woman going mental right in their faces was somewhat unnerving for them because they had put the pole away and gone inside.

The hospital was about an hour's drive way and we seemed to be catching every red light which annoyed me, but even though it was late on a Saturday night we knew they would be open. They specialised in wildlife so we knew they would be able to help our little possum. Dave drove and I nursed the little one on my knee, praying it would be alright. My sister was at home with Sarah and I'd told her not to answer the door if anybody knocked. I didn't want those guys getting a second wind and coming to our house to have a go at me and abusing her instead. She was ready to call the police if they started hanging around our house. But they never came, I think they had just gone inside and started drinking again.

We really wanted to save that possum's life but his injuries were too severe, he stayed alive all the way to the vet and they took him in right way, even though the waiting room was full of people, they rushed him in ahead of them, but there was nothing they could do for him, it seemed there was a puncture wound underneath his arm. The dog being so big and him being so small a lot of internal damage had been done, the best thing to do was put an end to his pain. They euthanized him and handed me the blanket. I sat silently holding onto that blanket on the ride back, I had a bloodstained blanket and a bloodstained heart. We came home so defeated, if we could have just saved that one possum I would have felt that some good had come out of all this.

I was so angry at those guys, sure possums can be annoying, we've all had them in our roofs. Nobody ever gets any sleep when there's a possum in the roof and where there's one there's always more. Still that's no reason to take their life into your own hands. You do what any decent person would do and call a professional to catch them and release them into the wild then find out where they are getting in and block up the hole before a new family of possums takes their place. Or even cut down your trees, if you don't want possums in your garden then don't give them a reason for being there.

I lay awake for a real long time that night going over what had gone on, it saddened me to the core that such cruel people were engaging in acts of such horror so close to our home, a home where so much love and devotion to animals was taking place. What a huge difference a few footsteps can make to the life of an animal.

I chastised myself for turning left instead of right as I walked out the front gate when taking Sarah for her walk, if I'd only just turned the other way we may have been able to prevent that possum from dying. Instead we didn't even get to save it. That thought played on my mind for days on end. Then one day about a week after the incident I said to David "Ok there was nothing we could do for that little possum but there is something we can do to make something good come out of all of this". He looked over at me no doubt wondering what was coming next. I then said "We have to find a needy animal and help it". To go on with our lives and forget about that night, act like nothing ever happened, well that didn't sit right with my heart. I suppose it was just my small way of trying to right a wrong, but I knew I had to do something, not just to help a needy animal but to help me as well. I had to have something positive come out of all this sadness in order to heal.

And so we set about looking for a pug in need, checked all the pounds and started looking at newspaper ads again, that's what lead us to Harper and there was no pug more in need of loving kindness and attention than she was at that time. The timing of going searching for Harper was perfect even if the reason we ended up looking for another pug in the first place was not. I would have gone looking for another pug somewhere down the track as I was destined to have more pugs, but my next pug wouldn't have been Harper and Harper needed me to go searching for her right there and then, she needed to be saved and I believe I needed to be the one saving her, I'm glad she came to me. What if she'd gone to somebody else, somebody who didn't understand pugs and their special requirements or somebody who didn't realise how ill she was. Or she could just as easily have gone to somebody who thought dogs belong outside the house not inside, she could have been cast out into their backyard. That would mean her entire life would have always been spent outdoors and I believe Harper deserved a lot more than that, I believed she needed to be treated as a true member of the family and be shown a better life. Because she was cheap Harper could have easily fallen into the wrong hands, fallen prey to somebody just looking for a bargain, we were lucky that we got to see the advertisement when we did. We were the first caller and I believe it was meant to happen that way.

Harper died here at Grace Farm in 2009. Although we never knew her real age we believe she was around 12 and a half years old when she passed away, although she could well have been much older. Harper had been sharing our lives for seven wonderful years when we lost her and we consider ourselves blessed to have known this wonderful little girl. We were also lucky to have had her for length of time we did considering the state she was in when we got her. In a way she probably should have died a year earlier. She was really ill the previous year, even our vet thought she wouldn't pull through, although the words were never actually spoken but he knows what our pugs mean to us and you could see it in his eyes.

Harper developed an abscess in-between the two bones in one of her front legs. She was so sick with it as you can imagine. The goo was just pouring out and pouring out and there was no stopping it, when we took her to the vet the goo was dripping all over the countertop, dripping down David's jacket as we sat waiting to go in. It came through the towel we had with us, soaked through it in no time. Lots of cleaning needed to be done, lots of strong antibiotics administered, she was on high doses of antibiotics for many weeks, and we used poultices to draw out the discharge and it just went on oozing and oozing. Dripped out for well over a week and she was just so poorly, it seemed to be affecting every part of her, contaminating her entire system. Even when the goo finally stopped oozing she was still very ill. She could barely lift her head and was unable to stand unattended, she couldn't put any pressure on that front leg and due to her having no energy she wasn't able to hold the leg up and hop about like she would have done if she'd merely just had a sore paw. She needed help with everything and I was more than happy to help her although I felt for sure we were going to lose her and every day I just kept cleaning her wound and trying to get her through the day as best I could. She was still eating which was a good sign, but eating very little, even chewing took it out of her. And that was hard to witness because Harper really did love her food.

But to her credit Harper pulled through those long weeks of sickness, the weeks and weeks of carrying her outside because she was too weak to walk and the hand feeding to encourage her to eat. We'd give Harper her favourite foods just to tempt her, but it made little difference, it was like they were not her favourite foods anymore. She slept a lot of those weeks away and in the mornings I'd dread opening my eyes just in case she'd passed away in the middle of the night. I'd roll over in bed and feel her body just to see if it was still warm and that she was still breathing, I did this just before taking the others out for their morning walk. I'd let Harper sleep in, then I'd come back and take her out for a wee on her own as I didn't want any of the others knocking her over. Even a slight brush against her would have sent her toppling she was just so weak and unbalanced. I'd stand half crouched down with my hands either side of her so I could catch her if she fell. She didn't want me holding onto her while was doing her business, so I just had to pop her down on the grass and be ready to pick her up quickly once she'd done what she needed to do. That's what I did four or five times a day, as soon as she woke up I'd take her out and then bring her in and offer her a drink, try and keep her fluids up. Added carrot juice to her meals as well just to get extra fluids into her, couldn't have it too sloppy because I was hand feeding her and you can't hand feed soup, so I added just enough to make her meals super moist and tempted her with special treats just to get her to take her antibiotics. I think she knew there was an antibiotic hidden in there, but bless her she'd eat them anyway because she knew how happy I became when she did. I'd see her swallowing and start praising her like crazy for doing so. Harper took a long time to come good but she wasn't ready to go then, she fought hard, she stayed with us a bit longer and we were so grateful to her for doing that.

All of this happened a few months before Horton came into our lives. I guess as Harper was going through all this Horton himself would have been being born. Born to a breeder who at that point wouldn't have known there was anything wrong with him, at that time he would have been just another tiny puppy in a litter, he wouldn't have stood out from the others in the slightest and when he did, well that's when his story started with us. Harper sure did love Horton a lot and he loved her right back. They were drawn to each other, gravitated instantly and got a lot of comfort from one other. I think they must have sensed one another's specialness early on because I remember they formed a close bond pretty fast. Harper got great joy from having Horton in the house. Her eyes lit up watching him, she sure did love babies that was clear to see. Looking back on it now it makes me wonder if perhaps she stayed around for him, did the little guy in fact give her something more to live for. Oh to Harpers great credit she'd gotten herself through the worst of it on her own with no knowledge at all that there was a little black pug puppy out there somewhere who very soon would come bursting into our lives and into our hearts. But she did take to mothering him very quickly and bless her because she still wasn't one hundred percent right herself. Maybe she wanted to stay around looking after him until she felt he would be alright on his own. She saw what he was, witnessed his transformation and maybe then thought it was ok to go. Certainly Horton noticed right away how lovely a dog Harper was, he chose her above all his other siblings to climb into bed next to, in the early days he spent a lot of time sleeping beside Harper and gained strength by doing that. I think he sensed she had a true mother's heart and felt comforted by that and I understood this because I felt exactly the same way when I was around my own mother. Mothers are just special, there's no denying that. And Harper was such a docile old darling, you couldn't help but feel good around her and when little Horton dragged his body in next to her she'd turn, lean down, sniff his ears and give the side of his face a little lick. Horton loved sleeping wrapped around Harper because there was so much loose skin, always a lovely soft warm spot for him to rest his little head on. Harper was treating him like her own pup. And in a way that was a nice thing for her to have happen wasn't it, to not have this puppy taken away from her like so many others had been. Harper got to see this one grow up, become strong, become healthy and I don't think there's anything greater for a true Mother's heart then bearing witness to that. And Harper, more than anyone, deserved to be able to witness what Horton became.

Harper started feeling unwell again about a week or so before Horton got desexed, she was slowing down a bit and just not feeling good in herself, both David and I noticed it. And we were readying ourselves for making the decision that all dog parents dread. When Horton came home from the vet after his operation Harper was delighted to see him, spent lots of time slowly sniffing him over, then she'd slowly sniff at him again. He didn't like the others sniffing him but he was fine when Harper was doing it, it was as if he realised she was checking that he was ok. Perhaps Harper knew Horton was going to have that operation when he was strong enough to do so and was waiting around for it to happen so she could see he pulled through. Harper stayed beside Horton while he slept. The two of them wrapped themselves around each other and snoozed the afternoons away. But being only a young dog Horton bounced back from his operation very quickly, he was back to his mischievous playful little self in no time and Harper lay in her bed watching him play.

Horton's stiches were due to come out in ten days but Harper wasn't there waiting for him this time when he was carried through the door. A few days earlier she let us know it was time for her to go. She'd had a really good extra twelve months and was healthy and happy throughout that year, never quite her old self though, but not too far from how she used to be so we'd hoped she would go on for a few more years at least. But that was not to be and she let us know that in her own gentle way, so we said our goodbyes, we thanked her for the love and joy she had brought into our lives then called the vet out to the farm to put her to sleep. We can at least do that for our animals, we can't do it for our human companions but we can make that phone call, bestow one last act of love and kindness on our beloved animals. We didn't want Harper to have to close her eyes for the last time in a strange place on top of a cold metal table so our farm vet came out on a Sunday morning.

That call is always going to be one of the hardest calls you ever have to make and it doesn't matter how many times you have to do it, it hurts pretty much the same. I don't know how people have their dogs put down because the family no longer wants them or they're a nuisance because even when you know deep down in your heart that it's the right decision, it does seem so wrong on some level that a phone call is made, a dog's life ends and you were the one who made the phone call. But the reality of the situation is this, if you know no more can be done for them, it is a blessing to be able to make a decision and have that pain taken away from them instantly, they no longer have to suffer, you have control over the amount of pain you put them through and you should never allow them to linger because of the pain losing them is going to cause you. That wouldn't be true love. It really isn't love in any form at all. It's selfishness if anything, selfishness in its cruelest form.

While David dug a hole I sat on the veranda with Harper in my arms. I remember I held her for the longest time because I knew after that day I wouldn't be able to hold her again for a long, long time. I looked down at her body laying cross my stomach, I was wearing an olive green t-shirt that day and her fawn fur stood out against it. I concentrated on her body, it looked broken, she looked broken, I honestly believe she didn't have even one more day to give. I hadn't noticed how worn she was when her body was in movement but as she lay still in my arms I could see how broken it was, years of over breeding at the hands of that greedy backyard breeder had taken a toll on her body. The fact that she got to 12 and a half years of age was a miracle in itself. But seven years as a loved and treasured member of our family, yes I was so very thankful and appreciative to have been granted that. When David said the grave was ready I took my t-shirt off and wrapped Harper in it because I wanted her to have something from me, of course she'd had years of love and kindness from me but I just wanted to envelope her in something that I'd been wearing, something that smelt like me. I felt comforted knowing she was wrapped in my t-shirt. It was almost like I would be hugging her forever.

And although I grieved for Harper in a way I didn't feel as if she had left me, I felt her presence beside me in a very real way, in life she was my shadow, a most loyal pug and in death I still felt her close. I'd be in the kitchen chopping food at the bench. Harper would always sit behind me when I did this and I'd turn around and give her a little treat, a little bit of what I was cutting up. Weeks after she died I was still doing this, still turning round with food in my hand for her because I could have sworn she was sitting behind me. I felt her there, her presence was so real. And I didn't think of Harper as being in the ground either, I'd walk past her grave and it hardly registered. I still looked for her as I walked across the paddocks when I took the other pugs for a walk and I'd get home and search the house for her, it'd take a little while for my mind to realise that she wasn't here anymore.

Everyone copes differently when they lose a dog, some want to be around people but I sort of go into myself a little. I want and need to be on my own, on the farm, with my other pugs, no contact, no phone calls, nothing. I need this time to heal, to hug the pugs that are still with me and just process everything that has gone on and of course cry bucketful's while I'm doing it. I find people want to help but really what can they say, what is there to say. Grief is a lonely road and we must travel it on our own, we all heal at different speeds and all have different needs while we are healing. But there is always light at the end of every tunnel even if that tunnel happens to be a long one.

CHAPTER FOUR

Ruby

Davison, Sarah, Harper and I had just moved into a townhouse, we had crossed over to the other side of the river. We now lived in a double story residence on the side of a lake, it was a beautiful home and the view was lovely and I could still walk the dogs by the same river, only we were now walking on the opposite side. The distance we had moved was not very far, but the other side of the river, well it was a completely different world living over there and a totally different lifestyle too. We were enclosed by huge architectural masterpieces of homes and some mansions. Our home wasn't one of them thank goodness because lord knows I couldn't have coped with that. I felt uncomfortable in my new surroundings. I couldn't settle within those walls, I wanted to but I just couldn't do it. I loved the house, it was double brick so it kept the pugs cool in summer, the bathroom was done up in those large Italian tiles that I had always admired and there were two spa baths one upstairs and one down. If ever I was going to do up a house it would have been exactly like this one, the tones, the light fittings, the kitchen, the layout of the house, everything was perfect apart from the privacy factor. There isn't a great deal of privacy when you live by the side of a lake. And I like my privacy a lot. The lack of seclusion was hardest of all. I felt as if I was on show all the time, like a caged animal clawing at the walls trying to escape. I now knew how animals at the zoo felt, people staring at you and no means possible of escaping it. Also the lake lifestyle was noisy and I've never been good with a lot of noise, I much prefer peace and quiet.

This tranquil haven we thought we were moving to ended up being not very tranquil at all. If we were set back a bit from the waters edge it may have been different, quieter, not so exposed. In summer it was a total madhouse, we spent most of the time with the blinds closed, just to try and regain some privacy. What was the point of having a lovely view if we couldn't even see it. It hadn't been like that when we were being shown around by the real estate agent. It was a Saturday afternoon and the lake was empty, everything was so peaceful, so serene and of course that's how we thought it was always going to be. But we were wrong and when we finally moved in the reality of what we had bought hit us hard, especially me. The lake lifestyle was a brilliant one if you are the kind of people who like parties and constant socialising but it was the wrong lifestyle for us.

Winter was a completely different story the lake was quieter then, it was like we were living in a completely different house. I lived for winter. I'd sit for hours watching the rain hit the water. The pugs were sleeping on a thick rug by the heater and I was happy then, content, so at ease. I've always loved rain and to sit by that vast amount of water watching tiny droplets fall was pure heaven for me. And not too many people went walking around the lake when it was cold and rainy and that suited me just fine. I could sit as close to the front windows as I liked and nobody was staring in. I wasn't an animal in a cage then, I was just me, and I liked that. But far too quickly the warmer weather returned and so did the people, the parties and the noise. It was hard to hear my own thoughts with so much noise going on. I have always been a deep thinker so this was a hard way for me to live. I just didn't know who I was living there. I lost my inner peace. And inner peace is very important to me.

Thank goodness for those twice a day walks, they kept me sane, the pugs and I could escape down to the river and things were back to normal again. I lived for those walks. I turned forty in that house and all I wanted for my birthday was to get the hell out of there. It was a sad time for me. David loved the place and I felt guilty for not loving it as much as he did, I wished I could have loved it more, if only for his sake. I missed my little home sitting all the way over the other side of the river and longed to be back there. I thought about the young guy we'd sold it too and wondered if he was as happy there as I had been. While I was sitting in my elaborate cage I used to imagine how much joy that tiny red brick home of mine was bringing him. I was really hoping our next move would be to a farm, but it wasn't we bought the lake house instead.

I thought things would improve in time, thought I'd get used to it, but I didn't. The lake lifestyle was perfect for people living on their own and a few of the townhouses were occupied by such people and it was fantastic for them because they never had to feel alone, ever. There was always a door for them to knock on or a conversation going on, even on a cold winters evening all they had to do was walk out their door and go tap on a door or window and instantly they weren't alone anymore. And I was glad for them because I can't think of anything sadder then wanting company when no company can be found.

David was away on business a lot of the time too and that didn't help matters either because I missed him like crazy and that made living where I was all the worse. He'd ring from overseas and I'd put on a happy voice for him so he wouldn't worry, he had enough on his plate with work, he didn't need the added burden of me.

My sister would come and visit once a week on her day off work and I couldn't wait to see her face. She made me laugh and when I was laughing life didn't feel quite so bad. I always felt uplifted after her visits. We were sitting in the downstairs spa one hot afternoon discussing a family member who' d recently been diagnosed with a terminal illness, we were saying how worried we were about them, how short life was, that sort of thing. I turned to her and asked if she was happy with her life and what she would do differently if she could, she rattled off a few things and asked me the same question.

"I'd be living on that farm I've always wanted and I'd be looking after elderly animals" I said so fast I stumbled over my words. I suppose I could have mentioned my house but at that point we'd been there well over a year and I was trying to love it, to make peace with the lack of privacy, so I let that one go. At the time that was my rule. As soon as a negative thought about where I was living came to mind I was replacing it with something positive. It helped a bit, made me more grateful for the things I liked about the place. Sometimes it was just the pretty old style light fitting outside the front door that brought me joy, so I'd concentrate on that and it helped me get through the day. I figured I had to do something to make life more bearable so I made up a little game to help me cope. I've always tried to turn a negative into a positive but most of all I wanted to be happier for David's sake, he'd worked so hard, done so much for me over the years I owed him that. Marrying David was definitely the best move I've ever made in my life, his wasn't my first marriage proposal, I think I must just have one of those comfortable comforting faces that men like to come home to at the end of the day, the other proposal wasn't right but David certainly was and still is in every way possible. If I had my time over I would have married him sooner than I did, David wanted to marry me two weeks after we'd been dating and I said I thought he should get some age on him first. I didn't think nineteen year olds should be asking such questions. I figured he needed to live a bit to really know his own mind. Being older than him I just wanted to make sure it was what he truly wanted to do. I didn't want him acting on impulse, being lured in by my peaches and cream complexion. I thought he needed to really think about things, and he did and he was persistent, he knew his own mind and never wavered, two years later his heart felt exactly the same way it always had.

David was 21 when we got married, I made my bouquet myself, twenty seven beautiful red roses went into it, one for every year I had been on this earth. I didn't want a fuss or a big wedding, one because my mum wasn't well at the time and I didn't want to be putting more pressure on her, and two because when you know deep down in your heart that something is this right there's no need to make a big deal about it. I've always been a quiet sort of a person, I like my days to be stress free and peaceful and my wedding day was going to be exactly the same way. I remember Mum had a hairdresser come to the house to do her hair. I did my own hair, again because I didn't want a lot of fussing. And I was sitting there in my night gown chatting away happily to the two of them, just slowly sipping a cup of tea enjoying watching Mum getting her hair done. After a bit of chatting the hairdresser made a comment about the bride, asked where she was and said that she was no doubt a nervous wreck. Me and Mum looked at each other and smiled and then Mum pointed to me and said "That's her, she's the bride". The hairdresser couldn't believe it, she said I was the calmest bride she'd ever seen. But that's because I took the pressure of a big wedding off my day. My wedding dress was second-hand and I didn't wear a veil or shoes. I was married at home and my 80kg English mastiff was part of the festivities. And that was it really, on the 10th of March 1992 David and I became husband and wife at eleven o'clock in the morning. I could feel the grass beneath my feet, my new husbands hand in mine and Tessa's wet nose as she leant against my dress. It was a really wonderful day.

I wouldn't change a thing about our life together because it was great. David was my rock and I loved him, that's why I made such an effort with where we were living. When we walked round the lake together I'd point out things that I liked and I made sure to be more positive when he came home. Not sure how convinced he was but I was making the effort and I think that pleased him.

My sister and I got out of the spa and had a nice lunch. We talked some more, not about anything important just how work was going for her and what she had been doing that week. After our serious conversation our mood was lighter, we'd had a few laughs, we always seemed to be laughing whenever we were together; it's been that way all our lives. She is one of the funniest people I know. As Alana left she mentioned something about some pugs she'd seen online, she was on the internet a lot more than I was, I didn't know much about the internet back them. Later that day she rang and read the ad to me over the phone. They were two old pugs that were looking for a home together, nine and ten years old they were, perfect I thought. Sarah was seven and Harper, we thought was around eight, I would have a seven, an eight, a nine and a ten year old how wonderful would that be. Alana said their names were Ruby and Grace, it just kept getting better and better, they were the best names I'd ever heard of for two little old lady pugs. There was a photo of one of the pugs, it was Ruby she thought, so she emailed it to David's computer. She gave me the phone number for the rescue group and before she hung up she said "You might not be on your farm yet Andrea but you can still help these two" and she was right I could and I did.

When David got home we went upstairs to the study and looked at the photo together. He sat tapping away and I hung over his office chair waiting for the computer to load up the image, it seemed to be taking forever, then suddenly there she was. A magnificent beauty, a petal, a rose, her little old body sitting slightly slumped over. Ruby was certainly a beautiful old pug, a sweet little silver fawn pug with big eyes and a graying face. All pugs have different faces and Ruby was the kind of pug I have always found to be the most attractive. I just fell in love with her from her photo. I turned to David and said we've got to take her. I think him seeing me so happy he didn't have it in him to say no.

Ruby looked adorable, the photo had captured her perfectly, old weary eyes looked into the lens, she was sitting on a small patchwork quilt in blue tones. We wondered what Grace was like, there wasn't a photo of her so all night I had images of various pugs flashing through my mind wondering which one she looked like. The suspense was killing me but we just had to wait until we got to meet Grace face to face, I concentrated on Ruby and contented myself with her, David printed the photo out for me and I stuck it on the fridge. By the time we'd finished talking about the two pugs it was late so I rang the rescue group the next morning and had a talk to the lady, she was nice, I liked her instantly, she devoted her life to helping unwanted pugs and I admired her for that. I told her I didn't know such a thing existed; she told me Pug Rescue had been going for a while. I'd rescued quite a few old dogs over the years by myself but I didn't know there were rescue groups out there for specific breeds. I thought it was a brilliant idea though.

I told her all about my life plans, for the farm and the elderly animals I wanted to take in. The she told me all about these two old pugs. I couldn't get my mind around the fact that somebody wouldn't want their pug but there you have it, takes all kinds I guess. We talked about Ruby, the ad said she had an unusual gait, I worried how she would go with the stairs, the lady thought she'd be fine and emailed me an application form, again waiting for David, always waiting for David when it came to things computer related. I didn't even have a computer of my own at the time, didn't know how to use one, didn't even know how to turn one on and had no interest in learning at that point. And when I did David was almost driven insane with teaching me. He has the patience of a saint. And is so calm and peaceful, but there were times when he'd be sitting there holding his head, well not so much holding it but massaging one finger along his temple the way he does when stressed. And I'd be there trying hard but just not getting it, he'd tell me to click on something and so I would and he'd be saying "No, no, double click, double click, you always have to double click when doing that" he'd gone through the same thing with me the previous day but that was twenty four hours ago, a lot had happened in that time. So I'd be yelling back "Well if you mean double click then say double click, how the hell am I meant to know if you want one or two clicks" and so we'd be forever going round and round in circles. I don't think David understood how something that came so easily for him was so difficult for me. It wasn't that I was stupid it's just that technological things baffle me. And I think the fact that I had little interest in them wasn't helping either. In the end in order to save my poor husband from ending up in a straitjacket I got myself a notepad and wrote his instructions down. That way I didn't have to bother him so much. And from those instructions I taught myself the basic use of a computer. Naturally I had to go back and ask for help when something new came up and there were many times were I almost gave up. I'd get so frustrated some days that I'm amazed the computer didn't end up at the bottom of the lake and if it had been my computer and not David's that's exactly what would have been its fate. I figured I'd lived this long not knowing how to use a computer and been quite happy, why go and spoil things now. But because David kept telling me about this amazing world of knowledge and information out there I persisted. And I'm so glad I did.

When David got home from work he printed the form out. I looked over the long list of questions, they were being thorough, I liked that about them, just because these pugs where no longer wanted by their families didn't mean they were going to hand them over to just anybody, and good on them for that. I liked how this organization worked. Even though I had pugs of my own I still had to prove that I was the right person for one their pugs. I mean I knew I was right but they didn't so were checking me out fully before allowing those two little treasures anywhere near me and I was full of praise for them for doing that. They were taking precautions, and I thought, excellent care of the pugs they were trying to find homes for. I had the highest regard for them instantly.

I remember the very first time I set eyes one Ruby and Grace, their foster mum had overshot our house, I didn't want to hassle the pugs by having her drive up and down the long street so I told her to stay put and we'd come find her, she said she'd start walking the two girls in the direction of our house. David, Sarah, Harper and I had been watching the street from upstairs, waiting by the window watching every car wondering if that was the car that contained our new pugs. When the phone rang we thought they weren't coming and my heart sank a little, but she was just lost that's all, so excitedly we made our way downstairs and out into the street.

They were about eight houses away from our place, I saw two ladies get out of a car and take two pugs from the back seat. I looked at the way the pugs were walking you can tell an old dogs walk a mile away, suddenly I couldn't see anything at all, not even David and he was right beside me, tears fell down my cheeks so fast. I loved them, right there and then I knew that I loved them, how could anybody not want these two lovely old darlings I said to David as we walked down the street. David grabbed my hand so I wouldn't fall. I've always been a faller, trip over an ant I would and knowing this and seeing my eyes watering he thought the best thing to do was hold my hand so that if I did trip he would be able to keep me from falling down and hurting myself. I kept wiping the tears away because the pugs were getting closer and I desperately wanted to be able to see their faces. See Ruby's beauty and finally glimpse what Grace's face looked like, I didn't want tears getting in the way, robbing me of that very first vision.

I felt like a total twit standing here in the middle of our street crying like a baby but I just couldn't stop. The two ladies were polite and didn't say anything, and god bless them for that because I felt like such a fool, I couldn't even get my words out. David was handed Ruby and they handed me Grace. Oh no David's got the good one was my initial thought, but I was wrong they were both good ones. The only reason I'd thought that was because we'd only seen a photo of Ruby so hers was the face I'd been looking at every day for the past few weeks and I guess in my mind she was the one I wanted to hold first. I stopped crying when I held Grace and concentrated on her face. She was the smallest pug I'd ever seen at the time, so very little, just a tiny old girl sitting there in my arms wondering what the heck was going on.

Although Ruby and Grace were only a little older than the two pugs I already had they both seemed so very old to me, perhaps I was just used to Sarah and Harper and that's what they looked like to everybody else except me. I looked over at Ruby and David, they seemed happy together, like they belonged.

We walked back to the house and Sarah and Harper came running out as soon as David turned the key. The four pugs sniffed each other and we all went inside. I'd spent the week sewing cushions so the new pugs had something of their own to sit on, I didn't put them on the floor until the two new pugs were in the house. I didn't want Sarah or Harper claiming them as theirs because I felt it was important for the two new ladies to have something of their own, something that didn't smell like it belonged to somebody else.

Ruby just looked at hers, she just stood in the middle of the room eyeing everything with suspicion, it must have been so hard for them, what they'd gone through in the past couple of months. Being thrown out of their home because the family was having a large gathering for Christmas and they didn't want them around. Grace looked across at her cushion then promptly ran over and had a big wee in the middle of it. "That's what she thinks of my sewing" I said and we all laughed. Poor little girl must have been holding her bladder and just couldn't hold onto it anymore. I wondered why she hadn't gone in the street but she must have just been flustered by the long drive and being put into a strangers arms. I put Grace's cushion in the washing machine and she watched what I was doing then walked over and claimed Ruby's cushion as hers, but Ruby didn't seem to mind, she was still standing in the middle of the room eyeing everybody and everything with distrust, I think she was a little shell-shocked. When the foster ladies left, we took all four of our pugs for a walk to the river. Our two new girls only managed to stagger a few steps out into the street before unloading their bladders and bowels, both of them must have been holding themselves waiting for a bit of grass to appear. Grace had already had a wee on the cushion but to be fair on her it was green. Our two new pugs seemed to enjoy being out and about, we didn't know if they were up to going as far as Sarah and Harper normally did so we cut the walk short. Grace wasn't much of a walker, she kept asking to be picked up so David carried her most of the way. But Ruby, funny legs or not, was really enjoying herself, it seemed she loved walking, well running really because there wasn't the slow amble I had been expecting, she had a very quick swift way of moving along, yes an unusual gait but that wasn't slowing her down any. And she loved all the new smells down by the river. Her little old face looked so happy. It did my heart good to see her happy after how she had been inside our home.

Ruby's gait made her shuffle along like a little penguin. I thought she looked absolutely adorable doing it and it made her more endearing to me but I also worried about her, was she in pain, how would she be when she got older that sort of thing and when she was running down the steep river bank on our twice a day walks I thought she was going to hurt herself. She had trouble walking backwards, in the hallway she couldn't back up due to her back leg weakness, I knew how she got arthritis in her neck though because she'd just put her head down and barge her way through the other three pugs to get to the end of the hall and then turn around. Her front legs were crooked and her back legs didn't function properly and that worried me.

First thing Monday morning I was on the phone to Pug Rescue asking what I could do to help this little pug. Was there some form of operation perhaps? There wasn't, of course Pug Rescue had looked into it, they'd taken Ruby to see a specialist, that's how dedicated they are to these pugs but I didn't know that at the time, that's why I made the phone call I just wanted to do whatever was in my power to make Ruby's life comfortable. She wasn't in pain, thank goodness, at least I had peace of mind about that. She had been born that way, lived like that for a very long time, Ruby was used to her condition whereas I was not. I just took more care of her on the walks, tried to help her legs. I carried her down the embankment when it was wet so she wouldn't slip. She hated being carried, she wanted to run, she'd wrestle with me until she was on the ground again then take off down to the water's edge penguin walking as fast as she could go just to get away from me.

She looked gorgeous doing it. I think she was scared I was going to pick her up again and spoil her fun, she wanted to be free, she just wanted to walk and wasn't about to let her new mum stop her from doing it.

Pug Rescue had said the river walks would help build up her strength so we continued doing the same route. Besides I couldn't have stopped even if I wanted to, Ruby loved those walks, she was like a young pup out there. Once I'd gotten her and the other three safely across the busy road we lived on and down to the river I'd take Ruby's lead of and she'd shuffle along quickly not stopping to sniff until she was a good distance away. I worried at first letting her off the lead like that, would she come back to me at the end of the walk. But she always did, she knew I was her mum now even though once we got home she didn't interact. The distrust was still there, her eyes told me everything she was feeling and I couldn't have understood her more clearly if she could talk. I didn't push her, I longed for her to settle, feel safe in her new home, but you can't push them, you just have to wait. But I told her over and over again how much I loved her whenever I was putting on her harness and taking it off again. And when I passed by her bed as I walked around the house I made a point of going over and gently stroking her head. Nothing forceful, just a gentle pat and then I carried on with the housework and her little distrustful old eyes would be watching every move I made.

Ruby at home and Ruby out walking were two very different pugs. Then again me out walking and me at home were two very different people as well. I did worry that she may have been getting bad vibes from me, dogs are very sensitive, extremely good at picking up on how us humans are truly feeling, was me not being fully at ease with where I was living making everything harder for Ruby. It was an awful way to live really and I didn't like that Ruby was picking up on it. I felt quite guilty about it to be honest. She was a very sensitive little pug and me being the way I was would have been making it harder for her to settle in. Grace was fine, she was a real little snuggler, made a beeline for you as soon as you'd sit down and when you picked her up she'd rub her face into your chest and lay like that sleeping for hours. But Ruby was different, she wasn't going to come anywhere near you until she knew she could trust you. So I just concentrated on doing things that made her happy and knew that one day she would come around. I loved seeing Ruby's face when she was walking by the river, she was at her happiest then, she loved everything about being down there and wouldn't turn back until we reached the bridge. That was our turn around spot and she knew it, she wouldn't even turn around if there was rain threatening and a few times we got caught out in heavy downpours because Ruby refused to come back until she got to the bridge. I'd call her but she'd pretend she couldn't hear me but I knew she could hear me just fine. I'd have Grace in my arms and Sarah and Harper standing next to me and the rain would be making my clothes and their fur soaking wet, but still Ruby soldiered on ahead. The rain didn't seem to bother her at all. So I'd get home and towel dry the little blessings first then leave them sleeping by the heater while I jumped in the shower and we'd all be there warm and dry cooking dinner when David got home.

David loved all our pugs and made a fuss of each one as soon as he walked through the door. If he sat down he'd be instantly smothered by three pugs wanting to be as close to him as possible.

And when they'd all settled he would ask about Ruby, she'd be on the other side of the room watching him with the three other pugs and he'd look over at her lovingly and ask how her day had been. I'd tell him mostly about her walking and how she especially loved those embankments. She was like a little kid at an amusement park, ran down them so fast I thought her funny little front legs were going to buckle under her but she never fell once and in time her legs did strengthen up quite a lot. I think running down the riverbank was a game to Ruby, she loved going down as fast as she could and would often let out a happy yelp at the top before taking off. The first time she did it scared the hell out of me, I thought she'd hurt herself and turned back to go help her, see what was wrong, I met her halfway up the embankment and held out my arms to her but she just flew past me with her mouth half open doing her happy pug face. The way she held her legs, not bending them, made her look like she was wearing braces, like her legs had invisible braces on them, but of course there were no braces attached it was just how Ruby's legs were. And she didn't want or need my help, she wanted to be on the ground, she wanted to fly down that embankment and she wanted to yelp, she wanted to live life her way and so I let her. Even though half the time I held my breath until she reached the bottom safely. On the way up to the river Ruby would lead the pack, be pulling on the lead, on the way back she was tired and lagged behind a bit so every so often the other three pugs and I would stand and wait for her to catch up. It was like she loved that river so much she'd used all her energy up on that. Once she caught us we'd carry on walking together as a group. She was a determined little thing, she was truly worn out but no way was she going to let you carry her. She refused your help because she wanted to do it on her own and I really admired her for that, would have dearly loved to hold her in my arms but couldn't help but be proud of her steely determination. I learnt a real lot from that little girl. Once we got back home Ruby would sleep the day away until it was time to go for the afternoon walk. And she'd rise slowly from her bed when she heard me getting the four leads and harnesses ready and she'd walk faster and faster as her little old legs came good.

Ruby was happy, she ate well and loved to walk but she wasn't interacting with us as much as Grace was. Grace was all over the house discovering every nook and peeping her little old oddly shaped face into every cranny, she was curious about the place, her funny shaped eyes darted everywhere. Ruby didn't do any of that she would just go into the lounge and stay there. Grace would come over and ask to be picked up, she loved to sit with you, didn't like to be patted too much but loved to be near you. Always wanting to sit on your knee when you were sitting down and was always rubbing her little face against you and grunting away happily to herself. With Ruby it was different, she took some time getting used to her new home and even more time getting used to us. She'd come in from a walk or come back inside from going to the toilet and head straight to her bed because she felt safe and comfortable there. It was her safe place. She came with this little blue beanbag that smelt to high heaven, it was her security, it had come from her original home so she had a connection to it. Grace had shared that same home, that same beanbag yet it meant nothing much to her, but to Ruby it was everything.

David wanted to throw the beanbag out because of the smell but I said "Oh no you don't, not until she's fully settled in" I thought it'd be unfair to take that away from her until she was ready to give it up. She'd had so much taken away from her already that I wasn't going to allow this beanbag to be taken away from her as well. I thought it would have made things worse for her, taken her longer to feel at home and she was already having enough trouble in that area. I wouldn't allow anything to make the transition any harder on her then it already was. David said "Well can't you at least wash it then", he stood in the middle of the room pulling his face with the stinky beanbag in one hand, only holding onto it with the tips of his fingers, that's how putrid he thought the thing was. But again I said no, because I knew the smell was part of the security, smells are very important to dogs, if I were to wash that familiar smell away then what would be the point. I may as well have thrown the entire beanbag out. So even though David wasn't too happy about it he put up with the smell and when friends dropped over they just had to put up with it as well. I think everybody was happy when Ruby no longer needed her smelly old beanbag for security. But again it was her choice because it had to be, nobody pushed her to give her security beanbag up, because none of us had any right to do that.

When the girls first arrived I placed Ruby's beanbag in a part of the lounge where she could get the best view of the house, see me in the kitchen, look out the windows that faced the lake and take in the entire lounge room. She could also see our legs walking up and down the stairs. Those little old eyes that I'd first seen looking out at me in the photograph now looked at me from across the room. Every move I made was noted, every word spoken listened to, my comings and goings all observed from the safety of her little navy blue beanbag. As I went about the housework I'd stop by Ruby's bed, stroke her little old head, tell her that I loved her and carry on my way. I really felt for how she was feeling, I've always had an understanding heart when it comes to the animals of this world and my heart went out to little old Ruby enormously. I think we really need to put ourselves in their shoes and try and imagine how we would feel if we'd been through the same ordeal. We can't take in an old dog and say "Ok I've rescued you, you should be grateful for all I've done, so snap to it and settle in" I would hope that should I ever find myself in the position Ruby was in that somebody would be as kind and understanding with me. They don't have to be grateful to you, they don't have to be instantly happy so you can feel alright about it. They have feelings and needs and it's up to us to give thought to how it must be for them, think about what they have endured and think about how you would feel in the same situation.

Ruby had lived with her family since she was a puppy, she slept on the bed and was their baby until a human baby came along and then she was cast aside, she then went to live with a foster lady only Ruby didn't know she was a foster lady, over time she grew to trust her and even thought that she was her new mother. Because nobody wanted to take in one old pug let alone two, Ruby and Grace were with at their foster home for four months. That's a long time for little pugs, of course they would have thought that was their new home. And now they had to get used to our home and accept us as their new parents and that's a lot for a pug to have to do. No wonder she wouldn't come off her beanbag, no wonder she looked at me with distrust, no wonder she was taking a while to feel at ease. She was probably reeling and needed to sort everything out in her mind first. Her little world had just been turned upside down and she needed time to adjust, time to figure out what the heck was going on. And so the only thing David and I could do was let her work things out and just love her through it until she was ready to love us back. I was just happy that Ruby enjoyed the walks so much, at least I had something I knew made her happy. It's important when bringing a dog, especially an older dog, into your home that you take the time to notice what brings them joy and make sure you give them plenty of that.

I've always felt sad when a dog is handed back to a rescue group because they are not fitting in, sometimes I wonder if the dog has just been through so much that all they needed was an extra bit of time to adjust. And if given that time they would have come good and still be in that home today feeling loved and wanted and very much settled, but due to human impatience weren't given the chance. Some things in life cannot ever be rushed, especially when dealing with trauma and emotions, there's no time limit on these things because how can there possibly be. Because you are not dealing with a one length of time fits all cases kind of thing, you are dealing with living breathing beings, beings that have emotions and who have all gone through different life experiences that brought them to you.

And even if two dogs have gone through the exact same experiences, like Ruby and Grace did, you are still dealing with two different personalities and each personality is going to have a different reaction and way of dealing with what has occurred in their life. Dogs, well, all animals really are just like us in that area, what will greatly upset one individual will simply just roll off another person's back. You have to keep this in the back of your mind at all times when dealing with dogs and show true empathy for them. And because both dogs are different they are going to heal at different speeds, put their trust in you at different times and open their hearts to you when they are fully healed and it takes as long as it is going to take. But I can tell you this, when it happens it's the most wonderful, joyous, rewarding feeling in the entire world and is very much worth not only the wait, but all you had to go through in order to get them to that place, and there is no greater happier feeling then knowing that their broken little heart has mended and that you have been allowed in.

Life with four old pugs was wonderful for me, I just loved taking care of them and suddenly where I lived didn't matter as much anymore. I tended to block my surrounding out a bit more and just concentrate of the four little souls I was now sharing my life with. Even the man next door and his opinion of my pugs didn't bother me. He was a real pain when it came to getting our neighbours permission to bring in two more dogs. I already loathed that we needed to have their consent. Hated that I needed to have somebody else's authorisation to do what I wanted to do in my own home. But there were 14 townhouses in our block and everything had to be run by the body corporate before getting the go ahead, and that was if they did give it to you in the end because a lot of things were knocked back I was told.

Lucky for me the people from either side liked us. One said yes right away and signed the forms without hesitation; the old man on the other side wasn't so easy and gave David quite a grilling. Flexing his geriatric muscle was how David put it. David thought he should be the one to go round to talk to the old bloke because he's more diplomatic than I am. We both knew if I went round things wouldn't have gone well and we really needed things to go well. I think David was a saint for putting up with this old man's attitude; even hearing about it aggravated the living crap out of me. Dave told me that the old man sat leaning back in his armchair with his finger on his chin wondering if four dogs in a townhouse would be a good idea. I think he was just playing with us, the way old people tend to do when they have nothing much else to do with their time. He knew the two pugs we already had went for walks by the river both morning and night. I know he knew that because I'd seen him at his upstairs window watching us coming and going. My dogs were healthier and living better lives then he was because I'd never once seen him out on a walk or leave his home much at all for that matter. He also knew our dogs were quiet, they only did little woofs at people on the lake and that was mainly Grace. But the old man next door wouldn't have been able to hear her, one because of the double thick brick walls and two because he was hard of hearing. When David walked in the door I tried to read his face, he looked completely worn out. David relayed the conversation to me. And there was a lot of "WHAT, WHAT, WHAT DID YOU SAY" and David would lean in closer so the old man could hear. "PIGS, DID YOU SAY TWO PIGS" another lean in, "No pugs, I said pugs, pug dogs, two more like the two we already have, only the two new ones are both fawn". David has a really soft voice as well so it would have made things all the harder, perhaps that's why he was gone so long. All the while I was at home worrying that the old guy would knock us back and planning the many ways in which I was going to make life difficult for him if he did. In the end he signed the forms which I think was always his intention, he just wanted to play with us a little bit before he did so.

The forms were for the council, they had some requirements before they'd give us the ok. Not only did we need our neighbour's permission, a home visit from a council worker needed to be undertaken as well. The man doing the home visit was a lovely guy, he wasn't in our home for more than five minutes, didn't even go upstairs, in and out in the blink of an eye really and it would have been even quicker than that if Sarah and Harper weren't harassing him for pats. And of course he obliged them, I don't think they would have let him out the door if he didn't. I'd seen his car pull up while I was upstairs and jumped down those stairs two at a time to beat him to the front door because I didn't want him ringing the doorbell. I knew if he did he'd set the pugs off barking and I knew noise was one of the councils concerns. He had his finger inches from the doorbell when the door sprang open, he laughed and said "Well that's service for you" and I thought, too right it is, I really want more pugs. As he was leaving he said that he had to give the ok because his nephew loved pugs and he'd never hear the end of it if he'd knocked us back. We had to pay an extra $100 a year on top of our regular council fees just to be allowed to own four dogs. That's what life is like in the suburbs, permission and extra payments every time you want to make a move. I found having to get permission to live the life I wanted to live very irritating.

While Ruby sat in her beanbag nest working her new situation out I started working on her health. This and walking was about all she would let me do for her at this point. And besides it's my job and I love being able to help their bodies heal. Nutrition is so important and I figured feeling better health wise would help her with everything else she was feeling. I started her right away on an improved diet and added glucosamine for her arthritis and flaxseed oil for health and joint function. After a few weeks there was noticeable improvement I was telling a friend about it one day and she said glucosamine being good for dogs hadn't been proven yet, and I said well try telling Ruby that. She doesn't know that I'm putting it into her food and yet she's walking like a little champ. Ruby was living proof that it worked, her life became easier, less painful in her neck area and that was good enough for me. But some dogs are different, what works for one will not necessarily work quite as well for another, and if this hadn't worked for Ruby then I would have gone in search of something else, would have kept trying different things until I found something that worked for her and I'll always go with the natural alternative before delving into heavy drugs that can at times be harmful to their systems and have nasty side effects too. Don't be too quick to cast aside natural remedies, they are much gentler on old systems and that's a very good thing. Yes it does take a bit longer for results to show up then with heaver drugs but I believe they are much safer and well worth using. I only go for heavy drugs when the natural way is no longer working and something stronger is needed or when time is short and you need something administrated right away, like say in pain management. You must never leave any animal in pain when you can take them to the vet and get instant relief. Natural remedies are great when an illness has time to respond, never for extreme cases, you have to use common sense with this.

One morning the five of us had just come back from a lovely walk along the river. Ruby was the only one to follow me inside, the others were sniffing in our little garden area, we'd only been gone an hour but you never know what may have occurred in our absence and Sarah, Harper and Grace always liked to check things out thoroughly before coming into the house. I left the door open for the others and picked Ruby up and carried her in. I normally let her walk into the lounge room on her own and shuffle her body onto her beanbag. But today she seemed a little tired so I thought I'd help her out, thought I'd pick her up and pop her on the beanbag myself and save her the job. She was stiff in my arms, one was due to the arthritis in her body and the other was because I guess she was wondering what I was going to do with her. It was the first time I had held her and I felt the time was right. I'd been desperately wanting to hold her ever since she first came but although I had been ready to snuggle Ruby had not, but today was different today was right. It was her second week with us and she'd gotten used to me a little bit in this time, knew who I was, knew I wasn't going to hurt her. We had a few moments alone one on one, I didn't want to have her in my arms any longer than she was comfortable with and I knew our first snuggle was going to a quick one so I made the most of it.

I just felt this huge outpouring of love for this little soul I was holding in my arms. I felt it so deep and powerful that I thought my heart was going to burst. But I contained myself, kept myself in order. I talked to Ruby in a low soft voice. I told her that she may not have been wanted in her last home but that she was very much wanted in mine. I told her how much I loved her and how overjoyed I was to be her mother. I told her that this was going to be her home for the rest of her life, for as long as she wanted to stay with me. I thanked her for coming into my life and told her how happy she made me. Then I kissed her little old head, told her that I loved her one more time then gently placed her in the middle of her beanbag and went to see what the other three were up to.

The entire time I held Ruby she never once looked at me, she couldn't due to the arthritis in her neck and back, she couldn't turn her head. To hold Ruby is pretty much like holding a brick, not being cruel, it's just the best way I can think of describing her to you. Her body is full of arthritis; she is like a solid brick of arthritis. That day I held her was a strange experience for me, my other pugs wriggle in my arms, give kisses, do something but Ruby did not respond, although neither did she try and get away which meant she was ok with me holding her and that was a good sign. I didn't know if what I said had sunk in, I had no way of knowing if she was even listening to me, she just gave a huff when I'd put her down then penguin walked on top of her beanbag bed, did a stomping little circle and flopped down.

A few hours later all the dogs were sleeping and I was reading a book when I felt unnerved, as if somebody was watching me. I glanced out to the lake expecting to see somebody standing on the water's edge looking in, but nobody was there. People were always walking by and if they were new to the lake and hadn't yet learned to be polite they would stop and have a good look in your windows. The fact that you were sitting in your own lounge room having a quiet cup of tea and reading a book didn't seem to bother them at all. They stood and they stared like you were a sideshow act or something and I thought it was so rude of them to do that. I was relieved that nobody was out there this time so carried on reading my book.

I took another sip of my tea and looked down and there was Ruby staring up at me and swaying on her little bandy legs. I was so enthralled in my book I hadn't even noticed she'd moved from her bed. I spoke to her like I normally do, asked her if she was ok, did she need anything, I was about to get up and freshen the dogs water bowl, Harper's tongue hung out all the time so when she had a drink she would often make a mess of the water, put fluff or a bit of dirt in it that sort of thing and I'm fanatical about fresh clear water for my dogs. I thought that's what Ruby wanted, she drinks a lot and I figured she'd been to the water bowl, saw it needed freshening and that's why she'd come over to me. But her little old chin wasn't dripping wet so she hadn't been near the water bowl. I talked to her some more but she didn't head for the door so she didn't need to go outside for a wee either. I honestly didn't know why she had come over to me, she'd never done that before, never in all the time she'd been here had she sought me out like this. I didn't know what she wanted but I thought while she's here and engaging I'm going to pick her up and give her another snuggle, may as well try and get one in while she's in the right mood. So I put her on my knee and stroked her gently while I talked to her, can't remember what I was saying, just babbling I think.

Dogs don't seem to care what you are saying half the time as long as your voice is friendly and you are focusing on them. I gently stroked her back and rubbed her little ears, did all the things she couldn't do for herself due to her funny legs and arthritic body. She was enjoying herself, leaned in to the ear rub, like I'd hit the right spot. She reminded me of somebody who has an arm or leg in plaster and they'd been itchy for a while and couldn't reach the spot. Ruby was delirious so I rubbed some more and babbled on a bit longer, sometimes when I run out of things to say I'll start singing, I sing to all my pugs. I like them to hear my voice in some shape or form when I'm patting them. It's a connection, makes them feel special, like I'm giving them my full attention, and who in this world doesn't like to know they have somebody's undivided attention. And besides I like talking and singing to them, the singing makes me happier than it makes them I'm sure of it. I love Christmas always have been a huge Christmas person, I start singing carols to the pugs as soon as December first rolls around. When a new pug comes into the house and they've not heard me sing before they'll tilt their head to the side trying for the life of them to figure out what I'm doing. I've not been blessed with the best voice, I'm first to admit that so I understand their confusion, I mean I'm not grating either, just somewhere in the middle I think, or am I being too kind to myself, maybe, but let's just go with that though shall we. A guy I used to work with said I had a lovely singing voice so it can't be that bad can it. I was working in a bakery at the time, early morning shift and was singing a Disney song. And really who can go wrong with a Disney song, they are such happy little melodies most of them aren't they. Anyway he was the pastry chef and I was the packer. He was a little guy from Sri Lanka, a truly lovely man, very shy and very quiet until he got to know you, he used to make me laugh with the things he had to say and the speed at which he could climb the racks when we needed more sacks of flour was remarkable. I would stand there with the trolley and he'd chuck them down, then we'd get back to doing what we had to do. I told him to join in with me whenever I was singing, but he said he didn't know a lot of songs. So I would sing and he would listen, pretty much what Ruby was doing with me now. Once a new pug has been here awhile they just look up at me, wag their tails and sometimes go back to sleep it depends how long I actually go on singing for.

I looked down at Ruby sitting on my lap getting her ears rubbed, it was a lovely sight to see and beautiful that she'd decided to come over of her own accord to say hello. My earlier snuggle and talk with her had not scared her off. I think it had encouraged her if anything. She sat with me like that for a real long time, I alternated between massage and rubbing her ears. She didn't try and escape she seemed contented to let me touch her and I was thrilled. She'd finally given me the gift of her trust. When a dog offers you that it's the most precious thing, no greater bequest, it's an honour. It was what I'd been waiting for, what I'd longed for since Ruby first came, it also told me that she was finally settling in, that she felt a little bit of inner peace for the first time in a long while and that was important to me. Seeing her sitting there like that made me think that perhaps she felt everything was going to be alright in her world from now on. That made me happier than anything. I love to know that my new pugs are doing ok. Ruby's back wasn't as sore for her now she was on glucosamine, but I was gentle and aware of how I was stroking her all the same.

After that day Ruby became a true member of our family. She continually asked to be picked up and held, she would now sit on the couch with me all the time when I was reading. As soon as she saw the book in my hand she knew I'd be sitting still for a while and would shoot out of her bed and across the room and be standing by the couch swaying waiting for me to walk over. She was the same with David when he got home from work. She'd follow the others to the door and be standing there ready to greet him. She'd sway for him to pick her up too and he always did, it was nice to see her being carried into the lounge room in his arms. Her face looked like it was smiling and her eyes would search the room for me and I'd let her know I'd seen her up there in her Daddy's arms. I'd go over and gently stroke her head and say "Well done darling" She was still steely determined on the walks to the river, still wanted to walk rather than be picked up, it was more when we were all in the house together that she changed, she became one of those pugs who had to be sitting on the chair with you. No more floor for Ruby, she'd sway to be picked up and if the swaying didn't get your attention it would soon be followed by a sweet little yap. An excited little yap, a yap that said, you are mine and I am yours so pick me the hell up will you I've been standing here swaying for the longest time. It wasn't really the longest time but in her mind it must have seemed like it was.

The change in Ruby was magnificent but the change she made in my husband was the most amazing and wonderful thing, she simply transformed him, turned him completely around and when I think of all that I'm grateful to Ruby for, and there are so very many things, this is the most beautiful one. She had given David a gift that would last him for the remainder of his life, one that many other pugs were going to benefit from greatly. She did what neither I nor any of the other pugs we had at the time could do. She turned her daddy into a pug person.

David loved all our pugs I know he did and he was so good, actually more than good he was wonderful with each one of them. He looked after Harper when she was unwell, he still carried Sarah over the stones at the river, he'd seen what she'd gone through with the operation and didn't want her injuring her one good eye, and he'd tuck Grace into his jacket when she was cold or when she no longer wanted to walk. But he was different with Ruby. He just fell head over heels in love with her. She simply stole his heart. I think at first he felt sorry for her due to her funny little legs. He would take special care in looking after her, make sure she was doing ok and handling herself alright on the stairs, that sort of thing. When he was home wherever Ruby was there was David a few steps behind seeing if she needed anything. He got used to taking care of her, looking out for her and her special needs and I think it all started from there, that was the foundation, and it just grew and grew and grew. They became inseparable and she adored him as much as he did her. She'd let me take care of her during the day but as soon as David walked in of an evening she only had eyes for him. She'd shoot out of her smelly old beanbag as soon as she heard his car pull up. She'd make sure to be right by the front door when he walked in, she'd shoulder the others out the way just to make sure she was the first in line for a pat. At times I'd have to pick her up so she didn't get knocked over as he opened the door. She wasn't too happy with me when I did this because she thought I was stopping her from getting to him. But I'd hand her across to him as soon as the others had said hello and she would go nuts in his arms. And that was it for the rest of the night as far as attention for me was given. Ruby would follow David everywhere he went, he'd be striding around the house and she'd be scurrying along after him doing her little penguin walk as fast as she could go. And I'd be watching on thinking it was the best sight ever. I mean how could I not, here he was over six feet tall and there she was tiny, silver, scurrying, waddling like a penguin. My heart was so full I could have applauded them as they went by. Ruby never even looked at me as they walked past my chair, her eyes were always on him, solely on him and keeping up with him. And the look on that little old face of hers was pure determination, she was going to keep up with him no matter what.

David made a bed for Ruby next to his office chair so that when he was at his desk, and when he was home he was at his desk most of the time, Ruby could be near him. She loved being around her Dad, she'd sit on his knee when he was watching TV and would actually be watching the screen too, she was a real card, she used to bark at the ads. She had her favourite ones and if she wasn't fast asleep when they came on she'd sit up straight and growl and woof in the ad breaks. At one time they were using meerkats to advertise just about everything and Ruby loved meerkats for some reason. While I was busy doing the housework I would put meerkat documentaries on just to see her happy. She sat there absorbed, totally fixated, if I spoke to her she didn't even hear me. But I couldn't leave her on the couch alone while she was watching them because she would have barked herself right off the couch and with her body the way it was that thud to the floor would have really hurt her. And I didn't want her to hurt herself not when she was doing so well, so I'd put her bed in front of the television and she'd watch her shows from there. Ruby was full of personality and a bit of a talker too. She went from being cautious and unresponsive to communicating with us through her special barks. Each one was for something different and it was up to David and I to figure out what she meant. David figured most of them out before I did because she talked to him the most, and he'd just let me know what she wanted. Her eyes sparkled when she spoke to him, sparkled due to both love and good health. It was nice to see the two of them together. She had single handily, or should that be single pawdly, taken his love of pugs to an entirely new level, well my level actually, and I couldn't have been happier about that. David now felt the same way about pugs as I did. He got it, finally he understood.

I thought he may have at some point wanted to go back to having big dogs in his life but after Ruby touched his heart he just wanted to stick with pugs. He thought bigger dogs may knock Ruby flying and that it wouldn't be fair on her, she had enough trouble walking as it was she didn't need to be bowled over by an overzealous Dane. I liked the change in David, he knew what I was talking about now, before he just used to listen to me going on and on about pugs, he thought Sarah was a crack up and had liked seeing the change in Harper's health, but now he joined in and had his own favourite pug things that he'd tell me about. And I thought that was just brilliant. There was genuine joy in his voice as well, you can't fake that kind of enthusiasm. I think his new found love of pugs brought us even closer as a couple.

One thing that did worry me about Ruby when she'd fully settled in was the fact that she now wanted to be with me everywhere I went during the day and while all of that was lovely it did cause problems when she started climbing the stairs on her own. I have never liked old pugs and stairs, I don't like puppies and stairs either because too much damage can be done. I see videos of small puppies attempting to come down high sets of stairs on the internet and my heart is in my mouth because I am so worried they are going to hurt themselves. I think the owners post them because they think they are cute but I never see them that way. I guess because I take in old pugs I see the way their bodies are, I bear witness to the results of falls and accidents that have occurred during their lives and how hard that can be on them when they reach double figures. It's just like us really, any injury that has occurred years in the past, injuries you may have totally forgotten about, well your body doesn't forget about them, they all come back to haunt you later on in life. Old age isn't kind to bodies and when that body has suffered damage and gone through trauma, well it'll come back to bite you on the ass later on in life and it's exactly the same with our animals.

Sarah and Harper were up and down the stairs all the time and handled them beautifully and Grace had followed me up a week into her stay but Ruby never bothered, she'd contently sleep in her downstairs bed while I went upstairs and showered. I never pushed the pugs to climb the stairs in fact I would have preferred they stayed downstairs until we were going to bed. I worried about all of them when they were on the staircase. We put netting on the side to keep them from slipping through the rails, Harper was never afraid of heights, about an hour after we moved in she came up the stairs behind me and danced all around the upstairs floor like she was proud of herself for being the first pug to discover what was at the top of those stairs. At times she'd lay long ways on one of the middle stairs and go to sleep, whenever I saw her I'd bring her down to the bottom level, what if she started jerking about having a dream, I'd just gotten her healthy I didn't want her to tumble down and break her leg or worse.

Sarah took a long time to attempt the flight of stairs, due to her eye she had trouble seeing in dark places and the hall and staircase were pretty dark. Sarah also had trouble with the slate flooring, it confused her, the lines where the slate tiles met seemed to trouble her greatly and I knew they would do because she was the same with the tiles in the entrance to our vets office, she always had to be carried in and it wasn't that she was scared of vets it was the tiles that bothered her, well not the tiles themselves but where they joined, where the grout was. We didn't last too long with that vet though because I didn't like his attitude and everybody in the family was happy when we found the gem of a vet we have now, but nobody was happier than Sarah was because there were no tiles in our new vet's surgery.

When we were first looking at buying the house by the lake I mentioned to David that Sarah wouldn't be pleased about the downstairs flooring. He said she would get used to it in time and that we'd just have to let her do it on her own, without pushing her, so that's exactly what we did. It was the same with the staircase, we never pushed her there either, just let her attempt it when she was ready to and it took a while for her to do that. We'd carry her up the stairs at bedtime and she'd be a totally different dog when she was up there. On the second floor she'd run around like a little puppy, but downstairs she sunk to the floor and gripped onto the skirting boards, she was terrified of the lines on the slate and there were a lot of lines on them. When we'd been for a walk I'd leave the door open and let her come in of her own accord. But gee I felt so sorry for her in those first few weeks. She'd keep peeping in and tapping the floor with her little black paw. Then coming a bit further in and tapping again making sure it was safe, each time she came in a little bit further until she reached the staircase then she'd run and hide underneath it, wait a while to get her bearings then shoot into the lounge when she felt brave enough. I could have gone and carried her in, it would have been quicker but then she'd never have gotten used to flooring and it would have made her more scared, she had to figure it out on her own, when she finally did we all stood around cheering and clapping and telling her how fantastic she was. She ran off and got her favourite lucky, a thing she always did when very excited, and we threw "Poo" for her over and over again. Each time she ran confidently over the slate retrieving her lucky like she'd never had trouble with it in the first place. When she eventually conquered the stairs again we clapped and cheered and again a lucky came out and was thrown. Sarah had luckies both upstairs and downstairs because I didn't like her using the stairs too much. When all the pugs had come upstairs we put a little gate across so they wouldn't fall down. This gave me peace of mind, especially at night time. I could go to sleep happily knowing none of the pugs were able to use the stairs. They had a bowl of water in the upstairs bathroom so there was no reason for them to go downstairs for anything.

Ruby shocked me the day she made it upstairs. I had all the other pugs with me while I showered, they'd followed me up like they did every day and lay sleeping happily on the thick bathmat. I dried myself off and walked out of the bathroom and just couldn't believe my eyes, there was Ruby laying on the floor in the landing area, she was facing the bathroom door and her little old eyes sparkled when I came out. I walked over and made such a fuss of her, thanked her for the honour, it was a big thing for her to have done. Her front legs were wobbly and her back legs weak and yet she had taken on those stairs because she wanted to be near me. I had talked to a specialist when Ruby first came because I was concerned about the stair situation but he said the climbing would strengthen her legs, he said the embankment by the river that she loved to fly down screaming was a good way of strengthening her legs too. But the stairs worried me a lot more than the embankment did so I was always mindful of her when she was using them. I allowed her to come up the stairs but never go down on her own, I always tucked her under my arm and carried her to safety. If her front legs buckled, which they occasionally did, she would have bounced all the way to the bottom and probably broken her neck. I wasn't chancing it, there was a double brick wall a few feet from the bottom step and I had visions of her slamming into that. I wasn't going to let that happen so once she was upstairs I'd put the baby gate in place and went and showered with peace of mind. And when she was coming up I would stand behind her holding my hands a few inches from her little saggy bottom, never making contact with her as I knew that would be off-putting for her and she needed to concentrate on what she was doing. But my hands where always there ready should she need me, I let her get the leg strengthening exercise and the benefit from that but never left her unattended while she was doing it. The only time she ever used those stairs unattended was the very first day she came up, and that was only because I didn't think she would ever attempt those stairs at all. She had always been contented to stay down stairs sleeping until I came back down again. But I guess for all I knew she could have tried to come up the stairs sooner and due to lack of strength simply couldn't manage it. Perhaps she tried every day while I showered until she actually made it up. But I think she wouldn't have been trying it during those first few weeks because there was simply no reason for her to, she hadn't fallen in love with me then so was contented to be on her sleeping bag and really couldn't have cared less where I was, but once she loved me that was it, not even a flight of stairs was going to keep her away from me. After that precautions were always taken, whenever we went out and the pugs weren't coming with us the baby gate was put at the bottom of the stairs to prevent anybody being tempted.

I knew those stairs were going to be a problem for my four girls as they got older, we looked into putting in a lift but it was out of this world expensive, way too much for us to ever be able to afford. David was concerned as well, especially about his beloved Ruby because she was the one whose legs were the worst, he said when the girls started having trouble with the stairs we would have no alternative but to sell the house. My face remained neutral but my soul leapt for joy. I could have run around that townhouse like a giddy little puppy when he said this, probably done a few laps of the lake as well I was that excited but instead I just nodded my head, looked over at Ruby and said "Yes, yes I think it's for the best" I was just hoping that we would get an excellent price for the townhouse when it came time to sell. Because what we got for the townhouse would determine the size of farm we could purchase.

The way things worked out I didn't have to wait until the girls started having trouble with the stairs to leave. Four months after adopting Ruby and Grace the lake house was on the market, it sold within ten days. It wasn't surprising that it sold so quickly, there was generally a waiting list for homes on the water. But the market was not good at the time the bottom had fallen out of it earlier in the year was what the four real estate agents we had value our house told us. And they were right it was a buyers' market not a sellers' market. I'd been keeping my eye on real estate prices for a while and all the houses in the area weren't getting good prices. We sold the townhouse for exactly the same price we paid for it two years earlier and I think we were lucky to get that as the townhouse next door sold for much less. But then we lost money with all the taxes and transfer fees. But that's just how it is with real estate. Of course we could have stayed longer until the market picked up, and a lot of people told us we were stupid for selling when we did. "Wait the market out" was what they told us. And we did think about it, but we also thought about overall happiness. Sometimes you just have to put quality of life above financial gain. Financial gain can't be what you make all your life decisions on, you have to lead with your heart sometimes because if you are always focusing on money, well that's pretty much an unhappy way to live. Money is only money, it isn't joyful or memorable, or able to give you the same feeling in your soul that following your heart does. It cannot buy time or true love or genuine happiness. Sure it may buy a bit of happiness for a while but nothing long lasting. It also cannot buy a life well lived only we can do that for ourselves, and it has nothing at all to do with money. David and I have never regretted the decision we made.

I felt relieved and excited to be leaving, I knew I'd miss the winters there, miss watching rain falling on the water. I enjoyed every second of that last winter in our townhouse because I knew I would never live on that lake again, when it rained I bolted over to the windows and stood there watching for as long as I had time to stand there. I took in each tiny, and sometimes not so tiny, droplet so I'd have that image imprinted on my brain forever. I mean I had to do that didn't I because it was the only true joy I'd gotten from living there. But I knew when the temperature rose I'd be so grateful not to be there, I knew there would be parties, I knew friends and relatives would flock and who can blame them really it's their own private swimming pool, the general public aren't allowed access to the lake, it's only for those who own property and those they invite.

Our neighbours threw us a big party when we were leaving. I thought it was a nice thing for them to do for us really. It was the only party we had ever attended there and it was a heck of a party too, lasted nine hours, we crawled home exhausted. Not being party people we didn't know what hit us. We did leave for a little while to go walk the pugs and we thought that may have been the end of it but they begged us to come back after our walk. So we gave the pugs their tea and a few extra treats because we felt guilty for leaving them and walked out the door. We staggered back in many hours later and collapsed into bed.

There was a lot of drinking done that night and then one of our neighbours on realising that David had only ever swam in the lake not actually gone for a canoe ride, decided to take him out. A canoe was dragged down to the lake before I knew what was going on. I had only been drinking mineral water so was the only one in the group with a level head about me, the others all stood round clapping and cheering the two of them on. The guy taking David out was incredibly intoxicated, but he drank all the time so could handle his liquor. Still he was the drunkest guy at the party, he had been drinking all day and it was nearing midnight when the canoe ride was suggested. How they managed to get in that canoe let alone row was beyond me. They were like two clowns putting on a show at a children's party, only there were no little kids in sight only two adult men acting like they were. There was a heck of a lot of laughing done before they finally disappeared into the darkness. I asked David not to go, told him how silly he was being, but the alcohol in his system made him think he was a superhero. So Captain Invincible took no notice of me. The other party goers went back inside but I stood on the shore for the longest time worrying if they were ever going to come back into view. It was pitch black out there in the middle of that lake and I was angry that they could be so irresponsible, as my eyes searched the darkness I started planning what I would do if the canoe came back empty and I had to run the farm on my own. I stood there arms folded, eyes fixated, jaw tight with rage thinking how could he do this to us now, just when we'd gotten hold of our dream. I had no idea how deep that lake was in the middle but I imagined it was pretty deep. If he wasn't dead already I was planning on killing him myself when he got back to shore. I was just about to call the emergency services when I heard a lot of laughing in the distance and the closer they got the louder it became. I think they would have woken all the neighbours up the way they were carrying on. When I asked David why he had acted so irresponsibly he said "Hey the party was in our honour, what's a guy to do?"

For a while I stayed in contact with a few of the neighbours. I made a friend or two there but none of them understood why we left and I didn't understand how they could stay. But when it's raining on the lake they say they always think of me. And I'll be here on the farm many miles away watching it fall on my front paddock and breathe life into the green hills that surround my little farm house. I know it's filling my water tanks to the brim, helping keep my sheep and horses alive. The sound it makes on my tin roof, well nothing can compare, I've waited my whole life to have a tin roof and the first time it rained here was like music to my ears. Rain in the country is everything; it's a lot more than just a pretty sight, its life and prosperity. It's hope for the future. Rain has always been dear to me but since living at Grace Farm it has never meant more to me in my life.

We looked at a few farms before buying here but this one had something special about it, it seemed like it was meant to be ours. It was already sold but the guy who bought it was having trouble selling his house, those were the terms of the contract he signed, so we had a two week wait before we knew the property was ours. Grace came everywhere with me, she saw this farm before our other pugs did, it was a long drive so we left the others at home with the air conditioner on and brought water and a bowl so Grace could have a drink. When we got here she went straight out and danced along the veranda, she liked the place as much as we did. The man we bought it off was a dog lover too, we sat at his kitchen table, him with his toy poodle on his knee and me with my pug on mine, over a cup of tea we talked about dogs. I felt like he understood what I wanted to do here. He must have liked the idea too because he threw in an old ride on mower and a beautiful marble coffee table into the deal. The mower caused more than a few headaches before finally dying, it lasted about three years from memory and was such a temperamental thing. Cost a small fortune to keep repairing in the hope of getting just a little bit longer out of it. Sure we would have liked a bright shiny new ride on like some of the neighbours had, but all our money was going into vet bills and other animal expenses, we had no other choice but to keep trying to breathe new life into that old mower. You looked at it the wrong way and it stopped dead in its tracks and refused to budge. I used to be scared of going out onto the veranda when David was mowing in case the mower saw me and got upset because somebody was watching it. Me and the pugs would sneak glances from the window when it had its back turned, then when David spun it round I'd dart over to the other side of the room trailing a pile of pugs with me before the mower saw us. Everything would be going fine and then I'd hear David out there muttering under his breath, doing all he could to get the thing ticking over again. There was so much frustration with that mower. I think it wasn't so much as a gift but a booby prize.

The coffee table on the other hand has brought us nothing but joy. It reminds me of this man's kindness towards us. It still sits in our lounge room today and looks as beautiful as the day it was given to us. The light apricot colour is stunning and I still marvel at it whenever I wipe it down. The man we bought the farm off passed away about a year after we'd been living here, I still think about him from time to time. He put his heart and soul into building this house. The house has flaws, it's no masterpiece, but because I was so in love with the place it took me a few years to see the roughness, the imperfections, the odd bits of wood glued together because he cut a piece too short. And yes the floor is slightly uneven too. Not like a house from a Dr Seuss book or anything like that, just a slight unevenness. I found that out the day the washing machine flooded. Stood there watching the soapy water slowing running towards one corner, it amused me actually, it probably should have freaked me out but nothing seems that bad when you are living in the country, well not for me it doesn't anyway, so I stood there smiling at it, watching it go, watching the pugs sniffing and pawing inquisitively at the suds before finally springing into action and mopping it up with thick towels. The laundry isn't a room, it's just a big cupboard with a few shelves and a washing machine and sink in it, but that's ok it's all you need really. And I don't know what on earth he coated those cupboard doors with but everything, and I mean absolutely everything stuck to them, fluff, dirt, dog hairs, insects, everything that floated by became drawn like a magnet. You'd wiped them down and think you'd gotten rid of it but then they'd dry and they are still sticky. I used to think that one day I'd walk into the room and find one of the pugs stuck to the doors like velcro. I'm not sure if John took the cheap way out or if he just simply had not much knowledge of what he was doing, or maybe he just used the wrong stuff on the doors and had no energy to try and rectify the situation. But we felt differently, the doors were quickly unscrewed, taken outside and sanded and stained beautifully by David. Now the pugs can walk by them any time they like and nothing happens.

I think that fact that my home isn't perfect gives it more character, gives it its own unique personality, it's got a soul, it's not one of these homes on a new estate where row after row of houses are all the same, same both inside and outside, you walk into one and it's a feeling of déjà vu. I find things like that a little creepy and unnerving to be honest. And not safe as far as burglaries go because the robbers know where all the rooms are located. And also my home being in a less than a perfect state seems kind of fitting doesn't it, fitting for the animals we take in, it's like everyone is the same here, a little bit flawed, but happy and full of contentment regardless.

The man was ill while he was building this house so I think that's why it's the way it is. But he sure was proud of the place the day he showed us around. I do worry about his dog, he loved that little thing deeply, she was all the family he had, I hope wherever she is that she's being well looked after and that they understand her needs, she would have grieved terribly over his loss I'm sure of it. You only had to see them together to know they shared a special bond. I noticed it within a few moments of meeting them and made mention of it too.

I like seeing animals when I'm looking around a home, I wouldn't not buy a place because the owners left their animals around while showing the property. Cats on verandas make a place homely. Cats are very soothing, they seem to ooze serenity. I'm twice as likely to buy a place if there's a cat sprawled out when I walk up the path or even better a dog wagging its tail in greeting. It's like if they can reach that level of happiness here then maybe I can too. Most people shut their animals away when a potential buyer is coming, they've no idea what assets they can be. Estate agents don't seem to get it either, I've found them to be animal lovers when getting you to sign them up to sell your house and loathers when you want to view a property with a pug in your arms.

"You can't come in here with that thing" one said to me once. "Well if she can't come in then I'm not coming in either" He rolled his eyes. "Well then don't let her on the ground" Why the hell did he think I was carrying her in the first place. We didn't stay long, the property was awful, lime green walls, out of date kitchen, bedrooms not much bigger than cupboards. He should have been begging me to put my pug down and let her wander around, Harper would have been the only decent looking thing in there. I reckon the agent earnt every cent of his commission on that place. It would have been near impossible to sell, probably had it on his books awhile and that would explain his less than cheery disposition.

When the other buyer had to drop out and this farm was finally ours we were beside ourselves with excitement, we couldn't wait for the settlement date to come around. We would have moved in overnight if we could have but naturally you have to go through the normal course of things. The wait to get here was an agony and it was made all the worse by a terrible incident.

I was walking my four pugs by the river one morning when a man with a small dog approached, the man was old and the dog was older. I smiled when they came into view. I thought they looked beautiful with their greying hair and old stiff joints walking side by side. But how wrong could I be. As the old man and dog got closer I realized his dog was getting upset, Sarah since her eye operation would have a go at an aggressive dog when she saw one so I bent down and picked her up. She was fine with most dogs, even very large dogs because she had lived a lot of her life with two Great Danes, but if a dog she met started getting nasty she would pick up on that negative energy and start going nuts. I didn't want her getting into a fight with this dog. The other three pugs had never shown any aggression of any kind. Harper loved the world, Ruby was too interested in shuffling along as fast as she could go, she was always on a mission to get down the embankment quickly, she wasn't interested in other dogs and Grace was a most placid little soul.

Sarah saw the old man's dog snarling and twisting on the lead. She heard its barks of aggression and started having a fit in my arms, she wanted to get down, be on the ground so she could sort this dog out, I knew that's what she wanted to do so I made sure I had a good hold of her and believe me it wasn't the easiest thing to do. Sarah was only small but boy was she strong, she pushed against my chest trying anything to escape. I was telling her to settle down but she wasn't for listening, so I put her on my hip, as close to my body as I could get her to try and make her calm down. I smiled at the old man as he got closer, to be honest I was a bit embarrassed by Sarah's behaviour, I may have said she was alright that I had a tight hold, can't remember, either way he could see she wasn't getting loose in a hurry. The man didn't look happy. Harper, Ruby and Grace started doing little woofs as the man passed by. The man's dog was showing its teeth and getting very hostile and of course Sarah would have equaled it if I'd let her out of my arms, my three on the ground where doing nothing other than woofing, barely interested in this old man's dog at all.

Then out of the blue the old man lunged at my group of three and started kicking out at all of them, I was screaming at him to stop, trying to tell him that they were not aggressive dogs but he wasn't listening, he was now having a violent fit that would put his own dog to shame. I was struggling with Sarah in my arms, by this time was really going berserk. She had managed to turn herself around and was now pushing her legs into my side as I struggled to hold onto her. Harper and Grace got out of his way but Ruby with her funny little legs couldn't move fast enough and he kicked her again and again, I was screaming my head off, telling him to stop, that she was a cripple but he took no notice he kicked her even though she was unmoving on the ground. There was a big double story house nearby, the people inside must have heard me screaming at the top of my lungs, they came to help, saw this man in a kicking frenzy and pulled him off, I think it was only then that he realized what he'd done to Ruby. He was like somebody possessed, the look in his eye was pure evil. A young man walking along the river came running to help us as well, he handed me his mobile phone so I could call David at work, get him to get Ruby to the vet as quickly as possible. I didn't have a mobile phone in those days so I was very grateful to the stranger who came to our aide that day.

I was sobbing and screaming and having a fit at the old guy, he said he was sorry, I told him I didn't care and carried on screaming at him, telling him Sarah was the aggressive one and that's why I'd picked her up to protect his dog. I told him the dog he had kicked hadn't done anything to him or his dog. While all this was going on Sarah was still struggling in my arms to get away, in that moment I wished she had been a bigger dog because I think I would have just let her rip that old man to pieces and enjoyed seeing her doing it. I would have picked up his dog to protect it but I would have let her teeth slice right through that old buggers arm if she'd of had the jaw strength to do it. Lucky she didn't though because although I wanted it to happen in that moment, it would have meant Sarah would have been put down. Because that's what happens to dogs who attack people, people who attack dogs on the other hand seem to just get a slap on the wrist and not even that most times. Still if I had let her on the ground she could well have taken this man's dog out. This old dog looked like it would have snapped like a twig with only the slightest bit of pressure applied. But I didn't want Sarah attacking some old man's dog and having it die, old people get very attached to their animals, sometimes it's all they have. I was respectful of him pity he hadn't shown Ruby the same kind of respect.

The lady from the big house stood over Ruby, cast a shadow to keep her cool, protect her from the sun, her husband ran and got a bucket of water and trickled it over Ruby's body, he tried to get her to drink but she couldn't lift her head. I was in shock, I don't know what I was saying or doing but that lady and her husband's quick thinking saved Ruby life I'm sure of it. I remember watching those two kind strangers taking care of my pug and being so incredibly grateful. I was still holding onto Sarah and had somehow managed to get Harper and Grace back on their leads as well. The old man stared down at Ruby and then just turned and walked away, I think he got that she couldn't have run away from his kicks but I can't say for sure, if he had been truly remorseful he wouldn't have just walked off, he would have stayed and helped her, offered to pay the vet bill, do anything other then what he did.

Perhaps he had heard me calling David and knew my husband was on his way, he probably didn't want David doing to him what he had just done to Ruby.

A lot of it was a blur I remember looking at Ruby asking if she was alive then sending a fast prayer to god to let her keep on living. I was worried about Ruby but I also had David on my mind, his voice changed so quickly when he heard what had happened. I was amazed I managed to remember his work phone number I was that much in shock. I worried about David leaving work and rushing home, I told him not to speed, didn't want him having an accident, but he didn't listen to me because he was there beside us in what seemed like mere seconds. It was like I'd only just hung up the phone and there he was running through the park towards us. I looked at his face as he picked up Ruby, saw everything he was feeling, it was all written clearly there, I prayed again for Ruby, that she would live, I mean how was David going to feel if this pug he had just given his heart to, fallen madly in love with, was taken from him.

I'd never been so pleased to see David in my life, he'd got there so fast I expected to receive multiple speeding fines in the mail but they never came, he got Ruby to a vet within thirty minutes of being kicked, it wasn't long before she was examined, given a painkiller injection and an anti-inflammatory. She was badly bruised and sore but nothing was broken. I was so relieved, but I couldn't believe nothing had been broken, I'd expected a few ribs would have been for sure, but perhaps the mean spirited old bugger didn't have much strength to put behind his kicks.

I stayed behind and walked Sarah, Harper and Grace back home while David rushed Ruby to the vet. Sarah was so calm once the old man and his dog had gone. Just a totally different pug, she started giving everybody kisses as soon as her little black paws touched the ground. I thanked the people from the big house for everything they had done for Ruby and asked if they knew who the old man was, the lady said she'd seen him around but didn't know where he lived.

When Ruby got home I grabbed the thick doona off our bed, folded it into four and she lay on that for days while she recovered. I spent the afternoon vomiting, going over and over the events in my head and vomiting some more. I knew it had happened but I couldn't believe it had happened. I'd never experienced anything like that in my life. I'd never been involved in any kind of violence. Ok I did get a kid in a head lock once for calling me names in primary school but that was about it, that's the closest I'd come to violence and the only time it had happened because once I sorted that kid out she was too scared to attempt it again and so I'd gone on my merry way without a single violent act disturbing me again until now. I'd read newspaper stories, seen things on TV, but when you live through it yourself, see it up close, it's totally different and it affected me greatly. I was like any other mother seeing their child beaten and not being able to prevent it. I blamed myself, if only I'd walked the dogs earlier or later or not at all that day this would never have happened. But we walked twice a day, we always went twice, that was our routine, that was our life and the pugs looked forward to it. I'd been walking all my dogs twice a day by that same river for many years without incident, different sets of dogs and different sides of the river but always a beautiful quiet peaceful enjoyable time had by all. I bet he wouldn't have attempted such a thing if I'd been walking the two great Danes. I'd met all kinds of people and dogs on those walks but nothing like this old guy. I couldn't possibly have predicted that that particular day was going to be different. The world had always been kind to me and my dogs, a wonderful place for us to live in. My world up until that day had been a good one, a safe one, but in that instant everything changed and I changed because of it. I became fearful.

David had to come with us on the walks now because I was too scared to go on my own, not scarred for myself more for my pugs, they were the most precious things in the world to me. I didn't want anybody hurting them again or worse, killing them, taking them away from me. So we got up extra early and walked by the river before David started work, then we'd wait until he got home again before walking a second time and that was usually in the dark which meant no river, only round and round the streets underneath the street lights. That was no fun for anyone. Being down by the river once a day simply wasn't enough for the pugs and it wasn't enough for me. Our entire routine was mucked up and the walks were always rushed because David either didn't want to be late for work or wanted to get home and relax after a long day, I felt there was no pleasure in the walks for the pugs or me anymore, we'd be dragging them back home with our eyes on our watches, but we did that for a few weeks until I felt ok being out on my own again. What snapped me out of it was seeing the pugs not as happy walking as they used to be. Ruby really missed being down by the river, her face was so different when walking around the streets. Yes still happy but not overjoyed and I wanted to see joy on her face again. The streets didn't have the same smells as the river did. The pugs loved that leisurely walk, they loved trotting along the sand and having a good old sniff at what had been washed up, and they deserved to be able to do that, they were dogs after all. For a few days we carried Ruby out for a wee and fed her all her meals on that doona. And when it was bed time David carried Ruby up the stairs wrapped in her doona and put her on the floor beside our bed. She was a little fighter though. Her eyes were bright after the first day but her body was sore. It took her a while to come good. For a few days she barely looked up when we took the other pugs for a walk, she needed to rest and heal, she slept a lot and I crept around the house keeping the other pugs as quiet as I could so that nobody would wake her. But I was so happy when she started to come on the walks again, almost as happy as she was. It didn't take her long, as soon as she felt just a fraction better she shot off the doona and was out there walking again and seemed so carefree doing it. I took a leaf out of her book, if Ruby felt safe after what happened then why should I be any different. Besides if we altered our life because of one incident, regardless of how terrible it was, it meant the old man had won, he'd have beaten us. He hadn't only taken that one day from us I was allowing him to take weeks, I couldn't let those weeks turn into months or worse years. So we went back to our normal routine again, the pugs were happy but my eyes constantly searched for the old man. I wasn't scared now, I had healed somewhat, but I was angry, I desperately wanted to run into him again only this time I would be ready. I didn't know what I was going to do but I knew I would do something, this time he was going to be the one to come off worse. I would never attack his dog I could never hurt an animal, it's not in me, and I would especially never hurt one that was acting the only way it knew how to. No, my rage was directed at the man. Old or not, no more respect, he was going to get what he deserved.

A few weeks later I thought I saw him in the street, and after weeks of planning what I was going to do to him I froze. I couldn't believe it, I was so terrified that I just froze on the spot, stood glued to the pavement, I couldn't move an inch. Seeing him again brought everything back, the images of that day were flooding though my head. I kept standing here willing myself to move, to go towards him but I couldn't, my legs wouldn't take one step. He was on the other side of the street and didn't look like he'd seen us; he was just going about his business walking his dog. I hadn't realized how much this old man had affected me, had taken from me, and I hated myself for not confronting him like I'd been planning to. All I could do was watch him disappearing down the street while I stood there with my four pugs on their leads all looking up at me wondering why we weren't moving.

Once he was out of sight I found I could move freely, so I raced the pugs back home and went after him while I could. I saw him in the distance and this time I ran, I found I could move without hesitation once I knew my pugs were safe. When I caught up to the guy I was so disappointed because it wasn't him. The dog was the same breed and color and the jacket he wore was the same one as the old man had worn that day but this guy was only in his late fifties and the man I wanted was in his seventies at least. I trudged back home disappointed, got the girls and took them for their normal walk.

Living in that house became even more difficult for me after that, I was so glad we were only a few months away from moving. I knew I could no longer live amongst people who thought behaving that way towards an animal was ok. But the truth was that I had seen more human kindness and compassion on that day then I had seen brutality, one man caused the problem, three kind strangers helped Ruby and me through it. But I wasn't thinking that way back then, what the man did to Ruby was so horrible in my eyes that I couldn't focus on anything else, his act of cruelty towards one of my pugs overshadowed everything.

I did a lot of research on this guy, talked to every one of our neighbours, talked to everyone in the street and down by the river as well. I told them what had happened, described him and his dog trying to find out if they knew him, people had seen him but nobody knew much about him, he and his dog kept pretty much to themselves. "Was he out there every day" nobody was sure. Then finally I ran into somebody who knew exactly who I was talking about. They said the old guy had cancer of the mouth and didn't have long to live, perhaps that was why he had attacked Ruby that day, maybe he just wanted to lash out at somebody and we'd come across him on a bad day, still no excuse. Ruby hadn't caused his cancer, cigarettes had and he was still smoking them I'd been told. Perhaps he had been in pain and wanted to inflict it on somebody else or he knew he didn't have long to live and had actually misunderstood my dogs actions and was trying to protect his dog while he was still around to do so. Honestly I don't know what was going through his head all I know is that if I was in his shoes I wouldn't want to spend my last days on earth inflicting pain on animals or other people.

The worst thing was when I found out he lived opposite our house, I couldn't believe it, I'd never seen him in his garden or in my street or anywhere other than down by the river that day. Or perhaps I had seen him and he'd been no more to me than some uninteresting old guy in the street, hardly worth a second glance. Now he was a monster that occupied my thoughts a lot more than I would have liked him to. Across the lake was an island and the big house that faced our townhouse was his. I just couldn't escape him. Every time I opened the blinds his house was right before my eyes. And even if the blinds were closed it didn't make any difference because he was constantly on my mind, always in my thoughts. I just couldn't get away from what happened.

One night I'd had enough, David had just arrived home from work, he came in smiling and happy like he does every day. But I barely spoke to him. I had been stewing over the old man's actions all day long and made up my mind to finally go and see him. Once my mind was made up I wanted to do it right away so I left David with the pugs and took off to the old man's house. It was already dark by the time I got there. I stood outside his house for a moment. Everybody on the lake seemed to leave their curtains open but me. I was always concerned about people looking in but almost everybody else didn't seem to mind it. I saw him and his wife in their kitchen cooking dinner. I felt sorry for them, well more sorry for her then for him, they looked so old and sad and pitiful slowly staggering around the kitchen like a couple of absent minded fools. They were only doing something as simple as cooking dinner but it seemed to be a huge undertaking for them, they kept going to bang into each other and having to side step in order to not cause a collision. They reminded me of a couple of old blind dogs in a small unfamiliar closed in area. Something changed in me as I stood there. I thought to myself what on earth are you doing here. I'd just walked out on a perfectly good life, left my lovely husband and darling pugs to go waste time on this old man. It seemed like a really stupid thing for me to be doing. Even if I went in and yelled at him some more it wouldn't have altered what had gone on. I may have felt better but that's about it, everything else would have remained exactly the same. And there was his wife to think about, she was innocent in all of this, she'd done nothing wrong. What right did I have to bring her into it, to upset her, she was just going about her business cooking tea. I had no right to ruin her evening. I figured if she was married to a man who felt kicking old crippled dogs was an acceptable thing to do then she would have had more than enough to put up with in life already. I doubted he'd have been the easiest person to live with. I reckon she would have suffered enough being married to him for as long as she had.

I was still undecided so I paused a bit longer. Watching them but not really watching them, I more had my mind on Ruby now and how happy she was these days. It seemed she'd healed from both her injuries and her ordeal. I decided to take my lead from her. And in that instant I knew I could finally let it all go. The anger, the resentment, the pain, the anguish, the torment I'd been living with, everything. In that one small moment everything seemed to just all slip away from me. He didn't matter to me any longer. I was finally free. So I turned around and went home.

As I was walking home I started thinking about all that had gone on and I released that from the moment he kicked Ruby I had changed, I began living my life in his cage, I had given him control over me. And that thought made me really annoyed, not annoyed with him, annoyed with myself that I'd give some mean spirited old jerk power over me. I wasn't responsible for what he had done, he was, that was all on him. I had yelled at him in the park, told him what I thought of him and then taken care of Ruby, got her to the vet, I had done my part and that should have been the end of it, but it wasn't because I wasn't letting it be. Instead I was allowing his actions to ruin my happy family life. I mean he seemed to be doing just fine, the old bugger wasn't standing outside my house fuming in the dark was he, he probably hadn't given me or Ruby a second thought since that day whereas I'd thought about nothing else and those thoughts had consumed me. I knew I couldn't allow that to continue, couldn't allow it to affect me or my family a second longer. So I just shook it off, almost like a dog does after a bath, you know just before you have time to put a towel around them they shake and water goes everywhere. Well that's what it felt like I had done with this old man and all the feelings I had about him. It was like I'd had a good shake and could now walk through my front door a different person to the one who'd walked out of it half an hour ago.

When I walked in the door my four babies and my wonderful husband all came to greet me, rushed at me like I'd been gone for weeks instead of only half an hour. The pugs must have heard my key jingling in the lock and were already at the door as I stepped inside and David was coming down the hallway as I glanced up, they were acting like I'd just gotten back from a trip abroad. David had a bit of concern on his face, I suppose he didn't know what state I would be in when I came through the door, but when he saw me smiling he started smiling too. I hugged each one of them slowly and completely, this time I was "All In" I had nothing else on my mind but them and in that moment I knew how lucky and blessed I was. Ruby had lived and was doing beautifully. We'd had a bump in the road but our happy little family was still intact and for that I was grateful.

I guess I could have kept the ball of anger rolling, kept the circle of hate rotating, may well have even ended up with my first criminal charge, but that night I chose not to. After that night I decided to be light hearted about it, and stayed light hearted about it until the day we left for the farm. When I opened my blinds in the morning I'd see his house facing me and in a care free manner I'd say "Good morning Beelzebub" then turn and walk away. It was the same when I was closing the blinds at night-time, I'd look over and say "Good night Beelzebub". The entire thing amused me if anything. I mean I had to have that attitude otherwise my last few weeks in that home would have been a nightmare and it would have had an effect on David and the pugs. I didn't want to be doing that so I had my little joke then set about my business of taking care of the house, the pugs and packing up all our stuff ready for the big move. The thing was I had been opening and shutting those blinds for over two years, been marveling at that house across the lake with its stunning architectural design having no idea of the evil person who resided there.

For a few years I stayed in contact with some of the friends I made while living in that house, but within five years they were all gone, the more involved with rescue I became the less I had to talk to these people about. And that's ok, no hard feelings at all, that's just how life is sometimes, not everybody who comes into your life is meant to stay. Some of the friends I've made in rescue have become family. They certainly understand how I feel about animals more than some of my real family members do anyway.

When Sylvia, one of my old neighbours rang and told me the man had died I didn't have a clue who she was talking about. "Who do you mean Sylvia" I asked. "Did I know him? I thought she was talking about one of the nicer older gentlemen that lived in one of our units and images were flashing through my mind trying to recall who she meant. She reminded me that not only had I known him but I hated him when I lived there, she spoke about a few other people and what they were now up to and I didn't remember them either, not all of them anyway, the names were familiar but I couldn't for the life of me put a face to some of them.

And as for the old man I didn't recognise his name at all and it took me a while to have an image of him come to mind and the image was vague at best. I'd simply forgotten all about him because he was nothing to me now and even less to Ruby. We had been living on our beautiful little farm a year or so by then and life was good, we were content and happy. Our lake life seemed like it had happened in a different lifetime, perhaps even in somebody else's life. The life we were all living now was total bliss. And I was blissful because of it. David noticed the difference in me from the very first day here. He said it was like somebody had flicked a switched. Everything about our life was different and better. I was a different person and the time I spent living on the lake was a distant memory, a distant memory for Ruby too I think. She took to farm life beautifully. The first night we arrived here she stood barking at the top of the hill, like she was announcing to the world that "The Comers" had arrived. She could hear the sounds, the animal noises that are all too familiar in the country when night shadows fall. I think farm life excited her as much as it excited me.

One moonlit night Ruby stood barking and swaying with delight. I stood beside her just letting her do it, and while she was doing it I was gazing across the open paddocks, I was in a trance at how beautiful they looked in the moonlight. Ruby stood by my feet and she was having a ball and I didn't have to rein her in or quieten her down like I used to do in suburbia to keep the neighbours happy. Here I could let her bark as loud as she liked for as long as she liked and nobody could hear her, all the neighbours were a good distance away, we weren't packed in like sardines here. It was so liberating for Ruby and for me, I felt happy not having to worry about somebody complaining. I mean Ruby didn't have a loud bark, she had that lovely growly bark that pugs have, barks like that are never annoying, but in suburbia it doesn't take much to annoy folk. Ok her scream was slightly higher and louder than her normal bark, but I still didn't have to try and keep her quiet, it was nice to be able to let her go and not have to worry anymore.

One of Ruby's favourite things to do was watching birdlife and listening to the different noises they made, she'd bark at them too. If we were on a walk and there was a Kookaburra sitting in a tree laughing then Ruby would have to stop and bark at it. I think the Kookaburra's laugh fascinated her, she would try and look at it but with the arthritis in her neck it was difficult for her to do, so depending on how interested she was in the bird at the time I would go over and pick her up so she could get a good look at him. She seemed to know what I was walking over to her for, and if she wanted a better look she'd stay put and start swaying with excitement and the two of us would stand there with this very obliging Kookaburra staring down at us, they don't seem to want to laugh when you are staring at them but Ruby was ok with that. She'd heard him laugh already, that's how she knew he was there, I'd gently tilt her on a slight angle so she could get a better view without putting any strain on her neck. On the days she wasn't overly bothered if she got a closer look at the bird or not she would start shuffling off as soon as I neared and we would continue on with our walk as usual. Ruby would also sit on the veranda and listen for birds. And when there were none for her to hear and bark at and get joy from David would go out there and start doing bird calls for her. He is really good at doing them too, he didn't just fool Ruby he fooled me as well. I'd hear the sounds and come shooting out of the house because I wanted to see the birds, time and time again he got me a beauty with his expertise. But shooting out the door was never a wasted effort because I got to see Ruby out there barking with delight, she, unlike me, didn't care if she could see the birds or not as long as she could hear them she'd bark away quite happily.

To be honest I wasn't exactly upset when I found out that Ruby had outlived the old man, because to me it was like she'd won. And I thought she deserved to win, after all, she was just an innocent little pug who had done nothing to provoke this old man and yet he'd set upon her all the same. In my eyes victims should win, that's fair isn't it. Karma they call it. It's the only time in my life that Karma has worked quickly enough for me.

Ruby died on the 6th of January 2011 the same day we lost Horton. Ruby died at eleven in the morning, she was 14 years old.

Ruby is buried here on the farm beside her lifelong friend and soulmate Grace.

CHAPTER FIVE

Grace

I remember our last day at the lake house, it was an early start of packing up the bedding before the removalists arrive. I wanted to keep the day as normal as possible as far as the pugs went because I didn't want to have them too disturbed. Almost everything else was packed, just a few bowls left out for the pugs breakfast. We fed the pugs as normal and then the four pugs and I stayed in our bedroom while David and the removal guys loaded up everything in the house. I didn't want the pugs getting trampled on or knocked about with the comings and goings, I also didn't want them getting out into the street with the gate being open. It was all a mad house really so the best thing for us to do was stay out of the way. The pugs lay on our bare mattress sleeping while I packed up a few remaining items. They could hear noise outside the door but after a few gentle woofs decided they were too tired to bother so settled down to sleep. I could hear thudding on the stairs, those removal guys were super fit because they were actually running up the stairs then running back down again with heavy boxes in their arms. I had this laughing giggle bag joke thing that sat in a box at the bottom of a wardrobe, I'd had it for years and it no longer worked but I couldn't bring myself to throw it away because somebody special had bought it for me. I was folding blankets when I heard in the distance the laughing bag going off, and it was soon joined by loud human laughter. It seemed the motion of the guys on the stairs had breathed some life into that thing and it was giggling all the way down the staircase and still going as it was passed from one guy to the other and loaded on the truck. I remember our couches couldn't go through the front door, they could fit well enough but due to the narrow passageway couldn't be turned so had to go out on the lake side and be walked round to the truck. I stood at the upstairs window watching these big hefty guys walking two cream couches along the waters edge. A few of the neighbours were out there watching too, if they had been in any doubt as to what day we were actually leaving they weren't now. A few moments later David appeared and said they were ready to load up the bed. So I put the harnesses on the pugs and took them for a lovely long relaxing walk by the river. It was a leisurely walk and we got to say goodbye to a few people along the way. The last people I said goodbye to were the husband and wife team who had come to Ruby's aid the day she got attacked. I thanked them once again for their kindness and they stroked Ruby's little old head and said how well she was doing.

We then went back and sat in the house while David dropped our keys off at the estate agents office. We were told to just slam the door on our way out and I thought to myself "It'll be my pleasure" I remember sitting at the top of the stairs with the four pugs looking around at the empty house and thinking to myself thank goodness we are leaving. The only thing I had with me was one dog bowl and a bottle of water in case the pugs got thirsty on the drive down, everything else was packed, loaded onto a truck and gone. The house looked so weird with nothing in it, but I held no emotions for it, it had never felt like a true home for me anyway but now it just looked like a sad empty nothingness. I started thinking about my little red brick house and how I would be moving further away from it. But even that didn't make me too emotional because it wasn't the same house anymore, the new owner had done it up, rendered over the bricks and repainted the roof tiles, it was like he erased any part of us ever having been there. And that changed my connection to it, it was like our time there was now only alive in my memories and I could take those memories anywhere with me. I could be living on the other side of the world and one walk down memory lane and I'd be back there in my little red brick home, I didn't need to stay close to it to feel part of it.

As I sat at the top of the stairs with the pugs sleeping around me I started thinking about my time in the house, the people I had met there, some good some bad, some not even worth mentioning. I thought about the day I was cleaning the upstairs windows and noticed a lady coming along on the opposite side of the road with a little fox terrier. I paused and watched her, she was unusual, not only in the way she dressed but in her actions too, I thought she was the most interesting person living here. I saw her a lot after that day, never when I was out in the street always from the upstairs window, her routine must have coincided with my cleaning routine. I used to wonder what her story was, what made her wake up each day and decide to kick every square on the garage door of the house over the road. Oh I knew it wouldn't have happened exactly like that, I knew there would be more to it. Was it a ritual that made some form of sense to her, something that would or wouldn't happen on the days she missed doing it? Was she like me having to always buy even pieces of fruit and not feel right if I didn't, or was it simply that the people who lived in that house had been mean to her or her dog. I often thought about going out and trying to talk to her, but what if she was in her own little world and my presence upset her. I certainly didn't want to do that. Didn't want to put her off her game or interfere with her routine. Still I would have given anything to have found out her story. And not in a nosy way either, I just find people like this fascinating. Regular types don't interest me all that much, I guess because I myself am not regular. Although having said that I wonder if anybody really is, maybe the ones you think are aren't but just putting on a front because they don't want people to see who they truly are. That'd be a hard way to live I think.

I also started thinking about another woman, she too stood out in my memory although not for quite the same reason. This lady used to be totally obsessed with my four pugs, she never walked by the river, I never saw her dogs running down there off their leads, she always caught us in the street. She had two dogs of her own and would quietly sneak up on us, get as close as she possibly could and silently walk behind us like she was part of our pack. The only reason I knew she was there at all was because Sarah would be going nuts because even though this lady was trying to be one of us Sarah knew she wasn't and that her walking with us like that simply wasn't right. She rarely talked to me, mostly to the pugs, it was like I wasn't even there half the time. I could tell she loved dogs but her dogs and Sarah didn't get along and yet she didn't have the sense to keep back, she would always cause upset amongst the dogs and didn't seem to care that her own dogs were as upset as Sarah was. I saw her in the supermarket one day and in a friendly manner said hello, she had no idea who I was and hurriedly scurried away. It seemed that without my pugs she didn't know me at all, I think it startled her that I'd actually spoken to her.

I also thought about the kids that used to follow me and the pugs when we were out walking, they were always riding their bikes up and down our street during the school holidays. As soon as they spotted us they'd fly over, dismount and walk their bikes beside us and talk, they were around nine and ten years old all of them. But they kept their bicycles wheels well away from my old pugs. It was a respectful thing for them to do so I would always make time for them, answer their questions and when all the questions had been answered they would just talk to me about themselves. They were really nice kids. I saw them in the supermarket one day too and they were all giggly and acting shy, like they'd spotted a celebrity or something and were too star struck to come over and talk, it was like they didn't think I did normal things like shop. It was the funniest thing, maybe I shocked them being in a place they never expected to see me, or maybe they were shy kids and their bicycles gave them confidence or something. Either way the next time I saw them in the street they were back to their normal selves. One of them had a turtle, he was telling me all about it, I had them myself when I lived in the little red brick house. I've always loved turtles and I told the kid I'd like to see his pet sometime. Anyway I'd only just gotten inside the house, didn't even have time to take all the pugs harnesses off when there was a knock at the door. I went to answer it and through the mottled glass could see this big turtle looking in at me. The kid could hardly hold the thing, it was massive, reminded me more of a sea turtle then a kids pet. He must have been so excited to have somebody show an interest that he barely gave me time to get home. I had no idea he knew where I lived, but they must have watched me a lot more than I did them. It was a beautiful looking turtle though, really healthy, so well looked after. And the size, no wonder he was so proud. The turtle didn't look impressed though, well their faces don't change much do they, but he was looking as unimpressed as a turtle could get. I could see the unimpressiveness even before I opened the door and he seemed less impressed to be inside my home. I felt a bit sorry for him, I imagined that kid racing in and grabbing the poor bewildered thing from its tank and racing out the door. I settled the pugs and offered to walk the boy home, carry the turtle for him. But he said he'd be ok and off he went smiling because I'd seen his turtle, well not only seen it but raved about what a beauty it was. But the thing that worried me was that he went and got on his bike, I thought he'd walked the turtle down but he'd ridden down with it tucked under his arm and was now taking it home the same way. I didn't like that but had no time to say anything, the kid took off so fast, riding one handed and weaving away as he went. He crossed the busy road and disappeared out of sight. I now knew why the turtle had looked so unhappy. The next time I caught up with the boys I explained to them about the best way to cart a turtle around, or better still not cart it at all. I said that next time somebody asks to see him, make them come to your house when your parents are home and bring him out onto the lawn. The more the kids got used to me the more they would hang around, they'd sling their bikes at the top of the embankment and come down to the river and walk with us. There was me, four pugs and six kids all walking together. I think they really wanted a dog of their own but the units they lived in didn't allow them so they made do playing with my four pugs. I'd bring a few treats along with me when I knew the kids were going to be about and they'd give them to the pugs just before we parted ways, they used to get so much joy out of feeding my pugs a few treats, I think they enjoyed it even more than the pugs did and that's really saying something. One of the kids had an older brother who was at that wanting to appear cool stage. He'd stand back and watch what was going on, his eyes letting me know he desperately wanted to join in but his body stayed where it was. I think he feared one of his school friends may catch him in the very uncool act of giddily feeding pugs and teased him about it. Feared they'd come along at the precise moment he was on the ground joining in the fun and he'd never hear the end of it. So he'd lean against the fence with headphones on, head nodding to the music, doing the toughest coolest pose he could muster.

I thought again about the going away party we'd been thrown, thought about the lovely meal we'd had that night. No food was organised because nobody thought the party was going to go so long. It was meant to be a lunchtime thing only. But time went on and people seemed to be really enjoying themselves. A few of the older residents left but the others stayed on. When we began getting hungry we all started planning what type of meal we would have. Somebody said they had a huge tin of tuna in the back of the cupboard they weren't ever going to use. Somebody else said they had a bag of carrots and ran to get them. Someone had half a bag of spuds they wanted to donate, somebody else had wholemeal noodles, another two tins of soup and we had a big bag of green beans in our freezer. Dave ran home and got those and as he dashed by our little chilli plant sitting innocently in its pretty pot he grabbed a few off and we chucked them in there too. Well Pete chucked them in because he volunteered himself to do the cooking and nobody disagreed, we all just kind of slowly backed out of the kitchen and left him to it. He didn't mind, he had a couple of bottles of beer to keep him company and was busily sorting pots and pans when I glanced back at him. In less than no time the house smelt wonderful and we all sat on chairs or on the floor with warm bowls of casserole in our hands raving about what a great cook Pete was. And he really was, he made the most delicious meal out of everybody's cast offs. I don't know what herbs he used to flavour that casserole but it had more than just our chilies in it. Everything he put in complemented each other beautifully. I overheard somebody asking him what herbs he'd used but he was too drunk to remember.

My mind then went to the new people living right next door, they, like us, kept to themselves a lot. The only difference between us and them was that we weren't thieves. Other than to say hello in passing we'd never had any conversations with them, they seemed to just shuffle off when they saw people coming. We had a few pot plants that used to sit outside the windows facing the lake and our chilli plant used to sit in amongst them. A real little giver it was and when I was cooking dinner I'd just walk outside, pick what I needed for that particular meal and add it to the food. David since traveling overseas had developed a taste for hot spicy food so a little chili plant was bought and I put it in a fancy pot. Well that chili plant sat there for well over a year without anybody touching it, there were no fences on the townhouses on the lake side, it was just an agreement of decency that you never took anything from your neighbours unless you were given the ok to. When we had extra chilies, which we did a lot, I would go round and offer them to the neighbours. Well one morning David opened the blinds and our little chili plant was naked, stripped totally bare, not only of chilies but they'd taken the leaves as well, taken everything off it and left it there like that. I often wondered why they didn't just steal the whole thing, pot and all. That would have made more sense to me. It wasn't an overly big plant and the pot wasn't too heavy either it could have just been picked up and walked off with, but then again I guess it would have been easily recognized wouldn't it. I would have definitely been able to tell the plant was mine if it was sitting in my pink pot. Thing is we knew it was the new neighbours that did this because one of the other neighbours saw them doing it. They'd done it after dark but the lake had these ball lamps all around for people to see their way, the lamp nearest our townhouse was broken and nobody bothered getting it fixed because it helped us sleep better. These new people next door must have thought they couldn't be seen due to the broken lamp, but they were and we got told about it. The saddest part was that the chili plant died after that, we had fully intended on bringing it to the farm with us but in the end it had to be tossed in the communal compost bin. Thing was if they'd done the decent thing and asked I would gladly have given them some chilies. The taking everything part was what upset me the most, well that and living right next door to dishonest people. But we didn't have to do that for too long because we already had our plans in action when they moved in. The cheeky thing was that when our house was put on the market and open for inspection, these same neighbours were the first people to burst through the door. I thought they were just being nosey, wanted to see what their next door neighbours had that they didn't that kind of thing, but perhaps they were casing the joint, maybe their nimble fingers didn't stop at chilies. Or maybe they wanted to see if our view of the lake was better than their own, it was, because we were closer to the waters edge and were positioned where the lake opened up. We had the best view of all the fourteen townhouse actually. Perhaps that had annoyed them and they'd taken it out on our poor little chili plant. Or maybe they thought we weren't using them fast enough so they'd help us out, I don't think they gave any thought to the fact that we were taking only what we needed on each particular day. And if they had done the same thing our little chili plant would have survived and been on its way to the farm with us now.

David coming in the front door shook me from my thoughts. He asked me if I wanted to say goodbye to the lake house the way I had done with my little red brick home, have a few moments alone with it that sort of thing, but I said no because I didn't feel the need to. No need for long farewells with tears running down my cheeks. I just stood up when David said it was time to go, picked Ruby up and carried her down the stairs with the other pugs following on, then walked out the door without a single glance backward. I secured the pugs in the car, made sure they were comfy in their beds while David did one last sweep of the place in case there was something we'd forgotten to pack, there wasn't and he was back in the car in no time. I heard him close the front door, you always had to slam it a bit to make sure it closed properly, he got in the seat beside me and started the engine, and that was it we pulled out of the driveway and I didn't even bother looking through the rear vision mirror for one last look at the place. My eyes were focused solely on the road in front of us, the road that was about to take us to our farm and I couldn't wait to get there.

When I think back to the lake house and I still do sometimes, very rarely but sometimes, distance and time have allowed me to see it differently to how I used do to. Now a days I think that maybe that house wasn't so awful after all, maybe it had a specialness about it, maybe it was the last place people go to before moving on to live out their lifelong dreams. And if that's the case it's a pretty magical place really. Perhaps the people who buy it do so because they are drawn to it somehow. Or it has a way of drawing those who need it the most in. It's the final step one takes on their road to happiness. Or maybe it's nothing of the sort, either way it gave me something to think about one day as I was walking the pugs around the farm. The thing I do know for sure is that it's been a stepping stone for at least two couples to go on and live their dreams. The man we sold the house to ended up doing the very same thing we did. And I know he definitely had to move there for his dream to become a reality. When we moved out I left him a bottle of champagne by the kitchen sink and a card wishing him well. He was a school teacher who loved making furniture in his spare time. He had lost his wife, that's why he was moving house, said he felt he needed a change. I found out from one of the friends I kept in contact with that he cooked breakfast for any neighbours who wanted to join in, did it every Sunday morning. I guess he was lonely living on his own and wanted to make some new friends and what better way to go about it really. He would have fitted in so well there, the most perfect place for him. I pictured the chili stealers loading up their plates, shoving people out of the way in the process and wondered if after a while they had been banned from those little get-togethers. Well a lady who lived in one of the other units used to come along to these Sunday morning rituals. She was nice, I remember her well, short, blonde, very artistic, always painting or making something, usually out of nothing and doing a really good job. Well those two ended up getting married and went to live in Queensland. He gave up teaching, became a furniture maker full time, which is what he truly loved doing and she carried on painting and the two set up a small business together. So the lake house is in fact responsible for at least two success stories and I bet there would be a lot more too if I bothered to do some digging. The ex-school teacher wasn't there as long as we were, he moved out within twelve months of moving in. And in a way he was lucky and in a way it didn't really matter because for us with Grace Farm the timing was perfect.

If there was ever a name more suited to a dog it would be this one and if there was ever a name more suited to a farm it would be this one. Grace fits her name perfectly because she is so very graceful, a real little lady, an elegant princess. Angel Gracie is what I often call her for she is like a little angel gracefully skimming the floor as she walks along. She was like a little ballerina actually the way she placed those tiny paws, just a special and unique way of moving about. Grace is a real tiny pug too, all the others are a lot bigger than she is so for this reason people often think she's my youngest which is a complement really because Grace is actually my eldest. People didn't just think she was the youngest due to her size either, it was the liveliness she had, just really marvellous for her age, she's fit and slim and healthy and full of energy. There's not much grey in her muzzle either so I understand how easy it is for people to get confused. They'd see this little girl in amongst the pack and she'd spot them and go flying over for a closer look doing her delicate jig as she went, then stand there looking them up and down with those big bug like eyes of hers. They'd bend down to get a closer look and if she liked them she'd let them, and they'd be there looking at this very small face with no grey on it. "How old is the pup" they'd ask and I'd say 13, 14 or 15 or however old she was at the time. Of course if she didn't like them she'd be doing her bouncy bark, up and down she'd bounce and at those times the question was never asked because Grace's face was never still enough for them to see it was free of grey. It all depended on her mood and if the person she met was to her liking. Some would want to pick her up and she wasn't having any of that. Whether she liked them or not it made no difference to Angel Gracie, she would never let a stranger hold her. With me and Grace things were a little different, we connected quickly and became closer over the years. Grace arrived with Ruby and where Ruby struggled a little at the start Grace got used to her new home fairly quickly.

I always think its special when we take in a pair of old pugs. And I have the highest regard for rescue groups who will not split up dogs that have spent their entire lives together. These are the rescue groups that truly have my heart. They will wait for the right home to come along, even if they have to wait a while, they will do it because they are not thinking of themselves they are thinking purely of the dogs and I am all for people who put the needs of the dogs before everything else. These are true dog lovers and these are the kinds of people I love seeing in animal welfare. I have taken in a few elderly pairs over the years and I hope to take in more, but Ruby and Grace were my first ones and so they are special because of this.

I feel honoured and privileged to be able to have a role in keeping those old souls together, because that's how it should always be. They have been uprooted from their lives and they are old, and sometimes they are unwell, to take them away from their partner on top of all this is an all-round heartless act. It's like putting a couple who've been married for fifty or sixty years into different nursing homes, and expecting them to cope, I believe such acts shorten lives, shorten them due to heartbreak, so I am always going to welcome elderly pairs into my home because of this. I may not be able to be able to prevent human pairs being separated but I can sure help a pair of old pugs. And I have so much joy in my heart when I know I have a pair coming into my life. My job is to take tender loving care of both of them for the remainder of their lives and then, when it's time, to put them into the ground side by side. Never to be parted again. Of course it's really sad seeing two little mounds of dirt sitting next to each other but I am always glad that they were allowed to live out their days together. They were able to walk together around my little farm, eat their meals side by side like they've been doing all their lives and then curl up together at night time. And of course they wake up the next morning curled around each other and the whole thing is repeated again and again and again. They don't have to go wait by a window, looking longingly down the driveway hoping that today is the day their soulmate will show up, they don't have to go to bed at night heartbroken either. And they don't have to pick at their food wondering why their little friend is no longer eating beside them. That's why elderly pug pairs thrill me so much, it's like I am involved in something very special and meaningful here. I am part of their final chapter and I know I can make their autumns and winters beautiful. Free of fear, blanketed in love and understanding, all their needs met and then some and I really love doing that for them. Well, I don't just do it for them I do it for me as well because it's something I truly love. Taking care of old pugs makes me happy.

I was lucky because I found out a little bit about Ruby and Graces old home. We are not always given such insight which is a shame because it really does help. The more you know the more understanding you have of them and why they act the way they do, the more you are told about their old lives the easier it is when helping them settle into their new ones. Although having said that all the pugs I have ever taken in over the years have told me a little about their past lives by their actions and reactions and sometimes it can break your heart. It's very easy to spot the ones who have received love and kindness and the ones that have not. The ones who were really part of the family, true family members, and the ones who were treated merely as pets or worse.

Grace was in the family first then a year later they got Ruby. Both had been bought as puppies by their newly married humans. They were doted upon for almost a decade until a human baby was born then they were quickly shoved out of the way. It always saddens me when I hear stories like this because it's so heartbreaking for the dogs, they've done nothing wrong and yet are cast aside and have no idea why. It was a shame actually because I believe at one stage Ruby and Grace had been that couples babies. Loved and treasured. Then when the newborns started arriving the mother began to think that her first babies, the ones with fur, were not clean enough to be around her human babies so Ruby and Grace went to live outside. I don't know how long the two of them were left outside for, but pugs don't do well living amongst the elements. They are house dogs and the only way you get long healthy lives out of them is to have them inside with you and look after them. Some people think I wrap my pugs in cotton wool and I guess I do to some extent and I do it because I want to give them the best shot possible of reaching lovely old ages. They are not going to do that unless they are well looked after and you can't overdo it when looking after your pugs as far as I am concerned. You are not spoiling them by letting them sleep inside the house, they need that, and you are not spoiling them with walks, you are beating off boredom, giving your dog something to look forward to every day and keeping their little minds active as well as their bodies. And you are not spoiling them by giving them the best food and taking time to prepare it, you are being a good parent when you do that. And none of this is any different to what you would do for your human children and nor should it be. I've had people with human children belittling me because of the care I give my pugs and I just say to them would you leave your kids outside at night, restrict their exercise and feed them junk food all the time, would you not put a coat on them when they are cold or keep them inside with the air conditioner on when they are hot, would you not bathe them, groom them and give them nice fresh clean smelling bedding. And of course the answer is always a big "NO" with shocked looks on their faces. Then I say "Well why should it be any different for my pugs" I wait for them to answer and of course they can never think of a good reason why it should be or if they can they are too scared to say it to my face.

I don't think Ruby and Grace were left outside for too long though which was a good thing, at least the mother decided to do the right thing by her pugs and rang a rescue group to come and take them. I'm grateful to her for doing that. She could have just left them in the outdoor kennel cold, lonely and confused, but she loved them enough to allow them to leave and have a better quality of life than the one she thought she could give them at the time. And God bless her for doing that.

She did have choices though, that's the saddest thing, she had choices even though at the time she may not have thought so. She could very easily have kept all her babies. Combined both human and animal babies together and still lived in a harmonious state. It is possible, it would have taken a bit of effort, a bit of thought put into it, a bit of planning, organising and a bit of getting used to but it can be done if one wants to put the effort in. The new mother could have had peace of mind and her babies could have grown up and older together. I think it's important for children to grow up with a respect and a love for animals, they need to be taught to be gentle from a very early age, that an animal is not a toy but a living being that deserves respect, love and kindness. They need to know that they are important family members, not lesser family members but are just as important as any other member of their family. And this new mother had a perfect opportunity to instill that in her children. And yes of course she could still teach them such values but they'd have learnt the lessons better if the animal isn't banished from the home. Of course if an animal is not going to be respected by a child, or worse still roughed up and treated as a play thing that has no feelings then I do think it's best for the animal if it goes to live with somebody who has better values.

As far as Ruby and Grace were concerned I think they would have loved to have been introduced to the new members of the family. And being old once they'd had a walk they would have easily settled down in their beds in an area of the lounge room and the child would learn to respect those elderly dogs just like they would do their elderly grandparents or great grandparents. I know a lot of dog rescuers who have young children, they make it work, and I'm sure would have many great tips to share.

Grace was most certainly more outgoing then Ruby was but she too showed me that she was a little anxious about what had taken place in her life over the last few months. Some pugs take a long time to heal and others don't give their past lives much thought, or if they do they don't linger on it, instead they live in the moment and are happy. And at first I thought Grace may have been one of those pugs that walked in the door and was more or less home. And in a way she was but there were a few tiny little things happening that let me know her mind was concerned and of course it would have been, she had gone through the same things Ruby had been through. Grace just reacted to the situation differently because the two of them had different little personalities dwelling within. Grace was full on for wanting to be near you. She wanted to be always sitting on your knee. Ruby wouldn't come near you but Grace chose to heal while being as close to you as possible. She loved rubbing her face into your chest and grunting away happily, sometimes to herself, other times she would raise her head and look you in the eye, just checking you were noticing her and then her head would go back down and she'd be off rubbing and grunting to herself again.

She would sleep peacefully in your arms then wake up and go pacing across the row of windows, the windows that faced the lake, sometimes barking at people other times just trailing, but always back and forth back and forth. I didn't know if she was just amusing herself, like it was her thing or if she was perhaps a little bit anxious. But she seemed more happy then anything so I'd just watch her and smile at her when she'd pause and look over at me. It took her quite a while to stop urinating in the house too. Most pugs they'll mark their new territory for up to two weeks and then that is it, they never wee in the house again. But some pugs do take a little longer to stop weeing mainly because of being unsettled and Grace was one of those pugs who took a while.

I've had a few pugs over the years who you think are never going to stop marking their new home, and you start thinking to yourself "Oh we have a lifelong wisser here" and you just accept that fact and live with it. Clean up the mess and move on because really it's not worth getting upset about, they are old and deserve a bit of understanding as all elderly beings do. You don't ever, ever shout or raise your voice even a little bit at them nor do you lose your patience with them, you just clean it up and carry on loving them throughout it all.

Some you have to make sure to carry outside first thing in the morning before getting the others ready to go out because you know they've been holding there little bladders for a while and they are about to burst. And some days this works, they'll trot off and wee and you'll praise them, other days they stand at the door doing nothing then run inside as soon as the door is open and wee on the rug and again you just clean it up. Dogs love their owners so very much, they will do absolutely anything to please them. You are their world, they idolise you and if they could work out right away that you wanted them to wee outside instead of inside believe me they would do it. And most will get to know what you want from them in time, but yelling at them is not going to make it happen any faster, it'll make the entire thing worse if anything because now they'll be weeing due to fear and how horrible is that. Put yourself is their shoes, would you want to be so scared of somebody that you pee yourself through fear. Also if their little old bladders could hold on for a long time they would do that for you. But sometimes this isn't going to happen and you just have to be ok with that because it isn't their fault. But I must also note that if you think their urination pattern is unusual and maybe not like your other dogs then please take them to a vet in case there are health issues happening. And sometimes there can be, and your vet will be the best person to sort this out. Untreated urinary tract infections can lead to all sorts of trouble, especially in little old dogs. Just go with your instincts really. But please don't make them go and live outside for the rest of their lives because you can't be bothered putting the effort in with house training and cleaning.

I've had one or two over the years that would urinate inside their entire life here on the farm. Maybe not every day, but some days and then sometimes they'll stop for a few weeks but then will keep relapsing if it's cold or they don't feel well or even if they just forget or just cannot hold themselves all night long. Winter is the worst for this type of thing because nobody likes the cold. And I understand fully because I don't like the cold either and the older I get the more I don't like it. We just clean the puddle up and get on with living our happy lives together because in the scheme of things it isn't important. Yes its extra work but you have to remember that they are elderly and deserve some kindness and consideration in their senior years. I mean we'll all be old one day and who knows what we'll be like when we are in our eighties and nineties. Let's hope somebody isn't going to yell at us for something that is beyond our control.

Certainly we would prefer them to be here with us then outside in the ground. Both David and I always say that we would rather be cleaning up urine then walking past a little mound of dirt on our daily walks around the farm and really that's how you have to look at it. It kind of puts everything into perspective then. And even on our busiest days we both have this in the forefront of our minds. And besides we've become experts at wiping up urine, if there was a wiss cleaning event at the Olympics one of us would win gold for sure. Actually one would win gold and the other one silver, it just depends who got to the little puddle on the floor in the fastest time. Like most things on the farm we just make a joke out of it, pat the little blessing on the head and carrying on doing what we were doing.

Of course we've taken in some pugs that we both thought were lifelong wissers for sure because some considerable time has gone by and they are still weeing in the house. But then you find one day that they will just stop doing it, nothing has changed as far as you can tell, it's just that they now start holding themselves until they are out the door. And it's lovely when it happens. Grace took around four or five months from memory to finally stop weeing in the house. She stopped around the time we moved to the farm.

Grace was a beautiful loving pug. The first moment she walked into our home she came over and asked to be picked up, just pawed at my leg and then sort of climbed it like a kitten, letting me know what she wanted from me. She stayed in my arms a little while and then indicated that she wanted to get down. So I put her by my feet and she quickly trotted off and went around discovering her new home and taking everything about her new lodgings in. Over the weeks she let me know she liked sitting on my knee but if I put my arms around her which I'd instinctively do she didn't like that. I'm an in your face kind of mum, I just love my pugs and sometimes I think I get to be a little bit too much for them to cope with, they think I'm too full on until they get to know me then it's like "Oh here we go Mum is hugging and kissing us again". Little Gracie had to get used to me before she allowed me to totally envelop her. I don't think she'd had a lot of attention for quite a while before coming to live in our home so I must have been a bit of a shock to her.

I understood this so pulled myself back a bit and allowed her to adapt. I touch my pugs often. I'm in love with them. So it was a real quest on my behalf to let Grace alone, at times I'd almost have to sit on my hands to remind myself not to overdo it. She was absolutely lovely and I just had to love her with my eyes until she felt comfortable enough with me touching her. We took things slowly, a lot slower than I would have liked but it wasn't about me it was about Grace. I'd sit with her perched on the end of my lap and stroke her gently, take my hand way, leave her a bit and then gently stroke her again, after a while she began to lean in, to rub her face against me in a cat like manner, once she was comfortable doing this I began planting gentle little kisses on her ears and the top of her head. She'd feel my kisses and pause, her little face would tilt up and her little old eyes would take me in. We'd spend a few moments gazing at each other and then her face would be down again rubbing and my head would be down again kissing.

That's how we became better acquainted, little tenderness's every now and then until she got used to me. Although I would have simply loved to have known what she was thinking when she felt my kisses gently falling on her head, as she was gazing up at me I tried to figure out what was going through her mind. Her eyes never left my eyes, so maybe she was trying to figure out what was going through my mind as well.

I can still remember how Grace looked walking along the street towards me that first day, she looked very old to me, a lot older than the two I already had at home. She was tiny and delicate a typical old lady. She seemed a bit bewildered by what was going on, she'd been in the car a long time and had now been put on the ground in a strange street. She didn't know what to do or which way to turn. I found out later that I wasn't the first person who wanted to adopt them, a month before they had been on their way to another home when the lady changed her mind. Just like that, the pugs and the foster lady were already in the car half way to what everyone thought was going to be their new home when the mobile phone rang and the lady said she no longer wanted them. That hurt my heart because if she was so indecisive then why didn't she just tell them earlier. She could have saved them the upheaval, although I do think it was better that she did it this way instead of having those poor confused pugs with her for a week and then sending them back. Of course the fact this woman changed her mind was good for me otherwise I'd never have had these two little blessings in my life. But I thought it was unfair that Ruby and Grace had been mucked around like that. The two of them and all their belongings had been loaded into that car, there were last hugs and sad goodbyes at their foster home, then they'd been driven half way to their destination only to have to turn around and go all the way back again. You can only imagine what was going through their minds at the time.

Ok they were not human children in an orphanage who'd been told a new family was coming for them and were waiting on the steps with packed suitcases by their side, but they would have sensed something was going on, dogs pick up on little things, they would have been aware that something was changing. People don't think about this when adopting a dog and they should. Dogs have emotions just like we do, they are not a car in a car yard that you've changed your mind about, they are living feeling emotional beings. Thought and respect should be given to them at all times, but sadly too often it is not, because more thought is given to human beings because they think their feelings are more important and they are not.

When I looked into adopting Ruby and Grace I had to go to the council and my neighbours on both sides to get their permission, had to pay an additional fee and have a home inspection. All this took time and while I was waiting I was asked by Pug Rescue if I wanted to have them for a weekend visit. But I said no. And it wasn't because I didn't want to meet them because I did, I desperately, desperately did. It was just that I didn't want to muck those two pugs around more than they had already been. If they came here and went back they would be unsettled again, they were too old and had been through too much already. I didn't want to have them here then have the council reject my application and have to send them away, that meant they'd have been rejected yet again and that wasn't fair on either one of them. Until I could offer a forever home I felt it was in their best interest to leave them where they were. I told the lady from Pug Rescue this and she understood perfectly.

Seeing Grace coming towards me that day, confusion written all over her face like that, I knew I had made the right choice. I knew they were coming to stay with me for good and that I was going to love them and be there for them for the remainder of their days. And that's what they both desperately needed. Especially considering the time it took for Ruby to settle in, for all they knew this was just another home on their way to their forever home, or maybe by this stage they'd started thinking a forever home was never going to come and that for the rest of their lives they were going to move from one home to another every couple of months until one or both of them died from heartache and exhaustion. These little darlings needed a home with security and I'm glad I waited until everything was well and truly sorted out before offering it to them.

When Grace first came she would only eat dry food, she started off eating what I was giving my original two girls but after a few days decided she wasn't going to eat it. She was hungry and she wanted to eat she just didn't want to be eating that. Ruby didn't have a problem with it, from day one she'd always been a good eater, most pugs are but Grace was different, she'd stand and stare at the bowl in front of her then stare back at me as if to say "You got anything better? And of course I didn't think dry food was better but if that's all she would eat then that's what I was going to give her. You can't change everything in their lives at once. Sure I was going to improve her diet but for now I'd just let her have what she fancied and introduce better eating gradually over the next few weeks. The dry food was top quality though, a very good brand, so I at least had peace of mind about that.

I could have starved her, fed her that same meal until she was so hungry she'd eat it but I decided to keep offering her different things until I found something she was interested in. I don't like to have them upset for any reason during that settling in stage. I think they have enough on their plate without adding to it so I pander to them a little bit. Then slowly bring them round towards what I'd like them to be eating, and Grace was not a fat pug either, she's always been slim, I didn't want her loosing condition so the dry food container came out until she began eating what the other pugs were thriving on. I'd introduce my diet along with her dry food at first, just slowly getting her used to eating a better quality of food. And I always add water to the dry food as I don't like it swelling in their tummies, I don't think that's good for them. So I'd put either water, tea or carrot juice on the dry food and let it soak for half an hour or overnight. Although with the dry food container I was always conscious of not shaking it around Harper, we found out the hard way that Harper in her old home used to have to fight all the other pugs for her food. I think the old breeder just chucked handfuls of dry food on the garage floor and the pugs would have to fight each other for it.

The sound of dry food rattling in a container sent Harper into a snarling, growling, vicious, fierce faced rage. It was like you had flicked a light switch, that's how fast she changed. She didn't even have to smell the dry food just the sound of it turned her from her normal peaceful happy state to the dark side in two seconds flat. And there she'd stand in the middle of the room puffed up and shaking with rage protecting food that wasn't even in front of her. To be honest Harper looked like a little bit of a twit doing it. I thought so and Sarah did too because when I looked over at Sarah she was standing with her head tilted to one side looking across at Harper with an expression that said "What the hell are you doing that for? Sarah would then look at the ground and go searching, sniffing all over the place just in case there was actually something there to eat, there never was but Harper was pretty convincing.

Perhaps Harper was just getting herself ready for when the food came out, like she'd no doubt done in her old home, but there was no need to fight for food in our house, Sarah had never fought for food in her life. The first time it happened Sarah took a few steps back from Harper. I think she was startled, scared even, she was top dog but the way Harper was behaving it was like she was demon possessed and that can be pretty intimidating for another pug. Sarah had never seen anything like it, and to be honest up until that point neither had I, I've seen it many times since but with Harper it was all new to me. Sarah probably wondered what the crazy girl was on and that she was not getting involved in it.

I pictured the old breeder lazily sprinkling handfuls of dry food on the floor and all the poor pugs fighting each other to get their bit. It would have been easier for the lady being so old and all but not a good way to feed any dog and especially not good for a breed that is food orientated and prone to food aggression. Actually that way of feeding is ideal for bringing out food aggression in a pug and should be avoided like the plague. Well not only avoided for aggressive behaviour but avoided altogether. I mean who wants to have to suck their food up from a dirty garage floor.

Harper must have been a good fighter though because of how fat she was when she first came. Then again she was fighting to feed her puppies a lot of the time wasn't she, it's what any good mother would do and Harper had been an excellent mother. It was a real shame though because as I've said before Harper was a great natured pug, one of the very best and to have been put in the position of having to fight like mad for every mouthful was an absolute disgrace. It took months before the snarling growing pre-meal performances finally stopped. But then when Ruby and Grace came along Harper started doing it again. I think she thought that even though two more pugs were now in our family that the amount of food given was going to remain the same, and maybe that's how the breeder did it but that's not how I was going to do it. Once Harper realised she wasn't going to have her food cut she stopped with all the nonsense and would dance around the kitchen excited at mealtimes. No more snarls only smiles.

We came a long way with Grace and her eating, not only what she liked but how it was served up to her. Like I've said before Grace was a very small pug, small frame, small paws, small face, a little tiny mouth and very narrow throat. We found out the hard way about her tiny her throat was, you'd be feeding her a meal and she'd keel over, totally pass out, at first I thought she was having a seizure but she wasn't jerking about, just laying on her side on the floor unconscious. So I'd pick her up and hold her in the standing position and she'd come good again. No food was trapped, she wasn't choking, for some reason she had just passed out, with cold food it was even worse, that seemed to make her airways close up even more. We took her to the vets but he couldn't find anything wrong with her. I talked to Pug Rescue but they hadn't heard of it either, nobody I spoke to had had a pug that did that. The vet asked what we were doing to prevent it, I said after trial and error we had begun rolling Grace's food into little bite sized balls, he said then keep on doing it and that was that, he sent us on our way. A bit of a wasted visit really but of course you have to get her checked out in case there was something seriously going wrong in her body, which at one point I thought there may have been. If her food was accidentally rolled into an even slightly bigger ball then she would faint, if you concentrated and kept the balls all tiny, not even one slightly bigger in the bunch then she had no trouble when she was eating. She only ever ate small meals anyway, for a pug Grace had an unusually small appetite, didn't take much to fill her, so I'd roll the food up and even if the pugs were getting impatient they were ignored while I took note of what I was doing. I'd serve her meals on a small plate and Gracie would dance around my feet until the plate was put down then she'd eat her meals quite happily. No more trouble after that.

I was just glad I'd been standing with Grace the first time it happened, if I'd put her food on the ground and walked away she would have been dead when I went back to check on her I'm sure of it, and I would never have known why. I may have just thought she'd had a heart attack or something, yet it would have been something as simple as being given the wrong sized food. Pugs are a funny little breed, full of oddities, they keep you on your toes, it's one of the many reasons I love them so much, I wouldn't have them any other way. You get a new pug in and they'll soon start showing you their likes and dislikes, working them out can be hard but once you have life runs pretty smoothly. Life is never boring with a pug that's for sure.

There was an incident once when we were walking by the river, people were always feeding the ducks and pelicans down there. And one day the five of us were cutting through an empty paddock to get to the river faster. We were running late and Ruby really did want to get down to that river as quickly as she could. I mean we weren't late by much but you could set your clock by Ruby, she knew when dinner was late and she was the same way with her walks, it was like she had swallowed a little alarm clock when she was a puppy and it was still working perfectly inside her. She was the same if David worked back late, once she fell in love with him she became well aware of the time he should be walking through the door. And became an impatient little Miss until his face appeared, I think if she wasn't so in love with him she may have given him the cold shoulder on the nights he was really late. But she never did, she may have wanted to, may have been sitting there festering planning it in her little old head while waiting for the sound of his car, but when she actually saw him all was quickly forgiven, she flew into his arms with a rocket propelled action. I've never known a dog to be more aware of the time then little old Ruby was.

So there we all were rushing through this empty lot and Grace oddly enough was leading the pack this day and I hadn't spotted her eating anything, I must have been concentrating on one of the others but next thing I looked up and Grace was on her side flipping around like a fish out of water. I raced to her, picked her up and checked her airways, I couldn't see anything so put her down and she was upright for only a few seconds before flopping on her side and flipping around again. I picked her up and looked inside her mouth again, this time I saw that there was a small bit of bread stuck to the roof of her mouth, I knew it was bread only because I'd glanced back at the other pugs and saw they had each found themselves a bit of bread too, but they weren't having any of the problems Grace was having, they were happily eating their bit and sniffing around in the hope of finding some more. I dislodged the bread from the roof of Grace's mouth and it took quite a bit of doing because she was really freaking out. Throwing her head around and panicking. She desperately wanted me to get rid of the bread but didn't want me to put my fingers in her mouth to do it and of course that's not how it works. She was really fighting me on it and getting herself quite upset in the process, and I had to be really careful with her because I didn't want to hurt her tiny little old mouth when prying it open. I chucked the four leads I was holding on the ground and put all my attention into helping Grace. Even when the bread was finally free and I put her down on the ground she fell over and started flipping about again, and it wasn't because the bread I'd dislodged was blocking her airways because I'd made sure I'd gotten it all out and once I did I'd flung that bread as far away as I could, flung it in the opposite direction of where the other three pugs were because I didn't want them getting hold of it. It was more that Grace still had the sensation of having it stuck to the roof of her mouth. That's what all the fuss was about. She'd be ok in my arms, I'd be rubbing the side of her shoulder and soothing her with my words and I'd think she was ok but the moment I put her down again she toppled. I picked her up once more and this time didn't put her down. I figured what she needed now was to be distracted. I needed her to forget about the bread and start thinking about something else so I called over my shoulder to the other three pugs and strode to the river as quickly as I could. I walked out of the paddock and down the embankment with Grace tucked under my arm. She wasn't freaking out now, she was looking around and I was looking around too making sure all the pugs were with me. Ruby flew down the embankment fast and was screaming so I knew she was ok, Sarah was a few feet behind me and Harper was the same distance behind her. We all got down the bottom safely and started walking along the waters edge, up ahead I noticed the pugs had all gathered in one area weeing, kicking their little feet and weeing some more. I caught up to them and put Grace on the ground in the area that was of interest to the others in the hope that she would be ok now, this time she just grunted a few times to herself, had a little wee, then carried on walking. The bread was a distant memory now, well for her it was anyway, but me I think I'll remember that day forever because it was just the oddest thing to happen, well not that a pug finding something to eat on a walk was odd but the way Grace reacted to it, or should I say over reacted to it, that was the odd part. The way she was acting I thought she'd gotten a fish hook caught in her mouth. But it was just a small piece of bread that had caused all the drama.

And maybe that was all that was wrong with Grace, maybe she just didn't like food of any kind touching the roof of her mouth, perhaps that's what was happening when I was feeding her her meals when she first came, that's why she was passing out. I thought it was her narrow throat that was causing the trouble but it was her little mouth all along. She just did not like how food felt when coming into contact with or even worse sticking to the roof of her mouth, and when her food started getting rolled into balls that must have solved the problem, or if not solved it made it a little easier on her, easier enough so she wasn't getting so upset. Of course at the time I didn't know any of this, I was just doing what we all do when a pug is acting strangely, keep trying different things until the problem is fixed, and because she was actually fainting, well I wanted a vet to look her over in case I was missing something. When that bit of bread got stuck it must have really pushed Grace over the edge and although I didn't like seeing her in such distress I was glad to finally be able to figure things out. If she'd not found the bread in the paddock that day I would never have had an answer to why she was fainting when she first came and me being the curious person that I am I really did want to know what was causing it. Ruling everything out and stopping it happening wasn't enough for me, I like to know exactly why things are taking place and now I knew. The thing is we all have quirks that are uniquely our own, it's what makes us who we are and our dogs are the same. The rolling of her food must have minimalised the roof touching and that's all Grace really wanted. She liked her food at room temperature too, if cold food touched the roof of her mouth she went nuts, head shaking and fainting. So her food was taken out of the fridge, rolled and sat on the bench for a little while before eating. Finally the mystery had been solved and I couldn't wait to get home so I could phone David at work and tell him. I started out trying to make him guess, the way one does when one knows they are never in a million years going to get it, but he was busy and in no mood to play, so I cut my little game short and just told him.

From then on Grace ate all her meals by my side. I made sure I was always watching her, watching every mouthful of food going down. Food touching the roof of your mouth is no reason to get upset, and definitely no reason to faint, only to Grace it was, it was very real and extremely important to her. She wasn't really overreacting because when you have a tick like this, and let's face it we all do about something, it is very real to us. I just wanted to make sure Grace was always going to be ok when eating and maybe having me stand with her helped her a bit too, made her feel less alone with her phobia. She would stand and eat her little rolled up balls of food and every so often she'd look up at me to see if I had anything else in my hands for her. Ruby would eat pretty much the same way she walked, head down in determination, never looking up until the job was done. David made Ruby a little platform to eat off, it helped with her neck, the arthritis made it hard for her to bend her head down, it was causing her some discomfort, I could tell that and I wanted to make her life easier so I came up with the little device. But she'd be hitting that food bowl pretty hard making sure she got every scrap and it kept slipping off the platform so we glued three strips of wood to the top and sat her bowl in there, after that Ruby could be as forceful as she liked, that bowl wasn't going anywhere.

All the other pugs had their food in bowls but Grace always had hers on a plate. From the first day she came she wouldn't eat out of a bowl and I guess that was all about the roof touching too, perhaps eating off a plate made it easier for her to pick up the food. I didn't know this I just knew that she didn't want to eat out of a bowl, she showed me that by head butting her food out of the bowl and picking it up off the ground. And well that ground was dirty I didn't want her eating dirt so I raced inside, got a plate, and put the rest of her food on it, too easy really, problem solved. And yet even though she was eating off a plate, an even surface, and her food was rolled into little balls, no food ever ended up on the ground after that. She had a way of eating that was very delicate and a little unusual too, she just hovered over a ball of food, sucked it up fast then moved slightly over and hovered over the next one and the next one until her entire plate was clean. The way Grace hovered there like that she reminded me of an alien space ship only instead of abducting people she was abducting her food. She certainly was full of character was little Gracie. I think if she was a human being she would have been eccentric. And if she was a rich human being she would have had a pile of servants pandering to all her needs. But she wasn't a human being and she wasn't rich and she didn't have a pile of pandering servants, she just had two people who truly loved her and did everything they could to make life easier for her and her little quirks.

The plate Grace ate off was beautiful, my sister bought it for her, bought quite a few of them actually because they were an end of line clearance and going for a good price. My sister works in a big department store and is always on the lookout for bargains that'll do nicely for the pugs. I still have a lot of those plates today. They are china and have small pastel coloured butterflies flying over them, pink, purple and mint green butterflies flickering across the surface in an artistic manner. I thought those little bread and butter plates were as beautiful and delicate as Grace was, it's like they were made especially for her. When the four pugs were eating together Grace's plate was always the last one to be put down because it had the least amount of food on it, that way all four pugs would generally finish together and that always works out best when it comes to feeding pugs. I couldn't have Harper gutsing down her food then coming over and stealing Graces. Sarah was a bit of a slow eater so her bowl was always put down first. Harper's and Ruby's bowls went down at around the same time because I knew even if Harper finished first there would be no problems there. The way Ruby eats no way known was Harper ever going to get her face in that bowl until Ruby's head came up and by that time it was game over, no food left to steal. I used to picture ways Harper would be able to steal Ruby's dinner and it'd only have happened if Harper could have stretched out her tongue, run it along the floor and up and over the side of Ruby's bowl and snuck a bit of food out through the slight gap Ruby left for breathing. I was telling David this one day when we were both standing out there feeding the pugs, I was next to Grace and he was standing in amongst the other three. He was looking down lovingly because he, like me, likes watching them enjoying their food, he glanced over at me when I spoke, laughed and said he wished he too could live in the cartoon world that I live in. And I just said "Well come on in, there's plenty of room"

I think any person with multiple dogs will tell you that feeding time is the time that normally causes trouble, like if you are going to have issues feeding time will be when they'll show up. If you don't work out their eating patterns, who likes to eat on their own, who eats best with who, who eats fastest or slowest and don't pair them up accordingly then you are going to have trouble. But once you sort it out its pretty much smooth sailing. Of course when somebody new enters the house you will have to adjust things slightly but that's no big deal. These days I'm feeding a lot more than four pugs and if my sister helps me and puts the bowls down in the wrong order then there's trouble. And if she gives a pug the wrong bowl or puts it down in the wrong place you quickly find out something is wrong. I do it twice a day so I'm used to it, I can have them all fed and off for a wander in such a short amount of time, but she's only doing it once a week on her day off so things do get confusing. To her a few of my pugs look the same so I'll hand her the bowl and instead of saying the pugs name I'll be shouting out things like "This purple bowl is for the big fawn with one eye" or "The one with the tongue, the one with the tongue" meaning the one with its tongue hanging out or "The one in the blue coat" or "This bowl is for the one standing at the end of the veranda glaring at you because he thinks you're going too slow" and she'll say she's going as fast as she can, then slumps on the couch exhausted saying it's all been too much for her. And I say ok then I'll just feed them on my own next time but then her day off work will roll round again a week later and there she is offering to help me once more because one, she likes being involved and two, because she's completely forgotten all about what happened a week ago.

"Hey lady your dog looks like an alien" if I heard this once while out and about with Grace I heard it a million times. Time and time again that all too familiar comment would go ringing through the air. The way they'd say it was like they actually thought they were telling me something new, like I hadn't even noticed my daughter's extra-terrestrial like features. Then again I can understand that one perfectly because I've seen many a human mother and child together and I look at the babies face and yet still the Mum is standing there smiling proudly like she's just given birth to the future Miss World. And I'll be walking away thinking to myself "Oh no you haven't", or maybe it was more that they got excited when seeing Gracie's alien like features and couldn't help but blurt it out, people would do a double take and I always knew why. But the thing was I wasn't offended by it and I couldn't disagree with them because she really did look like an alien. I thought it the moment I set eyes on her. I can clearly remember the first time I held Grace. In an instant I had soaked up her tiny weird elf like features and bug like eyes, she looked exactly like a little alien sitting there in my arms, a Martian, an extra-terrestrial or was that being too cruel. I looked down at her face again, nope not being cruel at all, just stating facts. Grace really did look like a creature from outer space. I had no idea what she was going to look like before she came as I'd only seen a photo of her soulmate Ruby. For a few weeks I'd tried to picture what little Grace would look like but of all the pug faces I'd had running through my head not one of them looked like this. I thought it was brilliant that she looked the way she did, she was unusual looking but terribly cute all the same. And the fact that she did look like a little alien made her even more appealing to me. I've always found oddities appealing. David asked me once "That's not what drew you to me was it" and I told him that of course it was, those enormous glasses that were trendy when we met made him look like an insect. I used to joke with my friends that I was dating an oversized bug.

It took David a few days to work out that Grace resembled an alien and I think it was because he was at work all day long and only seeing her at night time. One evening he was sitting with Grace on his knee while I was making dinner. I heard him laughing and just figured one of the pugs had done something amusing, he called me into the lounge room and when I saw it was Grace that he was looking at I knew exactly what he was going to say even before he opened his mouth. I turned the corner, saw little Gracie sitting there looking up at her new dad, saw the expression on his face and instantly knew what was coming, and we both laughed about it.

David and I spend a heck of a lot of time looking at our pugs, we notice all sorts of things other people don't. We actually thought Grace looking like an alien was our little secret, a thing only those who spent a lot of time with her would pick up on so it was really funny when people started pointing it out to us. Not everyone pointed it out though, some were too polite or may have thought they could of offended us, but we'd hear them laughing as they were walking away and knew exactly why. Although to be fair to Grace she doesn't look like an alien all the time, the alien face appeared when she was overly interested in something, when in full concentration mode or when she was barking. When she was asleep or chilling she looked like a very plush soft toy. And she could snap from plush to alien quite quickly and recoil to plush just as fast. Grace is the pug on the cover of this book and of course there's nothing the slightest bit alien about her in this photo. That photo was taken when we were walking back to the house from the back paddock one afternoon and Grace had asked her Daddy if she could have a lift home. She'd gotten tired of walking and settled comfortably into David's arms as soon as he'd picked her up. We'd stood talking waiting for the others to finish sniffing and I looked over at Grace and David and thought they looked so beautiful together. So I took a photo of the two of them then zoomed in on Grace's little face because I thought she looked stunning and so very sweet sitting there chilling out in the safety of her Dad's arms. There was a lot going on around her at the time. Birds chirping, cockatoos screeching, sheep and horses talking to one another, some of her siblings were barking at the birds and others there going from tree to tree sniffing and yet Grace took no notice of any of it. She was up in Dad's arms, she was resting and she was happy. If it wasn't for the motion of walking I think she would have eventually started snoring she was that contented being up there like that.

Grace by nature wasn't much of a walker she's always preferred short walks and straight home. She starts off with real determination then loses interest half way and wants to be carried home. She isn't over weight so her not liking to walk has never been a problem and she's extremely active in the home. Rarely sits still for very long, always patrolling the veranda, always going from room to room seeing if anything's changed in there since she last visited, it never has but it doesn't stop her checking and she likes to check on things so we just leave the doors open and let her. I think Grace is a real home body, I believe she would have been quite happy living in a small apartment in the city, as long she had windows to patrol and rooms to keep checking on then she would have been perfectly happy. A lot of land on a farm is not needed as far as Grace is concerned. Yes she'd come out with us, there was no way she would let us leave her behind, and she did enjoy following the others and sniffing about, but boredom would set in very quickly for Gracie. She'd tire and she'd start pawing at your leg, she thought it was marvelous when Horton and his pram came along because then she had an easy ride. And Horton never bothered that she was in there with him. After a while he kind of expected it. We'd set off on the walk and half way along he'd start peering over the edge looking where Grace was. Once she joined him, he'd settle back and the two of them would be all bug eyed, heads twisting from side to side taking in the scenery. They were both similar in size and I'd smile while pushing them along because it was like I had twins. Then Harper would want in and it became triplets. Harper liked to sit in the very front of the pram and with Grace and Horton directly behind her it balanced the pram perfectly.

Before we got a pram Grace had to make do with me carrying her, she'd walk a bit, wee, sniff, have her fill and that was it she wanted to come up and be close to your face. I'd pick her up and she'd rub her tiny little face into the side of my face and stay in that position for a lot of the walk. It was me and her, with our faces stuck together and I'd have to try and watch where I was going so I didn't accidently step on one of the other pugs, but I couldn't move my face because then we'd become unglued and I liked walking cheek to cheek just as much as Grace did. So I'd hold my head straight and just move my eyes down and step very slowly and very carefully so Sarah, Harper and Ruby stayed safe. On the warmer days walking like this with Grace was a good thing because she would be kept under the shade of my wide brimmed sun hat. Being up there like that was a bit of a wind shield for Grace as well, she was never found of the wind, bothered her eyes, so it worked out beautifully really. I think that's why she wanted to be picked up on the walks by the river when she first arrived, because it could get pretty windy down there as well.

People would get a real kick out of seeing our pugs when we were walking in suburbia. There were always people walking or fishing down by the river and when you have a few pugs they always draw a crowd. People wanted to know how old they were and how they came into our lives. Well that was the second question they'd ask, the first one was always if I was a breeder. When people see you out with a few pugs that's where their mind always goes, nobody ever asks if they are rescued. They also think they've all been bought as puppies. Nobody ever thinks they are all old and unwanted and that we took them in not knowing how long they will be with us but took them in all the same because we love them. People aren't used to you doing that. They don't come across too many people who live the way we live our lives, so I'll always stop and talk to them about what we do and why, and how wonderful old dogs are. Try and educate them. Try and make them see the value there. I do it in the hope of being able to change their way of thinking, in the hope that the next time they see an older dog in the pound or with a rescue group that they'll remember talking to me and give that old dog a home. You never know the impact you are going to have on people, or if not on them on somebody they are going to be telling your story too. So even though the pugs are getting a little antsy I will talk to them for as long as they want to talk. Sometimes they will even carry on walking with us and that works out best because then the pugs are not being held up and that makes me happy.

You don't realise who is watching you when you are out and about and I don't mean that in a creepy way. I remember when we first sold the lake house and went into the estate agents to sign some papers. A man standing at the counter talking to one of the agents turned around and on seeing me said "Oh you're the lady with the four pugs" I didn't know him, I'd never even seen him before in my life, but I smiled and said "yes" regardless. He then went on to say that he and his wife had watched us out there every morning while they were having breakfast. They must have been in one of the doubly story residences on the river's edge. He said he had been watching me for years, first on the other side of the river with two pugs and now on this side of the river with four. I said well you'll only see me for a couple more months because we are leaving. He seemed a bit disappointed, but I doubt it would have lasted very long, no doubt he and his wife would have soon found somebody to take my place. I wondered what their conversations would have been like when watching me. It'd be something like "Mildred", I have no idea if his wife's name was actually Mildred, but I think that name suits a woman who eats her breakfast while watching other folk walking, and besides he looked like the type of man to have married a Mildred. And to any Mildred's reading this book I am sorry if I've offended you. Although now I've written the word a few times I think I rather like the name and may even add it to my pug name list. So anyway it'd be like "Mildred, isn't that the lady who used to walk on the other side of the river" And Mildred would pause for a few moments, maybe grab the glasses she had hanging on a chain around her neck, pop them on for a better look and say "No I don't think it's her because she's got different hair and two extra pugs". And there'd be a similar discussion every morning over cornflakes until one of them figured out it was actually me. I bet they saw little Ruby shuffling ahead all determined like, saw Sarah and

Harper too and I bet they watched me every day carrying Grace all the way home.

It's no wonder that Grace lost interest in the walks half way along, on the way up the river she was all over the place, if she saw somebody on the top of the embankment, whether it was one person or a group, people with dogs or people without, it didn't matter to Grace she'd shoot up the embankment and standing barking at them until they were out of sight. Lucky for us she had little old lady eyesight otherwise I think we would have been standing there forever waiting for her to come back. Sometimes we did have to wait a while for her though, when she was having one of her happy barking days. I'd call the three other pugs back to me so they didn't get too far ahead and we'd stand waiting for Grace to wear herself out. Sarah and Harper always came back right away. Ruby on the other hand wasn't stopping for anybody when she was in full penguin shuffle mode, so we'd catch up with her later and the rest of us would stand watching Grace doing her joyful bouncy bark until she'd had enough. Then she'd turn, look for us, spot us and come trotting back happily and of course she'd be tired then so she'd want me to carry her for the rest of the walk. On the weekends when David was walking with us the majority of the walk home was done with Gracie's little alien like face peeping out of his jacket. She was like a baby possum in a pouch. He'd pull up his collars to protect her face from the wind and she'd pop her head a little further out if anything interesting was going on and give a small soft bark. She was still curious about what was going on she just didn't feel she had to be on the ground to enjoy it.

All the pugs seemed to enjoy the freedom of the farm, Ruby especially; I don't think she missed her old walking harness one little bit. It used to hurt her arthritic neck she hated me putting it on but loved the walks so persevered. I was always conscious of her wearing a harness but with the traffic in suburbia you just can't walk your dogs safely if they're not on a lead. Now all I do is open the back door and out we all go, shoot down the ramp and into the paddock, no cars, no roads, no harness, no leads. It's a fantastic way to walk, a natural and easier way to walk a lot of pugs at the one time so it suited us perfectly. They get to amble along at their own paces, take all the time they need sniffing and I can stand in the middle of the paddock watching and waiting knowing they are all safe. I no longer have to keep glancing all around watching out for other dogs, there were a few dog attacks down by the river I've since heard so I'm glad we don't have to walk there anymore.

We moved at just the right time as far as Ruby's legs went, they deteriorated a little bit with each passing year, it would have been an impossibility to keep living in a double story residence with older pugs, far too dangerous for the majority of my elderly crew. Grace is the eldest but funnily enough she was about the only one who could have handled those stairs her entire life, she was such a sprightly thing. And she was born with really long legs so that'd have something to do with handling the stairs with greater ease I think. But farm life suits us better for all sorts of reasons, we can do whatever we want out here, no body corporate, we don't have to ask somebody else for permission. If we need to modify something we just go ahead and do it and don't have to worry whether or not it's going to blend in with the street or having one of the neighbours banging on the door because they don't like what we have done. Country people don't care so much about that kind of thing. They tend to mind their own business out here too and I think I like that most of all.

About two years after we moved in we modified the kitchen cupboards to help Ruby get on her feet. She used to nestle her backside under the lower row of cupboards and when she wanted to get up again she couldn't, all she used to do was keep pressing up and down, up and down, it was no good for her banging her back like that, if I wasn't there to help her she would have exhausted herself trying to make the move and if she was moving because she wanted to go outside and wee she would have been sitting in a puddle by the end of it all and that was no good for her either. So David put a strip of wood all along the base of the cupboards now all she has to do is press up once and she's back on her feet again. And for a little soul with bandy legs like Ruby this was the most wonderful thing, it helped her tremendously. Her face changed the first time she attempted it after David put the wood there, you could see her getting ready to struggle to her feet but instead she sprang up, well not sprang exactly, but got up faster than she normally did, her little face softened, went from grimacing to almost smiling. I think it's important to make life as easy as we possibly can for our elderly dogs. If you would modify a house, put a ramp in for your elderly parents or grandparents, then why not do it for your elderly pets too. They need just as much thought, assistance and effort put in as elderly human beings do. And if you don't want to alter your house permanently, just do temporary modifications. Ones that can be removed once your old dog has gone on to their heavenly home. But for heaven's sake please don't leave them there struggling, that's not fair.

262 | ANDREA COMER

It does seem fitting that our farm was named after Grace because she was the first of our pugs to see the place, she came with us when we looked at it with the agent, Sarah, Harper and Ruby stayed home and slept. We never know if there are big dogs on the farms we go looking at and it's hard to keep an eye on our four pugs at one time, especially when visiting a strange place, it'd be a frantic sniffing frenzy, they'd be darting about all over the place. Enjoying themselves no less, pugs are natural discoverers, but if they wandered into a horse, sheep or cow paddock it'd be dangerous. We could have kept them all on leads but what fun would that have been, over an hour in the car then put on a lead for half an hour then a long drive back, it wasn't fair on our oldies, they may as well stay in the comfort of their home. It was a warm day so we left the air conditioner on for them and set off with Grace on my knee, a tank full of petrol and a whole lot of hope in our hearts. Would this be the day we would find our farm, I was excited to finally be looking. I mean seriously looking not just going on country drives seeing how the other half lived, envying them, then returning to suburbia.

David and I all our married life, generally at my insistence, had driven past old rickety farmhouses seeing cows, sheep, horses and chickens roaming nearby and marveled at them. Well I marveled mostly, David would often turn his nose up at some of the run down farmhouses and declare he wasn't ever in his entire lifetime going to live there. I on the other hand was already planning what colour I was going to paint the place when we did it up. I rarely heard a word he said. With my face pressed against the car window I imagined the faded farmhouse painted cream with green trimmings. It was always going to be cream with a green front door, green window trimmings and green veranda posts. No matter what house we saw it was instantly transformed into my cream and green farmhouse with brown chickens happily scratching at the earth outside. Perhaps I've seen too many Hollywood movies or the artist in me made me delusional but I've always been able to look at something and see something else. Looking back perhaps I was just young and stupid because some of the houses were beyond my help and imagination, a strong gust of wind would have been all it took to send some of them to the ground like a house of cards. Still visiting those places and imagining what they could become kept me occupied, each country drive gave me hope, in my eyes I was one step closer to finding my farm. I never went home disappointed, those drives spurred me on, fueled my fire, made me get up on Monday morning, go to work and be the first one with my hand in the air when overtime was offered.

Grace was ok on the way up to see Grace Farm she slept on my knee most of the way, although it wasn't Grace Farm back then, it was just a farm that David had seen on a real estate site. It looked promising, but the best part about it was that we could actually afford it. We had looked for so many places that were within our budget and because our budget wasn't as big as we would have liked there really wasn't a lot around for us to go looking at. Loads of huge farms and of course we would have loved one of those, loved to be able to save more animals but you do what you can do with what you have. You concentrate on what you can do not what you can't do, because if you keep thinking about what you can't do you'll end up never doing anything.

We met the estate agent a town away from where our farm was. We got out of the car and went to walk in the front door of the agent's office only to find it was locked and it looked like it wasn't even open today at all. My heart sank a little, but knowing that agents like a sale I knew she would be around somewhere and I was right. A dark haired woman in a blue skirted suit shot out of a shop across the road and yelled to us that she'd be over to see us in a second, then quickly disappeared inside the shop again to finish with her purchases. We decided to give Grace a walk up the street to stretch her legs while we waited. The agent dashed back over to our side of the road and yelled out to us again with instructions, she was only little but boy did she have a set of lungs on her. I later learnt that she was one of ten children, sat somewhere in the middle, so I guess she learnt to be loud at a young age in order to be noticed.

We followed the estate agents car along the winding bumpy country road, she was driving so fast we lost her a few times, we thought we'd never find her again but we'd veer round a bend and there she was again pulled over to the side of the road. Then she took off faster than a formula one race car driver and was out of view once more. She knew the road well so was going like the wind. We did not so we were traveling at a more sensible pace. In what seemed like forever we finally turned into a driveway. As soon as we got out of the car I checked for large dogs, none, just a tired looking charcoal grey poodle, so I put Grace on the ground and the two dogs circled one another sniffing. Grace went to the toilet then ran inside the house right past the owner and his poodle and investigated every room, if I'd done the same thing I would have been considered rude, dogs can get away with many things we humans can't. The poodle didn't try and stop Grace either, if roles had been reversed Grace would have been right on that poodles tail driving it from the house but the poodle just stared at her as she ran inside its home, then stared at her again when she ran back out. Grace saw this entire house before we did, not that there was much to see, our farmhouse is real tiny, long from certain views so it's deceiving but tiny all the same, Grace was back outside standing beside me in two seconds flat. The man who owned the place was ill, that's why he was leaving, I felt sorry for him, he'd built this place with his bare hands and now wasn't going to live long enough to enjoy it.

I liked the man but David had issues, but David always has issues with people he's never met, he's shy, it takes him awhile to get used to new people, so I didn't take any notice. I inquired about the name of the poodle, it was Molly, she was important to this man I could tell. Actually she was all he had in the world, no wife, kids living interstate, family arguments with the ones who lived nearby. He was alone and sick, although we didn't realize how sick he was at the time. David and I fell in love with the place, it was already sold, but there were problems with the other buyer, we knew all this before making the drive but decided to come and have a look anyway. They'd given him another week to get his act together, get his own house sold so he could honour their contract. Due to this we had to wait to make an official offer on the farm so we made an unofficial offer and left it at that. But that week was one of the longest weeks of our life. Being in that house by the lake counting down the days until we knew were we stood was taxing, it was like we didn't know what our future was going to be, did we finally have a farm or didn't we. I kept thinking about this little farmhouse, thinking about the land and the views from the lounge room windows. I'd try and distract myself but it was no use, my mind kept wandering back here. Back to our visit, going over everything in my head.

I'd learnt a lot about the owner of this farm in a short amount of time. He was a dog lover and they are always easy to converse with because you have so much in common.

I remember looking at a farm two weeks before seeing Grace Farm and the estate agent had warned us about what a nasty person the owner was. So we sort of all crept around the place trying not to go anywhere near her, we hadn't seen the kitchen, seen the rest of the house twice and because we knew the owner and her daughter were standing in the kitchen none of us wanted to go in there. But of course we had to at some point didn't we. The agent was lingering back like he was afraid to walk in there so I went in first and David came in behind me. There was a large piece of wood blocking the entrance to the kitchen, I was about to step over it when I saw the most adorable face sitting there looking up at me. It was a French bulldog and I just squealed with delight, I've always wanted one and until that day had only ever seen them in a photo. I instantly bent down and picked him up, gushed at how wonderful I thought he was, started showing David and rambling on and on about how gorgeous the little guy was. His owner and her daughter instantly stopped talking to each other and came over to talk to me. She was a really nice person, she showed me this dog had a puppy but of course the older dog was of more interest to me. She then offered to show me round the house. Yeah we'd already seen it twice but I was up for a third look because it meant I could hold her dog for a little while longer. She showed us the garage, the sheds and the paddocks too, she was now acting more like an agent then the estate agent was. He just seemed to keep dropping further and further back, I figured there must have been an argument between the two of them at some point but the lady was fine with me so I just kept talking to her. The shed was full of cages, and she had a few German Sheppard dogs in there. Clearly she was a breeder, the garage was filthy, dark too, only two small windows, not a very nice place for any dog to be locked up in let alone such a large breed to be locked up in. The Frenchies must have been allowed in the house, she was breeding them too but at least they weren't shut out there in that shed. I took a dislike to her after that. Nothing turns me off a person faster than the way they are treating their animals. We didn't buy the farm, I was instantly put off it when I saw the breeding shed, it was like there was a bad omen there and I didn't want that kind of energy hanging around a place I was buying so animals could thrive. The house was bigger than the one I'm living in now but it needed work done, needed a new roof, in all three bedrooms there were stains showing water damage. David had drawn my attention to it with his eyes but I'd already seen it. I didn't like the setup of the land either, didn't like the way it flowed or should I say didn't flow, the entire place was stifled. There was no harmony there. You get a feeling about places pretty quickly don't you and I'd decided early on that it wasn't the right farm for us and being that she was a backyard breeder kind of sealed the deal for me. We left fairly quickly after that, if I could have tucked that little Frenchie under my coat and gotten him out of there I reckon I would have done it. The owner was more interested in trying to sell me the puppy. She wouldn't let her best breeding dog go.

The man who owned what was about to become "Grace Farm" was different, clearly besotted with his little poodle, real proud of her, she was his treasure a true member of his family that was easy to see. I spoke to him for quite a while. Nothing was forced and there was no rushing, the conversation just rolled and went on and on and on. I talked to him about his poodle, my pugs, the dogs that lived next door, his past dogs, my past dogs, dog lovers are the easiest people in the world to talk to, but I guess you have to be one yourself for the conversation to flow. He proudly told me his dogs name was Molly, he'd already told me that but clearly had forgotten so I just made a fuss of her when he said it again. I didn't think it quite suited her but of course that was none of my business. Like it did suit her but didn't if you know what I mean.

I asked to hold his Molly, he was reluctant, she didn't go to just anybody he told me, yet for some reason he held her out to me anyway and I enveloped her in my arms. Grace didn't care that I was holding another dog, she wasn't jealous, by this time she'd discovered the veranda and was having a ball out there, I could see her through the windows running up and down barking. And she was delirious with all the new smells she smelt. While the owner was talking to David and the agent, I talked to Molly, she was a timid little thing wouldn't stop shaking, the owner kept glancing back at his precious little girl but if he was concerned it wasn't enough to take her from me so I continued talking and stroking the poodley fur. I was enjoying the differences in this dog and my own. I whispered to Molly that she had a beautiful house and that I bet she was happy living here. I told her we would take good care of her home if we bought it. I looked at the high cathedral ceiling in the lounge, glanced out the windows at the surrounding green hills and prayed to god that we would be able to live here. I looked out across the open paddocks and felt such peace wash over me. I walked around the house working out where I was going to put my furniture, hang my pug photos and where the best spot was for the dog beds to go. All the while rocking Molly like a baby and massaging her fur, I always rock and massage any dog small enough to fit in my arms. Don't know why, half the time I don't realise I'm doing it until somebody points it out. And when they have I become a bit self-conscious of it. Sometimes I actually think I look a little bit crazy rocking away like that, you know like someone's old aunt who zeros in on babies at family gatherings and sits there rocking them in a trance like state and won't let anybody take them off her, like perhaps I belong in a home somewhere. Well it's a tossup between that and having the feeling that it's the most beautiful, natural, special thing you can do when you are holding a dog in your arms that you are deeply connected to. I go from one to the other depending on how I feel on the day, but most days I love that I just naturally rock my pug babies. I don't think it has anything to do with not ever having human babies either because a friend of mine does it as well and she's got four children so perhaps it's more of a nurturing thing than anything else. And I've always considered myself a born nurturer. One day this friend and I were standing in my lounge room, she had Horton, she always has Horton when she visits because she just loves him, I had Grace and we'd been standing there talking and swaying for ages before either one of us realised we were doing it, then it was her who had to point it out, I could have stood there all day swaying away happily without noticing.

Molly and I came back into the lounge room and saw that David had gotten over his shyness pretty fast. He was now talking and having a laugh with the owner. They were in the kitchen talking about water tanks and the like. David was leaning against the kitchen bench with his arms folded. Not in a defensive way either, but more the comfortable way he does when he's relaxed and happy. David and I locked eyes and I smiled and he smiled back and it was a genuine smile too, not his desperate get me out of here as fast as you can smile. When you've been married as long as we have you get to know the looks and the smiles and all their different meanings. I knew David was alright so me and Molly took off again, Grace had come inside by now so she trotted along after us. This time I went looking for a spot to put shelving up for my pug ornaments to sit on. I found the most perfect spot, one with room to put more shelves up as my collection grew. Over decade later and that shelving still isn't up- "You can't rush these things" is what David says whenever I ask him about it.

Next thing I knew Molly was stretched out sleeping with her back leg up my coat sleeve. Just all chilled out and limp like. The owner couldn't believe it. He said she'd never done anything like that with anybody before, he said I had a gift, that I was very special, but I said no, dogs just know when somebody truly loves them. Besides it was nothing new to me, dogs had been drawn to me all my life, and I always felt blessed when they were because I think dogs are the most fantastic creatures ever created. I'd always been good at calming their nerves and earning their trust, some just happen to trust you quicker than others and little Molly poodle was one of them. She was a dear thing, so different to a pug with her face and the fur and all, I really liked her. If I'd have known how ill the owner was I would have told him that I would have taken her in. That way she may have lost him but she didn't have to end up losing her home as well, the home she had watched him build. The way it was she ended up losing everything and I can only imagine how much her heart would have hurt over that.

He did something strange the last time we saw him which made me think he may have wanted to leave Molly with me but as I didn't know how sick he was I didn't understand it at the time. Looking back its clear to me now, especially when we found out he'd passed away, I just wish he had talked to me about it. I would have gladly had Molly living here amongst the pugs for the remainder of her days. This was more her house then it was ours. I felt she deserved to be here. I've never owned a poodle but I would have worked out how best to care for all that fur. I tried to track down his family after he died to see what became of Molly and whether she was in need of a home, but I couldn't find them. I just hope she ended up being loved in her next home. Because she really needed to be, she would have been in deep mourning after her beloved owner died, I hope the new owners realised that and helped her through it. I think one of the saddest things is that he didn't talk to me, explain everything, have it out in the open and secure a loving home for a little dog who meant everything to him. We got on well John and me, he could have asked me anything, he could see how much I loved dogs and how his Molly had warmed to me, it would have been the most perfect solution for him and her and given him peace of mind too. The only thing I can think of is that he had no idea how ill he truly was, he probably thought he had lots of time to sort things like that out, but sadly he did not.

Well needless to say the previous buyer didn't end up buying the farm we did and country life suits us. It's not for everybody but it is certainly the right lifestyle for us. I remember the day we were moving here, the truck carrying all our earthly belongings was already on its way. There was David, me and our four pugs all in his little old sports car and I was sitting there watching the road in front of us and I was 99% sure we were doing the right thing. But there was a tiny little 1% niggling feeling that maybe we were not. And I think that was only there due to the negative comments we'd received when telling people of our decision.

David's Mum loved our home by the lake and I don't think she ever forgave us for selling it, well me and the pugs really because she knew we were the main reason we were leaving. She adored the water, liked coming over for lunch and sitting by the waters edge enjoying herself and she loved walking around the lake too looking at all those huge expensive houses. I think she would have loved to live there herself actually. I remember the day we told her we'd sold up, the townhouse sold so fast we hadn't even had time to tell her it was on the market. It was a hard thing to do and we were both trying to pick the right time to bring it up. She was sitting at the kitchen table having lunch and just outside the window was the estate agents board. It was the back of the board as all the "For Sale" signs faced the lake. Halfway through the meal she turned, noticed the board, looked a little puzzled and asked if it was a for sale sign. I think she was hoping it was for one of the other townhouses in our block. David said "No it's not a for sale sign" I watched my mother-in-law relax and carry on eating, "It's a sold sign" David said and my poor mother-in-laws face instantly changed and she looked straight at me and the look in her eye told me she knew it was all my doing.

We were going to play a little trick on her the first time she was coming to see the farm, but due to how upset she was we decided against it. I think the fact that we'd sold the lake house was bad enough, I don't think she would have taken too kindly to being the butt of a joke as well. Up the road from our place there is an old tin shed sitting by a rusty old gate on a flat bit of land. After you pass that shed the road starts climbing up and that's where the best views are. Our plan was to pull into the driveway near that old tin shed, get out of the car and walk towards the rusty old gate pretending it was our farm and that the tin shed was where we were living. David and I had laughed a real lot when working out the little charade. We'd planned on both shooting questions at her, asking if she liked our new home and what she thought of the place. David and I knew we wouldn't be able to look at each other while doing this for fear of cracking up and giving the game away. But in the end we couldn't go through with it, we couldn't do that to her it would have been far too cruel. I think she would have burst out crying and we didn't want that.

But when she saw our real farm I don't think she was any more impressed than she would have been with the tin shed. And it was ok, if you love water you are never going to be happy with land and that's where David's Mum was coming from. I think if she'd owned a property by a lake she would never have left the place, ever. She said she liked the farm but she loved the townhouse and could never understand why we had left such a perfect place. But it wasn't a perfect place for us, this farm was. I think after a while she came to realise how happy we were here and that made her seem to like the farm a little bit more. And she got to name one of the new lambs so she was pleased to have done that. We just tried to involve her in the place as much as we could. And I constantly went out of my way to cook something special for her when she was coming over for lunch. But I think she would have always preferred it if she was still visiting us at the lake house.

And we understood it because she wasn't the only person who felt that way. Our neighbours thought we were nuts moving all the way out here, I think they would have been in a panicked state if they had been us. I reckon they would have expected to receive a million dollars if they made it through the first twelve months without losing their minds. They were used to having local conveniences, shops, shopping centers, restaurants, take away food outlets, movie theatres and the like. Here there is only a post office and a milk bar, the pub closed down years ago due to lack of punters. They were used to noise and crowds and nonstop partying, loads of social activity. I think this would have seemed like a prison sentence to them because they were not the same kind of people we were. I think it'd be a nice place for them to spend the weekend but they would be more than happy to pack their bags and head back home at the end of it.

A few of the old neighbours came to visit but they only came once. And that was probably just to see what we'd ended up buying, just wanted to satisfy their curiosity I suppose. They seemed a bit bored with it all actually. Their eyes glazed over when I told them how much I loved living here and they seemed equally disinterested when I told them of my plans for the place. The house tour didn't hold their attention for long, it was over and done within seconds because of its size, one was even rude enough to ask where the rest of the house was and David and I just laughed about that, I think they could have been trying to insult us, but we were deliriously happy here, you couldn't have insulted us if you tried. Most rubbed their eyes and asked if I had any hay fever tablets, I did, and I think that's the only reason they didn't just turn around and walk straight out the door again. Even the views from our wrap around veranda didn't interest them all that much, they said it was nice, but then they had to didn't they because that view looks like a marvelous oil painting people pay good money to hang in their suburban homes. If they'd said it wasn't nice they would have been lying.

That wrap around veranda has brought us so much joy over the time we've been living here. It's a special place to sit at the end of the day and watch the clouds passing over the hillside. Watch the patterns they make on the landscape, the changing light on the trees. See the cows over the road grazing contently and the pink galahs pecking at the ground. Hear kookaburras and cockatoos, watch rosellas sitting in your trees eating your olives and not care because there's enough there for everyone and besides you yourself don't like the taste of them. You glance across the paddock and see your sheep and horses wandering about. There are crickets chirping in the background sounding more like a symphony orchestra than mere insects. You get to watch the sun going down and the sky changing, bronze, gold, pink, crimson, purple, yellow and tints of orange, every hue is a feast for your eyes and makes your heart sing. Makes you feel alive and part of something exceptional. The show mother nature puts on is priceless. You don't get out there to see it as often as you'd like to so when you do you just can't take your eyes off it and nor should you because it's fleeting and changing all the time, you look down even for as short a time to rub a little old pugs tummy and when you look up again and it's like you are now viewing a completely different sky. You can smell the cypress trees, the eucalyptus trees and the hay. There's a pile of pugs at our feet snoring away contently, a cup of tea in your hand and a peacefulness dwelling within. A slow conversation is happening with the one you love or not happening at all and you are both completely comfortable with it. Sometimes there's simply no reason to talk. Absolutely no reason at all to fill every silence with a sentence, words are not always necessary, especially if they are meaningless. You can miss a lot of what's going on around you when engaging in mindless chatter, sometimes silence is a better option, there's plenty of time for talking later on when all of this has gone away for the day. Your love of the country runs so very deep, it's like each year you are here your roots seem to seep deeper and deeper into the soil and you know you wouldn't feel this much joy living anywhere else. You think you've only been sitting out there for a few moments but before you know it it's gone completely dark and if you're lucky tonight's sky will be crystal clear and the stars will be twinkling down like precious stones. Big diamonds, little diamonds, clusters of diamonds and diamonds over there twinkling on their own, and you feel a bit sorry for that one because your heart feels that nobody and nothing should ever be on its own. So you mention this to your husband and he tells you it's not alone, that no star ever is, it's just that we cannot see all of them from where we are. His answer makes you smile so you go back to star gazing again. Each one is magnificent and beautiful in its own right. Your husband then begins pointing the clusters out to you and naming them and you try as best you can to remember them all so that next time he asks you'll be able to let him know you've been listening. But you won't remember them as well as he does but that's ok because you'll enjoy the sound of his voice as he's telling you their names once again.

All the pugs love being on the veranda but Grace loved it most and at times became rather territorial about it. I think because she discovered it first she thinks it's hers, built specially for her. She patrols backwards and forwards a couple of times a day. In winter she'll go to the windows and check how things are going out there and if there's a bird of some sort, generally a blackbird, but even if it's something as small as a sparrow hopping along the edge it's enough for her to go into full bark mode, front paws lifting off the floor, until she's frightened it away. Grace is the boss of the veranda, I think if she had better sight and could see the ants she'd bark like mad at them too, tell them in her funny little old lady way to get off her property quick smart. She prefers summer when she can actually be out there scaring the birds off properly, she'll stalk them. At least she thinks she's stalking them but with the amount of grunting Grace does I'm pretty sure they know she's there. But it's still her favourite game, they let her get close then fly off just before she reaches them. Occasionally one of the other pugs beats her to it, she'll have stalked that bird for a couple of moments then just as she's about to bark and scare it off one of her younger siblings trots right past her and scares them away. Grace goes absolutely nuts when this happens, it gets to her like nothing else in the world does because if the veranda is her domain then so are the birds hopping along it. And so she and nobody else has the right to chase them away. She swings round all fierce faced and tells the offending pug off. Goes all psycho granny on their heads. Truth is Grace may think she looks fierce, and scrunches up her little face so tightly it's got to hurt, but the reality of it is that she's no more threatening than a fly. And the other pug has no idea what's going on because the fact that they chased the bird away was a complete accident, when one is not as bird obsessed as Grace is they more than likely have no idea there's even a bird there or if they do they have no interest in chasing it, all they are doing is merely walking by looking for a nice sunny spot to lay down. And in doing so they've disturbed the bird and set Grace off in a granny style rage.

Still being the veranda boss and having an interest in what was going on out there made Grace happy and kept her active and alert and right up until the end of her life Grace resembled a dog half her age. Not just in the face but in her sprightly movements as well. Little Gracie died a few days before we lost Ruby and Horton. She was just over fifteen and a half years old when she died. It had been a hot day and she was eating her dinner and started acting like she was choking. I thought I'd not been concentrating and rolled her food into too bigger balls. I checked, and no they were all the right size, the perfect size for her little mouth and throat. Both David and I checked her out so see if there was any food caught, there wasn't, again she did the same thing, walked away from her dinner and seemed like she was chocking. Again her airways and roof of her mouth was checked, nothing. It was after hours but we still called our vet, he said to take her to an emergency clinic, so we then called our country vet just in case they were in the area. They were, they'd just delivered a calf that was round the wrong way and were now on their way to help a bull that'd gotten caught in a fence. David worked out a place to meet the vet and took off down the driveway fast, kicking up a dust storm as he went. I stayed with the other pugs watching them while they ate their dinner and changing Horton's nappy after he'd finished eating. David and the vet were meeting somewhere in the middle of the vets next house call, they knew what car he was driving, what model and colour to look out for. Not that seeing each other was going to be hard, they were both on a quiet country road not a four lane highway. The vet was looking out for David's car and pulled over when she saw him flying up the road in the distance. They were the only two cars out there on that long country road. Grace was gently put on the bonnet of the vets car and worked on for a while, it wasn't choking as we'd first thought, she'd actually had a heart attack. David said she breathed her last breath as he was flying down that country road towards the vet. She was on the passenger seat beside him, he was watching the road but keeping an eye on Gracie as well, he said she was doing ok and then just let out one final breath and she was gone.

Her little old heart had just given out. The vet did try to bring Grace back but said that sometimes when they go like this at a good age it's probably best they don't come back because they are never quite the same again after that. I was really sad that Grace didn't get to pass at home, in the place she loved, the place that was named after her, a place that is peaceful and serine. It did hurt my heart a little that she was to die in a car speeding down a road. But I have since made peace with it and I now think to myself that at least it was on a quiet country road beneath the scattered shade of gumtrees with her Daddy beside her, yes driving fast but also holding and stroking her tiny paw. I think it would have been worse if she'd been by the side of a noisy highway with people who couldn't have cared less about her speeding by. I wouldn't have liked that for Grace. At least she was with her Daddy and a vet who loved animals enough to devote a career to them.

David had left in such a hurry that he'd forgotten to take his mobile phone so I had no idea what was going on, I heard the front gate open so left the pugs inside and raced out to the driveway. David pulled up just inside our gate and when he saw me at the top of the hill went and got Grace out of the passenger side of the car and began carrying her up to me. I was walking towards them and I smiled because I thought I saw Grace moving in David's arms. And I was so relieved in those few seconds and really happy too. But as I got closer I could see the look on David's face and that threw me a bit because I was still sure Grace was moving her legs, but I now know it was because she was being carried along that made her look like she was moving. Just the motion of David's footsteps making Graces legs move. My heart sank to the ground when David shook his head. I covered the rest of the distance with tears running down my face. David handed Grace to me and I just cried and cried, told her I was sorry and kissed her sweet little old head over and over again as my husband explained to me all that had gone on.

Of course that night was so incredibly heartbreaking, but it was only the start of the agony we were going to experience that week, the week that altered my life and me as a person. I worried how Ruby was going to react when she found out Grace had died, Ruby had been going downhill for a while, David and I were both aware of it, and with the loss of her lifelong friend, her little soulmate, well Ruby just didn't look up after that. Again I must stress how very important it is to keep pairs together, to not part those old souls who have lived together all their lives. We had eight pugs at the time and Ruby and Grace interacted beautifully with every single one of them but their own bond was incredibly strong, their little hearts loved each other to the point that Ruby decided she simply couldn't live without Grace. She shut down and died a few days later. If Ruby and Grace had been parted when they were first put into rescue I believe they would have both died within weeks of being separated. But they were kept together, got to live on a farm, share a bed and all their days and nights. They got to live together, walk together and eat together, eat side by side right up to the very end. And that's a thing that brings me a real lot of joy. When I think about Ruby and Grace and I do think about both of them so very often, I am incredibly grateful David and I could give them that.

CHAPTER SIX

Steffy

Steffy was the first pug we took in once we'd moved to Grace Farm. But she wasn't old and I suppose it does seem strange in a way that the very first pug we took in when living on a farm we had bought for the sole purpose of rescuing elderly animals was only a young dog. But although she wasn't old she was needy all the same and I just thought to myself "Well she needs us" and I wasn't ever going to turn my back on any animal that needed me, especially a deaf one. And with her being deaf, well she had my heart on knowing that. I thought Grace Farm would be the perfect place for a little deaf pug to live. I mean we are pretty peaceful and quiet here but of course that would have made no difference to Steffy because her world was even quieter. Her sight was perfect though and I figured she would love watching everything that was going on around the place and the smells out here in the country are very lovely for a dog and with Steffys sense of smell being heightened I figured she was really going enjoy herself here. I knew the smell of sheep and horses and hay being cut would thrill her no end, every day there's something interesting going on, every day something new to be sniffed at. I pictured her little flat face in the air when rain fell on the green paddocks in winter. I love the smell of rain on rich green grass and pictured Steffy right there beside me when the first rain of the wet season fell, and I pictured it right too because that's exactly what happened. We have a massive row of floor to ceiling windows in the lounge and I love to watch the hills, see the changes in them as the seasons come and go. You are more aware of nature living out here and I'd stand there watching, cup of tea in hand and Steffy would come and stand beside me, she didn't lose interest either, it was like she saw what I saw. And I think that had everything to do with her being deaf. She was just more aware of what was going on around her. She'd watch me like a hawk and if I took off fast she took off fast. And when I stood on the veranda sniffing Steffy did too. And when I'd walk back inside she'd walk back inside with me and jump up on the couch and sleep with one eye open so she didn't miss out on anything I was doing.

I was told that Steffy had gone deaf due to an untreated ear infection but I didn't think that was right. I felt that she had been born deaf and it had just taken her owners a few years to realise, and of course once they did they decided to get rid of her because she wasn't perfect. But she fitted in well with the elderly pugs we were already sharing our life with, who I suppose to the rest of the world were not perfect either, I mean Steffy not being able to hear was not a big deal to us, no issues there at all, I felt she belonged here, was a part of the "Not 100% Perfect Club" of which I consider myself an honourary member, so Steffy arrived and quickly became part of our little family.

The reason I thought Steffy had been born deaf was because of the noises she made, a hearing dog that had gone deaf over time would not have made those unusual sounds, they were the sounds of a dog that had never been able to hear a thing. They sounded a lot like a friend I had when I was little, Ian had been born deaf too and the sounds Steffy made reminded me an awful lot of him. And also my nana was deaf and she could pronounce things perfectly because she had gone deaf at the age of twenty one so she had years of hearing before it was lost to her. I mean I could have been totally wrong about this but I don't think I am. I just think Steffy's world had always been a silent one, but it was a happy one never the less and Steffy was a happy little pug, but boy was she a loud one. She could hit the highest of volumes, I'd never heard a pug reach those heights before. I didn't even think that they could.

She never barked, in all the years she's lived with us I've never once heard a bark coming out of her mouth. She would feel or see the other pugs barking and take off after them to see what was going on, she stood in amongst the pack with all those around her barking their little old heads off but she never once joined in. And I think that was because she didn't know how to. So I suppose in having said that, I believe barking to not be something dogs do naturally, but a language that is learned just like human language is learned. Steffy did scream though, that was her voice, they all barked and Steffy would scream, screamed very loudly at the top of her lungs whenever she wanted to communicate with you. She'd scream to say hello, scream to say I'm here, scream when she was hungry, scream to be let outside, scream when she wanted to come back in again and was standing at the wrong door, she'd scream when she wasn't allowed to join me in the horse paddocks, scream when David got home from work, scream when she woke up in the morning until she found where you were, scream when getting a treat because she thought you were going to not see her and she'd miss out on having something special but I honestly would have given her the entire pack of treats if she would only just shut up. Steffy just screamed, screamed, screamed all day long and never ever quietly either, but always on loud volume, I think she thought just because she couldn't hear us that we wouldn't be able to hear her, we could, but there was no way I could get that point across to her so she just went on screaming. And there were many days when I thought this little pug was going to be the death of me. It was a noise like nothing I'd ever heard, and of course never wanted to hear again but the next day she'd wake up and the amount of screaming remained the same. Even the other pugs would to stop barking and look at her. Pugs have a human way of looking at people I think and the looks they'd give Steffy it was like they couldn't believe that such an awful sound could come out of something that looked exactly like they did. They'd stop and stare and then walk off back to their beds, I think after hearing Steffy scream they'd completely forgotten what they had started barking at in the first place. I think that god awful noise blew their minds as much as it blew mine. They were confused by it, couldn't figure out why she was doing it and probably wanted it to stop as much as I did. And Steffy was equally confused by her four new siblings, but for very different reasons.

I don't know what the rules were for the dogs in Steffy's old home but I don't think they were allowed much freedom. They couldn't have been otherwise she wouldn't have thought my pugs going about their everyday lives needed reporting on, she seem to think they were doing something wrong all the time and that such things needed to be brought to my full attention. So instead of following them and enjoying herself, which is what I most wanted her to be doing, she simply watched on then ran back to the house to get me so I could stop them from doing it. I felt kind of sad for her really, all that worrying over nothing. And this behaviour was making it harder for her to fully settle in, making life less enjoyable for her then it could have been. Her being the self-appointed Pug Police was not a fun way to live, as all those who merely watch on in life while others are out there living it would know. All I wanted was for Steffy to run off and have a great time with her new siblings, discover the farm, sniff around a little and peep though the fence at the sheep and horses, but the rules in her old home were preventing her from doing it. She thought my lot were always doing something they shouldn't be and her worried little scrunched up puzzled face told me everything she was feeling. It really saddened my heart seeing her this way.

My nana had a neighbour who was the same way. I never met her because we had migrated to Australia by then so I had no idea what her face looked like but looking at Steffy I now had a face to put on that lady. I grew up hearing stories about this next door neighbour and assumed she must have been pretty bad for her to be remembered long after my nana came to live with us. "Ruined her face with worry" was what my nanna used to tell me. And I'd look down at Steffy and find myself saying the exact same thing to her, and of course she couldn't hear me but even if she could I doubt very much she cared what state her face was in, all Steffy cared about was bringing some form of order to our unorderly home. Well she must have considered it unorderly mustn't she otherwise she wouldn't be putting so much time and effort into trying to make it right. It's funny because in all the years I've been taking in pugs I've never once had anybody think this wasn't a fun house and that living this way wasn't the best thing ever. I could only imagine what poor Steffy had been subject to in her last home. Some dogs are just not allowed to be dogs and I find that incredibly sad.

No matter what the pugs were doing Steffy stood staring at them with a puzzled look on her wrinkled little face, she'd be staring at them like she couldn't figure it all out. And after watching them for a while she'd then glance up at me and search my face for answers. And well, I had nothing, because they were doing nothing wrong, so she'd look at them again, then back to me as if to say "What are you just standing there smiling for new Mummy, why aren't you telling those naughty pugs off"

I'd stroke her head and then go back inside to what I was doing, I did double check whether all the animals were alright before I walked off just in case Steffy had actually been trying to draw my attention to something that needed to be seen. Then I'd go about my business as usual and get lost in what I was doing and forget about Steffy and her worries and find myself jumping ten miles in the air half an hour later when her ear piercing screams rang out again. She was always going outside to the pugs then back inside the house to me and she'd try and position herself so she could see all of us at the same time. And sometimes that worked out for her at other times the pugs would move on and she'd have to get up and go have a look where they were and what they were up to. A lot of the time Steffy was outside when she screamed and I was grateful to her for doing that otherwise I'd have to start wearing earplugs during the day because you needed something to muffle it. And I did at one point think about resorting to earplugs, but then I wouldn't have been able to hear if the other pugs needed me, and besides I would still have been able to hear Steffy. So the earplug idea was rejected.

A lot of the time Steffy's scream sounded like the scream of an animal in pain. I'd instantly drop what I had in my hands and race out to see what was going on, fearing the worst and wondering who it was that was hurt and I'd race round the door and find poor little Steffy racing down the hall towards me, she was fast, she'd meet me halfway down the hall after running all the way from outside. And she'd have that extremely worried look on her face, a real face full of distress. So I'd pick her up and we'd both rush outside to check on all the pugs. But nobody was ever hurt and nobody was even awake most of the time. They'd all be there sleeping peacefully on the deck, the sun's warmth lulling them into the most wonderful slumber and me and Steffy would be standing in amongst them all spinning round and round to see if anybody was bleeding and had passed out from loss of blood. With Steffy tucked under one arm I'd tiptoe in-between the sleeping pugs, checking on them and trying so desperately not to wake them all at the same time. And that was hard to do because at times it was done with Steffy still screaming. And not only that she didn't like being picked up so would be squirming in my arms, pushing her head and neck against me trying to free herself. And she'd start doing the dog paddling thing whenever she was in the air, did it until you put her down, it was like she was getting her legs ready for when the time came so she didn't miss her chance of getting away from you. I suppose we looked like quite a sight to anybody looking on, old dogs flat out sleeping and a middle aged woman creeping gently in amongst them all holding a screaming pug who was doing the dog paddle.

Thing was I had to pick Steffy up otherwise she would have gone ploughing right through the cluster of happily snoozing pugs. Trodden on their heads and even squashed their tummies. I would have been tiptoeing but when she followed me in she wouldn't have had the sense to walk gently, such a thought wouldn't even occur to her. Steffy wasn't yet used to living with older dogs and she especially wasn't yet used to Ruby and her bandy little legs, she wasn't used to how slow moving they could be and she'd walk towards them and if they didn't get out of her way she would bang right into them. It took a while for it to dawn on her that she should actually be the one moving out of their way. So for everyone's sake she had to be picked up and she wasn't happy about it at all. Steffy just didn't like being held, and that wasn't just when she first game, that was how it has always been with her. She appreciated it when you lifted her off the bed or couch, went ballistic kissing the side of your face as you lowered her to the ground. And you'd appreciate those kisses and wished they'd have lasted longer, but you take what you can get because as soon as she was down that was it she scurried off at high speed, had a bit of a dance around and then came back and stood looking up at you wagging her curly little tail. And you'd put your arms out to her in the hope of another snuggle but she wasn't having any of it, it was like thanks for the lift down but no I will not be tricked into letting you pick me up again, not even for a snuggle.

I thought she was real cute doing that, but all too soon she'd be back to screaming and oh the noise, the noise, the noise was pure agony to my ears. She was beginning to get me as nervous and stressed out as she was. I knew I had to put a stop to it otherwise we'd have both ended up ruining our faces with worry. But it wasn't just the screaming it was the constant interruptions for no reason. I had to think of something to let her know what was and wasn't considered an emergency in our house. When David was home she would do the same thing with him, come running in looking for one of us, run into him first and try and get him to follow her so she could show him what she'd found. And he didn't quite know what she wanted, what she was doing and he'd look at me for answers, so I'd say "She thinks somebody is doing something they shouldn't be and is telling you about it". And he'd say "Why" and I'd say "Because she doesn't understand our lifestyle yet".

After a few weeks of this behaviour I would stroke her head and give her a gentle massage as way of uncrumpling her worried little face. But I no longer followed her out and by not doing that she came to learn the rules of our house and what was acceptable behaviour for everybody living here. I felt not following her out every time, not making a big deal out of it lessened the importance of what she was alerting me too. If she saw that I wasn't worried about what was going on I figured she would learn not to worry about it either. I think those first few weeks of following her out was only adding to the problem, making it worse, making her feel that she needed to be doing all this important reporting back to me. It was hard with her being deaf because you couldn't talk to her and tell her "No" when she screamed or that "It's okay, there's no need to panic". I couldn't calm her down with words so I had to use actions instead. She took her Pug Police thing very seriously but all she was ever telling me was "Hey new Mummy do you know there are a pile of pugs asleep on the deck? Or "Hey new Mummy did you know an old pug just went for a walk to the front gate and back" I mean she must have followed them far enough to see what they were doing but just couldn't relax enough to go and have a sniff with them and enjoy a walk. I would sometimes be looking out the window at the right time and see her standing there at the top of the driveway watching the pugs going about their business and I'd see her turn and come galloping back to the house at lightning speed with the most worried look on her face, so I'd go out and cut her off as she was coming up the ramp, I'd stroke her head and then walk off as if nothing had happened, acted like I didn't know she was rushing in with a face full of concern. She'd stare at me for a few moments as if to say "Well are you coming out to see what's going on or not" When she saw I was not she'd immediately come walking in the house after me. I'd stay inside a while, finish what I was doing then go outside, Steffy followed me wherever I went and when I was outside with her she would go off and enjoy a bit of a sniff. Always looking back at me to make sure I was there but she'd sniff never the less and that was good for her. It was another way of teaching her that it was ok for the pugs to be outside sniffing about, it was ok if they wanted to lay in the shade of a tree and go to sleep and it was ok if they wanted to bark at the sheep and horses when they came near the fence. Once she got to know that the pugs here at Grace Farm had a whole lot of freedom Steffy finally started to wander off with them and my heart felt such peace when she did that.

In those first few weeks I came to learn that Steffy was a nurturer. I realised this with all the reporting she was doing, the look on her face told me that she didn't just think they were doing something wrong but that she was actually really concerned for them, concerned about their safety. I think she liked to know where they were so she knew they were safe and it was a hard time for her because she was torn with wanting to be with me "Her New Person" and wanting to look after her siblings as well. No wonder her little face was crumpled. She was getting herself upset a lot of the time and it was all for no reason. She didn't realise that everybody was going to be ok. That she didn't have to ever worry about them that was her mummies job, that's what I am here for. Still, I thought her nurturing side was beautiful, loved that she had taken these old siblings into her heart so quickly. I thought that was so sweet of her. David said she was the "Me' of pugs because I'm like that, a born nurturer. And I'd say to him "Yes but I'm not as noisy as she is, if I was I doubt we'd still be married". I think any man would have walked out long ago if their wives were as loud as Steffy was.

David and Steffy bonded fast, a lot faster than me and Steffy did, and it was me who was the problem and I felt riddled with guilt because of that. I mean she came and fell in love with me from the start but it took me a while to warm to her. I was ok when she was quiet but once the screaming began I just wanted to get as far away from her as I could. And that isn't a good thing for any pug that's trying to settle in and especially not good for a deaf pug who is trying to settle in. I knew she would be feeling that I was rejecting her and I loathed myself for making her feel that way, but I just couldn't bare the noise she made. Well not all the noises because her quiet voice was really nice, a little sort of muttering hum done when she was sucking on a toy, she seemed to go into a dream like state, just her and her toy, usually a monkey because she liked monkey's a lot. We think it's the shape of the face so we made sure there were always plenty of monkey's in the house. But when they are hard to get hold of a rabbit or a teddy bear takes its place and Steffy is fine with that, she'll drag the bunny around the room by its ears and settle into a bed then suck on it contently with her eyes closed. It's like she goes off into her own little world and I wish I could join her sometimes because she seems so blissful in there. Even if she's pulled half the stuffing out of her special toy she'll happily carry it round by its head. I think the sucking on them is a really beautiful thing for her to do, she just loves them so much to the point where we started stocking up on favourable toys for her so when one was old, frayed and worn she always had another one to take its place. But the first one was never thrown out until she'd bonded with the new one, and once this had taken place the old one would be sneakily crept across the room, gotten and disposed of while she was humming and sucking on the new one with her eyes closed. We had to wait until the new monkey, rabbit or bear was fully broken in first though because for a while she would go from one to the other. Or have the two of them in the bed with her at the same time. But once the old toy stopped getting any form of attention I felt it wouldn't be missed if chucked away and it never was.

I really like watching Steffy bonding with a new toy. She'll carry it off to one of the unoccupied beds and lay for ages with her eyes closed doing a chewy sniffy type of bonding thing with an arm or a leg of her new monkey in her mouth. I'll put the new toy on the floor and let the others have a look at it, some may pick it up once or twice but once Steffy has taken an interest in it the others seem to know to leave it on the ground for her, there's never a fight or anything it just seems to be something they have always done. Maybe it's just an unwritten pug rule or perhaps they know how much Steffy's toys mean to her and besides there's always a dozen or so different toys lying around on the floor making the place look like a childrens play group. Everybody has choices here so there's no reason to fight. In a way Steffy treats her toys like family members, well a family member that you enjoy pulling the stuffing out of then carrying around by their heads. And to be honest I think we've all been there, well I know I certainly have anyway.

296 | ANDREA COMER

I liked Steffy's humming sound, loved it actually, I found it quite comforting and peaceful, whenever she was doing it I'd pause and listen to it for a while before carrying on with what I was doing, it was just her screaming that bothered me. It affected me to the point of tears some days because she was just so very loud and relentless. I had honestly never heard something so disturbing and grating in my life. It was a harsh unpleasant high pitched ear piercing sound that just went on and on and on.

I've never been good with loud noises. I've always shied away from loudness of any kind no matter whom or what is making the noise. I've been like that all my life. Noise sensitive is how I've been described. I am especially sensitive to high pitched sounds, they really upset me. I get panicky and anxious and want to flee, the reaction isn't how most people react to noise I'm sure of it. David wasn't as bothered by Steffy's screaming as I was but a few friends who dropped by didn't stay as long as they usually did once Steffy entered the house. She was quieter in the paddocks or maybe she wasn't but being outdoors made it that little bit easier to deal with. So if it was a person I liked spending time with who had dropped by then we'd walk the pugs round the farm and take our cups of tea with us and have a chat out there. If the person dropping by was a pain in the ass know it all as a few of our neighbours at the time were, then I would stay inside the house and sit at the kitchen table with Steffy screaming in the background. Those cups of tea where sucked down pretty fast and I'd have a smile on my face when waving them goodbye.

I suppose I could have lied and wrote a beautiful sugary love story here about Steffy and me, I could have bent the truth and with my words have you conjuring up images in your head that would do any Hollywood movie proud. But I can't do that because like I said it would all be made up, a huge fabrication just so I didn't have to go back and hurt my heart again by reliving how things really were between me and Steffy at the start. It wasn't that I didn't like Steffy because I did, I just couldn't bear the noise and of course the two went hand in hand, if she'd come with a mute button it would have been so much easier. Problem solved really, but she didn't come with a mute button, there was no way of turning her off.

Steffy to me personally was a huge challenge, a challenge that at times I didn't think I was up to and if I was up to it I honestly wasn't sure if I wanted to do it. And did I ever think of giving up on her? Yes I'm ashamed to admit it, but yes, there were many times I felt like giving up on her, in that first week, that first month, that first year even, I reckon I could have very easily thrown the towel in on the really bad days. She would have been the first pug I'd have given up on but the truth is I could have done it and I may have done it if it wasn't for my husband. You see David fell in love with Steffy right away and there was no way he was ever going to give her up. I liked her because she was a pug. I just didn't fall head over heels in love with her like I had done so many times before and that fact bothered me hugely. I felt like the most horrible person in the world. And going back to that place in my mind now, recalling it all, I still feel exactly the same way. All this little girl did was love me and all I wanted to do was escape from the loudness and I knew she couldn't help being so loud and that made me feel all the worse. David would come home from work and go sit on the veranda with Steffy on his knee so I could have a break from the screaming. I lived for those daily breaks from Steffy. Looking back I think they were the only things that kept me sane.

David knew the screaming was bad too but isn't as sensitive to noise as I am so it didn't affect him so much, plus he wasn't here all day long with Steffy like I was. Luckily we were on a farm if we were still in the townhouse we would have had so many complaints from the surrounding properties. I was grateful for our land. Grateful Steffy had a place to live where she could be herself. Yes it was hard on me but at least I could be happy about the fact that she got to do what she wanted to do. And what she most wanted to do at the time was scream. It was so hard to be around her because just when you thought you'd gotten her settled with a toy, just when you thought there was no reason at all for her to scream and start to relax in her presence, she would scream loudly again and you'd almost jump through the roof. I was living on the edge of my nerves.

David was so lovely with Steffy, he'd stroke her and talk to her, even though she couldn't hear him, she sensed him, she knew that he loved her and she was at her happiest then. And I really wanted to give her that too. I knew if only I could take to Steffy and love her, not just like her and take care of her and merely try and tolerate her, but well and truly and completely and deeply love her then she would start to settle down and be ok. But I knew that while she was still screaming at the top of her lungs I would never be able to fully relax in her presence so round and round in circles we went. I lived for night-time, waited for Steffy to fall asleep and reveled in that beautiful, peaceful, awesome silence. My home was back to normal then, I could hear the pugs sleeping and life was good, I was fully relaxed and happy. I'd wake up every morning and vow to not let the noise bother me but as soon as I got out of bed Steffy would see my feet touch the floor and start screaming and I'd become anxious and tense. I mean she was doing nothing wrong, most dogs dance about and get excited when their people first wake up in the morning and their day together begins, it's just that where most dance around a bit and get overly excited for a few moments then settle down, Steffy would not. And that's because it wasn't only when she was overly excited that she'd be screaming.

Our neighbours met us as we were driving in the front gate a few months after we took Steffy in. They were going out as we were coming in and we pulled over for a chat as you do, and everything that happens in the country gets round to being discussed if you're talking long enough. They began chatting about a weird noise they'd been hearing of late, we all stood around trying to think what it could be. "What's it like" I asked, "Animal or machinery? There are all sorts of weird animal noises out in the country once it goes dark and they are acceptable. But loud machinery noises are always frowned upon for disturbing the peace. We had a neighbour once who used to get to drinking heavily on a Friday and Saturday night, his way of enjoying the weekend no doubt, and that was fine, we all have a right to do that, but when he was fully drunk, which was normally around midnight, he would go speeding round his paddocks on his ride on mower shouting and swearing at absolutely nothing and nobody at the top of his lungs. So there you'd be sleeping peacefully then suddenly be jolted awake by the sound of a ride on mower choking because he was treating it like a racing car, and a drunk guy cursing and very loudly voicing his opinions on the world. We got to hear about everybody he loved and especially about everybody he hated, everybody who had done him wrong and his political views as well. Then just as he was about to finish the mower slowed down and he would start singing. We'd be laying there just waiting for the singing to begin because you knew then that it wouldn't be long before you could roll over and go back to sleep.

So the next door neighbours stood there by our front gate thinking, trying to describe the noise they had heard but neither one could say exactly what it was like, only that it was a bizarre unusual sound and very loud, they both leaned towards the fact that it could have been an animal, an animal in distress perhaps, but what sort of animal they had no idea, they said we must have heard it at some point because they were sure it was coming from our way or beyond us, the farm next door perhaps. They said it was really loud last Sunday, they even heard it above the chainsaw when cutting wood, they told us they'd turned the chainsaw off to try and figure out what it was. But even then it didn't dawn on me that they were talking about Steffy and you'd think it would have because she was always on my mind, I was so full of guilt and always trying to figure out how I could make things better for her, make myself feel differently towards her, be a better mother to her. But it didn't dawn on me or David about Steffy so the four of us stood around trying to figure out the sound.

I mean I knew Steffy was loud but to be heard above a chainsaw that was something else. "What time Sunday" I asked knowing we were home on Sunday washing the dogs and trimming their nails. When I said about the nails it hit me that they must have been talking about Steffy. She hated having her nails done, worse than any pug I'd ever known, so was having a total screaming fit on Sunday afternoon. I told them this and they looked at me like "Noooo Waaay". Neither of them believed the noise they'd heard could come from a dog and a small dog at that. They looked at me as if I was making the whole thing up- I wish- then we explained about Steffy's screaming problem and told them about her being deaf so she didn't realise how loud she really was. And still they looked at me like I was making it all up. In the end they believed me though because it was a good year or so before Steffy stopped screaming so loudly so they got to hear it a real lot over that twelve month span. I mean she was still screaming daily many years on, but not hitting the heights she once did, she seemed to mellow out a bit. I can't tell you exactly when her pitch lowered I'm just very happy that it did. It's like any irritating noise, you only think about them when you are hearing them, if you're not hearing it any more it no longer crosses your mind.

The neighbours popped theirs heads over the fence a week or so after our conversation, Steffy was at her worst that day and no doubt had become very irritating, they said their son had a deaf dog once and it didn't scream like Steffy did. Then they popped their heads back over the fence and never mentioned her again, well not to our faces they didn't anyway. But I have a feeling that she was very much being discussed when we were out of earshot. And I'd say they were as happy as we were when she finally stopped screaming so loudly. All I can say is thank goodness for lovely neighbours because Steffy is a true testimony to the decency of country people and a real test on a friendship. I was thankful and grateful to them for their understanding, and told them so, they could have very easily behaved differently and I believe a lot of neighbours would have. They were an older couple who had moved to the country for early retirement, moved for a peaceful quieter lifestyle, but they knew what we were doing for elderly dogs on our side of the fence, they knew we'd moved out here to rescue the ones nobody else wanted so they persevered and let us get on with trying to help Steffy. And I'll always be appreciative of them for that.

There were times when Steffy would be laying on the couch watching me as I went about the household chores, she barely closed her eyes in those first few weeks. I think she was terrified I was going to leave her. And I could understand how she felt, her world was a soundless one and she now found herself in a strange place it must have been frightening for her. With the others all fast asleep I'd use this time to have some one on one time with Steffy. She never liked being held so I never did that, didn't like being picked up at all and sometimes when they are like this it can be due to abuse but I didn't feel that was the case with Steffy, it may have been because she was deaf too but I don't think so either, what I think it was is that some dogs just do not like being held. It's rare but it does happen. And it does not mean there is something wrong with them, it's just how they are and you can't, nor should you try and force them to change. You can't change them by forcing yourself on them either it just makes things worse. Some dogs just do not like being enveloped in your arms, end of story. It's the same with people, some people are huggers some are not, some people don't mind you getting right up in their faces, invading their personal space, others don't want to be anywhere near you and it's ok, we are all different. And we are allowed to be different and so are our dogs. It's just an individual thing really.

Steffy liked being stroked though so I did that a lot and she liked sitting beside you on the couch, squashed herself in between you and the couch's arm just to be close to you but she didn't like being held on your knee or in your arms so I respected that.

I'd walk over and sit beside her and gently stroke her head and I can honestly say that in those moments I did really and truly love and adore her. I looked into her eyes and talked to her even though I knew she wouldn't be able to hear my voice. I'd stroke her wrinkled forehead and felt such tenderness towards her, she'd roll on her back and stretch out full length, back legs flexed and I would sit next to her and massage her stomach. With the lack of hearing her other senses were magnified and I thought massage was a good way of connecting with her. I felt peaceful and at ease in her presence, nothing was forced, it was all natural, the way I wanted it to be all the time. And in those moments my heart opened up and I felt a true mothers love towards her. I told her I loved her over and over again. Yes she couldn't hear a word I said but I feel that when one is expressing genuine love like that it's a spiritual connection and with all spiritual connections there is no need for words. I wished those moments could have lasted longer but they never did, something outside would catch her eye and she'd fly off the couch screaming and slamming into the glass sliding door, the moment was gone, the peace shattered and I would once again tense up.

But those moments were a starting point, not that Steffy needed to have a starting point, but I did. I believed they helped us build a foundation. I connected with her little by little in those few stolen moments while the others were asleep and Steffy was still. I knew it was very important for her to feel my love, so I would give it to her in the times that I truly felt it. I so desperately wanted her to be happy in her new home, not just because I felt she would finally stop screaming, although that was a big part of it to be honest, but I wanted it for her because this was the whole reason we had bought the farm in the first place, so animals could come here and heal, feel loved, feel wanted and feel totally secure.

David made Steffy feel loved, wanted and welcome all the time which was great I'm grateful to him for that. I made her feel loved and wanted when I could genuinely feel it, it was the best I could give her at the time, besides it's no use trying to fake things with a dog, they are far too intelligent to be fooled. And a deaf dog is even more in tune with your emotions, one sense goes and the other senses become strengthened, there was no tricking Steffy. Those quiet bonding moments were golden for us. Steffy is a much better dog then I am a human being because she kept on loving me even though she would have known I didn't always feel the same way about her. She loved me day after day until my feelings changed. And they did change I'm happy to say, it just took a lot longer than I wanted it to. It wasn't Steffy's fault she was a screamer and it wasn't my fault I am noise sensitive it was just one of those things.

Ok so I've told you what I didn't like about Steffy now let me tell you all the things I adore about my daughter. Steffy is a loyal and loving dog, she has some beautiful qualities that the others don't have and I think this is due to her lack of hearing, she uses her eyes more to compensate and she's an asset and a help to me because of this. Steffy is kind, caring and so very sensitive, she's taken it upon herself to look after the other pugs, to mother and nurture them. I don't think she felt they were actually her puppies, there was absolutely no confusion there, it was just that her heart was so loving and giving that the only way I can describe it is to call it a mothers heart, a true mothers heart that overflowed with love and concern for her family. And she took on that role as soon as she arrived in the house. Somebody suggested that perhaps because she had lost her first family she was now being overly protective of her new one, but I didn't think that was right, I just thought Steffy had been born with such an incredible depth of love in that little heart of hers that she couldn't do anything else but share it around, spread it evenly between all the members of her new family.

Her eyes were always on us, on me, on David and especially on her elderly siblings. If one of them dropped back on our walks Steffy would run over and guide them back to the pack and I thought that was a lovely thing for her to do. She did it from the moment she first arrived, well once she realised that walking around the farm was what they were all meant to be doing, and she is still doing it today. Although today Steffy herself has very little vision, so little in fact that it's really not worth mentioning and yet she still tries to help her siblings, sniffs them out and takes off after them with her stiff walk and God bless Steffy for doing this. Many a blind pug has been helped by Steffy's caring ways. Arthur, Buddy, Ruben, Billy, Amber, Nemo, and Casey all benefitted from Steffy and her incredibly kind heart. I never trained her to do this she just decided to do it all by herself. I think such a thing would be hard enough to train a hearing dog to do let alone a deaf one. What I think happened was that because she cared so deeply for her elderly siblings, her loving eyes never left any of them, and if one dropped back, she was the first one to notice, saw it even before I did, and she'd scream and run back to get them. At first I thought she was screaming to alert me to the fact that somebody was lingering sniffing, and wanted me to do something about it. But I soon realised she was just screaming to let me know she was leaving my side for a little bit and would be back soon with the wayward sibling. Because she worried about me when she couldn't see me, she thought it was the same for me if I wasn't able to see her. She was letting me know what was going on so I wouldn't stop and worry. And I thought she was beautiful for doing that. I mean I never did stop and worry but little Steffy didn't know that. And the reason I didn't over worry was because I knew all our fences were secure and nobody could get out, so if one was missing I'd pause, my eyes searching across the paddocks until the little soul was spotted and then we'd all wait for them to catch up. I was a lot taller than Steffy I could search the paddocks quickly and easily, but with Steffy being so close to the ground she didn't have that advantage. So she'd take off sniffing the air until she found what she thought was her lost sibling, and yes some of them were in fact lost and some of them were just enjoying an extra bit of sniffing but she'd guide them back all the same. When she brought them back I'd make the biggest fuss of her for doing it. Never picked her up, although I truly wanted to, but just bent down cupped her little chin, looked deeply into her eyes and smiled and told her "Thank you, thank you". I also patted her head and ran my hands down her body stroking, rubbing and massaging, my way of letting her know how well she'd done. And she'd scream and rub herself against my leg in a cat like manner. And when more and more pugs joined our family Steffy was a great asset to me. Between the two of us we always knew where everybody was at all times.

Steffy also became very good at sensing when one of the other pugs was feeling ill, she'd go and sit beside them with a face full of concern. And I'd see her there and go over and check the pug next to her out. I'd also check Steffy out too just in case it was her who wasn't feeling well, but she was always fine, the pug next to her wasn't though and I was grateful to Steffy for having brought it to my attention. It can be anything from ear infections that she's picked up on to a small tumour growing. She becomes aware of things so quickly and is intelligent enough to let me know when something isn't right. Sometimes she'll do it by screaming and running over to the pug once she's gotten my attention, other times it'll be that she never leaves their side and I'll quickly become aware of the fact that she's shadowing somebody. I'll notice her sitting there looking almost as miserable as the pug that's under the weather. Steffy takes everything they are feeling upon herself, she always has, it's because she's so sensitive and worries about them so much, and she looks so unwell that I'm convinced there is actually something wrong with her too that's why I'll always check them both just to be sure, how awful would it be if I only took notice of the pug Steffy was sitting next to and left her there unwell and unchecked, I never ever want this to be the case so both pugs are always thoroughly checked out. Because of her being so in tune with the other pugs, she'd sometimes pick up on things before I did. And it was a real asset to have somebody in the house doing this, because her sense of smell was better than mine she'd pick up on infections fast. I would have found the infection myself, but it could have taken me perhaps another day or so to do it whereas Steffy's super-duper sniffer nose found it right away. Which is wonderful because then I can get on with helping the sick pug, either on my own or by making an appointment with the vet, it all depends on what's wrong. And once Steffy knows I know, well, her face soon goes back to normal and her posture does too. It's like "Ok Mummy is onto it now" and she stops slumping and seems so much happier in herself. She is very loyal though, many a time she'll have her face close to mine as I'm crouched on the floor inspecting the pug, it's like she's making sure I get it, making sure I see what she's seen and once I've got it right she relaxes. And if it's something like a graze and I take off to get a face washer to clean the area, Steffy sits there watching me go, her eyes are on me as I come back with a towel to dry the area off and she sits there all eyes as the antiseptic cream is applied. Only then will she get up and leave the pug, she can be desperate for a drink but until everything is sorted she won't be thinking of herself, only them. I'll be at the sink washing my hands and I'll hear Steffy at the water bowl lapping up water as fast as her tongue will go. And as I'm drying my hands I'll be thinking to myself "Oh bless her"

Steffy was very good with Horton as well and seemed to be as in tune with his needs as I was. She'll also let me know if somebody has had an accident in the house, a few of the oldies can have accidents at times and Steffy's sense of smell is fantastic. She gets a whiff and is off the couch patrolling the house until she finds what she's looking for then comes and tells me so I can clean it up, although it'd be great if she didn't think it was important enough to wake me in the middle of the night for. I've lost count of the amount of times her little crumpled face has appeared at the side of my bed, never David's side either, always my side, it was like she figured out that her Mum and Dad had different roles. Him breadwinner, me wee cleaner, but there were times when I was so exhausted I'd be wishing she'd gotten the sides of the bed mixed up and gotten her Dad up instead of me. Still she takes her job seriously and that can only be a good thing. But it's not like she tells me quickly then goes away so I can roll over and go back to sleep which is what I desperately want to be doing. She insists on pounding on the side of the bed, at times even gripping to the side of the mattress with her font legs letting her back legs swing free. She's fallen a few times doing this, hits the floor with a thud but it doesn't discourage her she's back on her feet again clinging to the side of the mattress very quickly. She doesn't scream all the time at night though, sometimes it's more of a yelp, which is good otherwise she'd be waking everyone within a five mile radius and I don't think our neighbours would be too happy about that. Day time screaming is one thing night time screaming is a different story entirely isn't it. Anyway Steffy will not go away until I get out of bed, no matter how many times I try and ignore her she doesn't get the hint. She stays and she yelps and she swings on the mattress until I'm fully awake. As soon as my feet touch the floor Steffy feels she'd played her part in the process so shoots of into the darkness while I fumble around on the bedside table trying to find my torch.

About a week after she arrived I got to realise just how much Steffy loved being in cupboards. I learnt this the hard way after accidently locking her in the walk in wardrobe, hearing her scream, then having to follow the noise until I found out where she was. At those times I didn't mind at all that she was a screamer because it made her easier to find, if she'd been the silent type she could have been in that wardrobe for quite a while. It was the same with the kitchen cupboards, you leave one open, even if it was only for half a second while you walked to the sink, she'd watch you move away with a pot in your hand and scamper in there while your back was turned. She didn't care whether there was room for her or not, she'd still try and get in and make an awful racket doing so. And she'll sit in amongst the pots and pans banging and crashing away every time she moved around. She's fine because she can't hear it but it would wake some of the old pugs up and they'd come staggering over for a closer look, the noise would spark their curiosity so although they were sleepy they still wanted to see what all the fuss was about and there would be Steffy's head peeping around a saucepan. She'd be looking at them like she was thinking "What are you staring at me for" and the bewildered pug would stand gazing into the cupboard for a few seconds before finally going back to bed. In the end they just stopped getting up when they heard the thunderous crashing of pots and pans because they knew exactly who it was.

I never understood why she liked going in the kitchen cupboards though, I mean pots and pans are not the most comfortable things to be sitting amongst. She was the same with the laundry cupboards, and I understood that because folded bedding is very comfortable. But she wouldn't always like the way things were stacked so she'd push the contents around, move things to the side. Sometimes even drag things out if it wasn't to her liking and I'd come along and see one or more of the other pugs sleeping on the discarded bedding. They'd have a nest outside the cupboard and Steffy would have one inside. They seemed so happy there like that so I'd leave them to it and rewash everything once they'd finished their nap. It was always the others who came out of the room first though, Steffy wasn't so quick to leave her little nest because she knew once she did the cupboard would be closed and she'd no longer have access. The laundry cupboards are the ones she's been locked in the most, if I'm rushing or if I'm intently talking to one of the other pugs and not paying attention that's when she'll get locked in. But she didn't always scream for me when she was locked in the laundry cupboards, she seemed happy to be in there. It made me think that perhaps she used to sleep in the laundry in her previous home, maybe she didn't have a dog bed but just slept on all the dirty clothes that were waiting to be washed. Perhaps she came from a big family and the mother didn't bother putting the clothes in a hamper, either because she was too exhausted or because the hamper was always full. I pictured an over flowing hamper and little Steffy going in the laundry each night and making a nest for herself out of the piles of clothing. She sure did love our laundry cupboards a lot, maybe she was trying to recreate her old bed. I would notice Steffy missing and always knew exactly where to find her. I'd head straight to the laundry cupboard and there she'd be either asleep or sitting up waiting for me to open the cupboard again. She never looked scared, never bolted from the cupboard, never sprang out like a jack in a box. She always seemed quite contented, well she must have been mustn't she otherwise she'd never relax to the point of falling asleep. Sometimes I'd have to coax her out, go get a treat so she'd vacate the premises peacefully. I felt like a nasty landlord evicting somebody for not paying their rent. We did try setting up a dog kennel inside the house for her, we figured if she felt happier when enclosed instead of on our open dog beds then we'd try and create a little area for her, but she never took to it. Never even stepped one paw in there, peeped in, sniffed the air then walked way and never went near it again.

Something that Steffy has always done which David and I both think is rather cute is that she'll talk to herself of a night before drifting off to sleep. She'll do it during the day as well but not all the time mainly it's just done at the end of the day, a special night time winding down ritual she does before falling asleep. In winter she sleeps by the fire in the lounge room but in the warmer weather she'll sleep in our room and we'll lay there at night listening to these funny little noises coming from my side of the bed. The noises are a bit hard to describe actually because I've not heard anything quite like them. I guess you could just say that Steffy has this special little deaf girl language all of her own. It does occasionally resemble other animals, then goes back to being completely Steffy again. The best noise she makes, well my most favourite one is when she sounds like a Kookaburra. She'll be doing her own sounds and then out will come something that sounds very much like a Kookaburra's call, and seeing as Kookaburra's are my favourite bird I love listening to Steffy when she's doing this. I wish there was a way to make her do it more often, and if I thought such a thing was possible I'd try and train her to do it, but there isn't, it's just one of the many noises she makes. And you can't try bringing out just one noise, that'd confuse her, she wouldn't have a clue what I was trying to do. And besides she stops when she is interrupted. You go near her and she'll stop and stand up like she thinks we are going somewhere and she's getting ready to follow. So the Kookaburra's call is just tucked in there with all the other noises that are uniquely Steffy and it comes out when it comes out and you just have to take great joy in it when it does. So far none of the Kookaburra's here at Grace Farm have ever answered Steffy back and that's probably because although it sounds very Kookaburra-ish to us it doesn't to them. They are probably sitting in the trees thinking that somebody in our house is taking the micky out of them and are very ill amused.

But I'm not ill amused I love that she does this, makes her kind of special doesn't it, she's done it from day one and I remember the first time I heard it. Steffy arrived here in Spring and we were still using the log fire because Spring here on the farm gets pretty cold at night. We'd load the fire up just before we went to bed so it'd last until the wee hours of the morning and the pugs would stand watching David shoving those big logs in. Once the door to the coonara is closed they know it's time for bed. And that door can take a bit of shutting too because there's so much wood rammed in there, if it wasn't so hot David would be putting his foot on the door to help shut it I'm sure. Steffy stood around with all the other pugs watching the goings on, at that time the wood heater was our only form of heat. When Steffy saw the other pugs turn and walk towards their beds she went and jumped up on the couch and David and I looked at one another and I said "Well I guess she's chosen where she wants to sleep". They normally go where they feel most comfortable and happiest so we just let them choose. Steffy hopped on one end, thought about things for a few seconds then ran the length of the couch to the other end, the end which is nearest the log fire. We went into the bedroom and began loading the pugs that sleep on our bed up and once they'd stomped around and gotten comfortable the lights were turned off. We were laying there in the darkness getting ready to go to sleep when all over sudden these unusual little noises began floating in from the lounge room. David and I started discussing them then stopped because we didn't want to miss out on hearing anything Steffy had to say. We thought it was a beautiful thing she was doing, it also showed she was happy, it was her first night after all and she was deaf and apart from the fires glow the house was in darkness and it was a strange house to Steffy. But she didn't seem bothered by any of it, she was just in there kind of humming away to herself in a contented fashion. Well half humming and half talking and switching back and forth all the time. After that we used to lay there every night and wait for Steffy's little performances to begin. Each night was slightly different, but all totally Steffy, listening to her made us happy. We'd never had a dog do that before, and each night was different in the length of time it lasted too. But the more sleepy Steffy got the softer her tones became until she stopped talking altogether then we'd hear her snoring. It's only then that I roll over and go to sleep. I always wait until I hear her snoring because I think if I fall asleep before Steffy does that'll be the night she does the Kookaburra and I really don't want to miss out on that.

If I didn't already know Steffy was deaf I certainly would have been able to figure it out within a few days of her being here and it was all due to the way she'd take in a room with her eyes, she reminded me so much of my Grandmother. My nana was deaf too and she had the exact same way of absorbing a room, noting everything in it with her eyes in one long slow glance. My nana had been gone fourteen years when we got Steffy. I think it's the little things we forget when our loved ones pass. I mean you'll always remember the big things, the major events, the lessons learnt, encouraging words spoken when you needed them the most, things like that stay embedded. But the little personality quirks, the traits, the gestures, hand movements, facial expressions and in my nana's case the eyes, these are the things time takes from you. They fade too quickly but with Steffy's help I had gotten something back, something I'd lost and if not for Steffy may never have remembered again. And you know what, I realised how much I missed seeing it. I had a huge lump in my throat the first time I saw Steffy doing this. In a flash I was right back there standing next to my nana, it was like I was watching her eyes not Steffy's. It was beautiful and precious and yeah a little bit sad too. My nana never complained about being deaf, in all the years I spent with her I never once heard her being anything other than positive about it. She always used to say that being blind would have been so much worse, but I had a feeling that if she'd been born blind she would have said being deaf was so much worse, because that's just how my nana was and I loved her for it.

My grandmother was a remarkable woman and I had a real lot of admiration for Annie Harper. She'd lost her only son when he was twenty, he came back from the war only to be killed in a motorbike accident a few months later, she lived through a great many things in her life and was always so courageous. And she had all the time and patience in the world for me. Taught me to knit, no easy task, it took me a while, I could never pick up crochet and she put a lot of time and effort into it in the hope that I would. But I never got it and she never lost patience with me. She'd just say "Come on then Andrea lets have another try shall we" and we'd try and I still didn't get it, just couldn't wrap my mind around it. My nana made it look so easy. But me, well the will was there alright but I just couldn't pick it up. Her hands used to be full of arthritis but she still made them move, move real fast, whether knitting or crocheting she was super speedy and worked with such ease, it was all so natural for her, like she was born to do this, like this was her talent, her skill. She whipped up blankets in no time at all. I love the way a crocheted blanket looks, and Nana would go in very slow motion for me so I could clearly see how her hands worked that wool and yet when I tried I just couldn't make the wool do as it was told. And it bothered me a lot, bothered me something fierce back then actually, most artistic things I picked up on so easily, just not this. Today it doesn't bother me half as much as it used to. I think I've lived a bit, been through a lot and you just come to the realisation that not being able to crochet isn't worth getting upset over. But I admired my nana tremendously, she made the most beautiful things, I'd sit there with fascination watching her hands moving and these glorious creations appearing. Appearing from something as simple as wool and a stick with a little hook on the end, I used to watch her hour after hour, how those bent arthritic fingers could produce such beautiful items in such speed was beyond me. I was a teenager when I first started working, wasn't earning much but I wanted the two pugs I had at the time to have beautiful things. Every pay day I'd buy the loveliest softest wool in all sorts of beautiful colors and my nana would crochet dog blankets for me. They were really not the right kind of blankets for dogs, their nails plucked the neatly crocheted mounds and twists but I thought crocheting was so much prettier than regular knit and pearl and I wanted my pugs to have the best.

My nana lived with us after my grandad died, Dad went to England and got her, I can still remember picking her up from the airport. She was the nicest person and of course Mum was really happy to have her with us. I had the warmest and most loving childhood due to having not only my mum but my grandmother under the same roof as well. A little extended family. And I think living that way with that kind of love and security builds a foundation, it sets you up for life and I feel truly blessed because of it. I'd get home from work, have a chat with Mum then go off to say hello to Nana and see how much more of the blanket had been done. When I walked in the door she would hold it up proudly for me to see how far it had come along and I'd make the biggest fuss about it. Those blankets Nana made where true works of art, just masterpieces really. But the pug nails did pluck them so every couple of months they went back for fixing and when she handed them over to me again they'd look brand new. Nana never minded that she had to fix them either or that my dogs had ruined her masterpieces, she just took them out of my hands, slowly walked over to her big wool drawer and found the right shade to fix it. And I'd sit talking to her while she did so. I still have one of those crocheted blankets to this day, it's a hot pink one and when one of the pugs is feeling unwell I'll wrap them in it because it's like not only am I looking after them but my nana is too. And I really like the idea of that.

Nana made hats, scarves and cardigans for all us kids, she was fantastic because she never could follow a pattern, didn't understand them, said they made no sense, so she just made it all up in her head and they turned out brilliantly. I'd marvel at her, I thought she was wonderful for being able to do this. Other kids grandmothers knitted too but they always had a pattern by their side and referred to it regularly and yet my Nan never did. So my adolescent mind reasoned that out to meaning my nana was a lot smarter than any other knitting nana's I knew. And I didn't just marvel at her for that but also because my nana could knit without having to look down at what she was doing, she was like some kind of specially programed robot, one that never made a mistake ever, and never lost count. I felt she was a superstar. She'd be there watching tv and knitting away like crazy. Even when she was talking to me, she didn't have to look down at her knitting, no need to keep track, instead she'd have her head turned towards me, watching my lips move and keeping up with her side of the conversation without missing a beat. She never dropped a single stitch or lost track of what we were talking about. And what we were talking about was usually what was going on in my little world at the time. A lot of nanas would have dozed off but not my nana, she was interested in everything I said and remembered things too, like the names of all my friends and asked about them regularly. Nana was a great sewer too, again no pattern needed, just a brilliant mind and a strong determination, how magnificent she was.

My mum couldn't knit at all, not sure if she didn't want to learn or just wasn't interested in it, but it didn't really matter because she had her mother there to do it for her. I guess she more or less just figured there wasn't any need to learn and she was right. With the mother she had there wasn't. My mum had other talents. Mum had a true gift with words, songs, poems, stories. All made up at lightning speed and always fully entertaining. Just the most brilliant quick witted mind and clever, a real skill with anything like that. She could rhyme too and made up funny rhymes for me and my sisters when we were growing up and she always had a twinkle in her eye while reciting them because she knew how much we were going to laugh and she was never disappointed, we always doubled over. Mum had a coffee table near her lounge room chair and it was chock full of books with book marks and odd sods of paper sticking out of them. Books half read, about to be read and fully read but kept close in case she wanted to read them again, on top of the stack sat a well-worn bible. That was for her daily readings and I never knew her to miss a day. Mum read a lot as a kid although you couldn't call her a bookworm. Reading was done at night time. She wasn't one of these kids who never went outside and played, she was a bit of a tomboy in some ways and I think I get that from her. Mum would have a go at anything and normally had a few friends following her when doing it. She had a little club for all the neighbourhood kids, Mum was the leader and made up songs for the kids to sing and took them on adventures. She just liked being around people and people liked being around her. That was a gift that lasted all throughout her lifetime. I didn't read much as a kid but I did enjoy Mum reading me bedtime stories. She got as much enjoyment out of it as I did, you could just tell how much she loved books and how important they were in her life. From the time she first learnt to read I don't think there was a day that went by where she wasn't reading something. But the sad thing was she would never get to read my books, none of them. Mum died before The Joy of Horton came out in print, it was a real bittersweet moment for me, I was so proud of Horton and his story but I knew the person I wanted to read it most in the world never would. And I hurt a real lot over that. It upset me for quite a while actually. I chastised myself repeatedly. I wanted to go back in time and change things so very badly. Wanted to have another shot at it, one where I'd told Mum about it every step of the way, but of course that could never happen because we don't get to go backwards in life, only forwards. I carried that hurt around with me for a very long time and still do in some ways. You see I had written The Joy of Horton while Mum was still alive and never told her I was writing a book, she never knew anything about it because I wanted it to be that way. Of course she knew about Horton and all my pugs, I talked to her about them all the time, but I never mentioned the book and the reason I didn't tell her was because I wanted to surprise her. I wanted to one day walk into the room with The Joy of Horton behind my back and give her a lovely surprise. I wanted to see the astonishment and joy and pride on her face, I wanted her to read it and talk to me about it, but of course now that was never going to happen and yet it so easily could have if I'd acted differently. The thing was I didn't think Mum was going to die so soon, she was doing really well in the nursing home and she was only seventy four years old, far too young to die, her death came as a shock to everyone. If I'd known how things were going to be I would have shared everything with Mum from the very beginning, I felt stupid for wanting to surprise her because in doing so I had lost the chance for Mum to be part of Horton's book, of my very first book. I could have easily printed out each chapter as I finished writing it and sat beside her as she read. From that little white chair beside her bed I could have watched her face, witnessed her reactions to what she was reading, seen her emotions, I would have been on the edge of my seat those first few pages hoping she liked it. Would have been sitting by those blue curtains eyes fixated on Mum waiting for a reaction. I reckon Mum would have paused at certain bits and we could have discussed them together and I would have loved to have been able to do that with her. How special to me that would have been. I think for the rest of my life I'm going to be kicking myself and be full of regret for the decision I made there. Then again if it had all gone to plan and I'd been able to surprise her like I wanted to I would be sitting here now telling you about the look on her face and for the rest of my life I know I would remember exactly what that look was like.

I was sharing all these feelings with my sister one day when we were both talking about Mum. My sister said how proud Mum would have been about Horton's book, she said Mum would have been telling everybody about it. And I knew that was the truth because I had a little write up done about me and one of my dogs in a magazine and Mum showed that article to everybody she knew and even people she didn't know. She showed it to all the nurses in the nursing home as well. After Mum died I found that magazine amongst her belongings, it was crumpled and the corners were all curled up, clearly well thumbed through. I could tell just by looking at the state it was in how many people she'd made read it and how many times she had read it herself. I could only imagine how she would have been with a book. Even now writing this my heart is still stinging because Mum reading a book I wrote would have meant everything to me. But even though we may desperately want to, we don't get to rewrite the past so I just have to be grateful for the things I did get to share with Mum, and there were so many of those, a lifetime of memories to look back on. So much love and so much laugher and you can't ask for anything better than that can you.

I consider myself lucky to have had not just one but two creative beings influencing my childhood, well not only my childhood my entire life really. I think I got my creativity from both my mum and my nana. They both, merely by just being themselves, gave me these incredible gifts and I'm enormously appreciative to both of them for it. And it's not just the creativity either, it was them, who they both were as people, how they looked at the world and how they showed love. You grow up watching that and it sticks with you for life. I often think about how it would have been for Mum growing up with a deaf mother. I'd hear all the stories of what Mum would get up to when her mother's back was turned. They were pretty funny stories. But I also think having a deaf mother gave my mum a special skill and uniqueness about the way she took in the world and it has affected me and how I take in the world around me as well. Both Mum and Nana got joy and a whole lot of comfort from the special little things that life has to offer, not money, that was useful to get by on but it was not the most important thing. They saw life differently. And I believe that's how Mum was raised, not being deaf but seeing things from a deaf persons point of view and that's an incredible asset to have, I know because I've got it too. Both these ladies stopped and watched and lived in the moment. They saw the wonder and the specialness of everything that was going on around them. They were observers. And I am an observer too. And just like them I get tremendous joy out of it. Just this morning I was walking the pugs round the farm and saw some yellowing leaves getting caught up in a gust of wind and beautifully floating down from a tree. That sight was magical to me. I stopped and watched and smiled and got enjoyment out of it. I felt lucky that I'd been coming up to that tree at that precise time otherwise I would have missed it, I like seeing things blowing in the wind. Flowers in pots by the back door when I'm coming up the ramp, well I seem to notice them more when the wind is blowing. I'm the same with horse manes and the cypress trees that line our property. But even when there's no wind I still see things, truly see them, concentrate on everything around me and it's a marvellous way to go live. Seeing the beauty and specialness of life that others sometimes fail to notice, those are things Nana and Mum left me with and they, to me, are more precious than gold. Mum's joy came from watching washing blowing on the line. She said that sight made her heart happy. And if I see my own washing blowing I go straight back to hearing Mum's words and the sight makes my heart happy now too because it reminds me of her. And as I write this an image popped into my head of my mum's washing blowing on my washing line here at the farm. I used to bring it back from the nursing home, there was a laundry service there but they kept loosing things, so I brought her clothing home with me. And just before I took it back I'd spray everything with perfume so that Mum would feel joy when wearing the items. I used a few different types of perfume so that she didn't always smell the same, all perfumes that she liked of course but each day she smelt something different because I felt she would like doing that. I can't recall what sights made my nana the happiest and I so wish I could. Even better if she was still around for me to ask, or if not her, if Mum was still here so I could ask her that question because she'd definitely know the answer to it.

Nana had a way of making everything you did special and everything you said interesting. She was a gem who knew how important it was to make kids feel significant. I remember with my first ever pay I bought Nana this little gold dragon brooch. It was cheap, not even a dollar, ninety nine cents to be exact. But Nana didn't care about prices. She took it out of the box and held it up in the air admiring it, it had small red and blue jewels stuck to it and she showed me how pretty they were when catching the light. I hadn't thought to hold it up, but Nana had a way of making everything more beautiful and again I think it was due to her being deaf. Back to that dragon brooch, well my nana wore it with such pride, she had plenty of expensive broches and other jewellery, she had gone to a lot of dances when she was young. I saw photos and she was always the best dressed one there. The photos were in black and white but I could tell her outfits matched. She was always standing there in very high heels with this strong proud look, held herself beautifully, very straight back, even though she was tall she never once hunched over. She had self confidence that was very clear to see. When my younger sister was in concerts at school out would come the dragon brooch. Nana could have put any one of her more expensive brooches on yet she wore my cheap little golden dragon with no less pride then the ones she had that cost a hundred dollars. She'd seen the joy in my eyes when I'd given it to her and valued it on that.

As a teenager my nana had an ear ring ripped from her ear splitting the lobe in two. I don't know why she didn't get it stitched at the time, perhaps she lived too far from the doctor or her parents didn't have the money, or maybe she just couldn't be bothered, she was the type of person that wasn't entirely fussed about a lot of things other people would have worried about, and I loved that about her I really did, but if she had of gotten stitches it would have healed beautifully. Instead she'd be sitting there with that split ear lobe and didn't seem to care. I guess she'd learnt to live with it by the time I came along. When I was little I used to sit on her knee and study it, it fascinated the hell out of me to be honest. I'd never met anyone whose ear was like that. I thought it was the most incredible thing I'd ever seen.

When I was very little she'd tell me the story of how it happened and that story got bigger and better each time she told it. I'd hear it a hundred times and still ask to be told it again, I guess she was sick of telling the story in the end, perhaps that's why she kept adding bits, to keep herself amused more than for me. I'd sit there all bug eyed staring at the ear listening as she told the tale. At the end she'd say "Touch it Andrea" and I would, when she said the same thing to my sisters they'd run screaming from the room and Nana and I would laugh. She'd say "They're not like you are they Andrea" and I'd shake my head and touch the ear lobe again. I thought it was a good way to get rid of them actually so brought it up even when we weren't talking about it. I did it just to be on my own with this wonderful lady. Those two weren't like me and Nana they were scared of things, my older sister more than my younger one, I think my younger sister was just too young to understand so when she saw her big sister running she figured the best thing to do was follow. Nana would hand me back her earring, a round half ball like thing, not as pretty as the one that did the damaged she'd tell me but that was all she could find to wear that covered the ear back then. Nana loved beautiful earrings, the ones we have today are great, and whenever I'm out shopping and see a pair I think of her again, I bet she would have loved them. I was so gentle putting that earring back on my nana's split ear lobe because I didn't want to hurt her.

Having the Nana I did helped me a lot with understanding Steffy. Steffy seemed to be contented in her little silent world, and I knew that you could be deaf and happy regardless because I'd seen how happy my nana was. There was no self-pity in my nana and no self-pity in Steffy either. I had a friend who used to feel very sorry for Steffy because she was deaf, she'd drop round for a cup of tea and always spent a lot of time stroking Steffy and giving her plenty of attention. Steffy would never allow my friend to pick her up and yet that was the thing this friend of mine wanted to do the most, but she'd try and Steffy would react badly so she learnt to be satisfied with just being able to give her head a little stroke instead. She'd comment on the unusual noises Steffy made. Of course Steffy would be screaming the first half hour somebody came to the house but then she would find her special toy and go off to a bed and suck on it contently making her lovely little deaf girl noises. And those were the noises my friend really loved. But there were many times when she would almost be in tears due to Steffy's deafness and I'd talk to her and tell her that Steffy's world didn't seem like such a terrible world to be in to me. But this lady had a great love of music and I think being unable to hear would have been a punishment for her and so of course she was projecting all of this onto Steffy. And I'd say to her that Steffy has never been able to hear anything so she wouldn't be missing that which she had never experienced. To Steffy life was how it had always been, silent, yet content and happy regardless. This used to pacify my friend for a bit but after a while I'd see her looking over at Steffy with sadness spread all over her face again. I'd look at this friend and I'd look over at Steffy and there little Steffy would be, over in the corner bed sucking contently on her toy being totally unaware that on the other side of the room a human heart was breaking for her.

I think because I like things to be quiet and I'm contented with my own thoughts that I was able to have a good understanding of Steffy. And I could see the joy she used to get from everyday things, Steffy wasn't a sad dog, far from it, and her lack of hearing didn't hold her back either. Yes the settling in period was hard because she didn't understand how things worked round here but once she wrapped her head around it all and got used to our home everything changed in her world. I think Steffy had been an only dog but once she got here she soon realised what assets her elderly siblings could be. They became her ears, in a way she didn't really need to hear, she just had to keep her eye on them, which she was always doing anyway, they'd hear something, be alerted to it, bark and scurry off and Steffy would see them scurrying and jump off the couch and be at their side screaming with her little curly tail going ballistic. And if they left the windows and ran out the door, she'd run out too and scream and her tail was rarely still. You can judge a dogs level of happiness by their tails and Steffy's little tail told me everything I needed to know. She was happy and that made me very happy too.

With Steffy being the first deaf dog I'd ever owned I did worry about how best to deal with her around the farm. But I'd had dogs in my life for almost forty years when Steffy came along and if I didn't know how to communicate with a dog, any dog regardless of the disability, by that time then I never would. And besides we seemed to be communicating just fine, the fact that she never took her eyes off me was an asset, because with a deaf pug it's all about the eyes, if they aren't looking at you then you are not going to be able to let them know what you want from them. I figured Steffy and I had to work out our own little sign language. And it could be any sort of hand movement really because we were the only ones who had to understand the meaning of the gestures, what we looked like to everyone else didn't matter, it didn't matter if others couldn't understand it as long as Steffy and I did. What I wanted to do most was work out how to get her to come to me from across an open paddock and most importantly for my own sanity how to get her to quieten down before the sound of her screaming drove me from my own farm. Thing is I didn't want to be this sergeant major standing there issuing out orders, although to be honest I would have looked more like a traffic cop than anything else what with all those hand movements and all. I just needed to work out a few simple gestures to make life on a farm with a deaf dog easier for me and less dangerous for her. Really all she needed to learn was to come and to stop. In a small suburban back yard such a thing wouldn't be an issue, and when walking in suburbia she would have always been on a lead, so no problem there either. But with all these wide open spaces and vast paddocks things were different. And the stopping her screaming, well I had no idea how I was going to accomplish that, or if I would ever be able to.

I spent a few days watching Steffy, paying extra attention to how she reacted to things, trying to figure out how her mind worked, I thought if I understood her more I could best work out how to communicate with her. I didn't want her getting hassled or upset because she wanted to please me but had no idea what I wanted her to do. I thought I'd take it slow, we had all the time in the world to learn our own language. Steffy wasn't going anywhere, I'd long ago realised that I had rescued this pug, I was her mother and she was my daughter, it was up to me to make things work, to find a solution. By this time I no longer held thoughts of rehoming her. I hated the sound but I loved the pug it was as simple as that. She was an easy dog to train because her eyes were always watching what I was doing, it wasn't like I had to get her attention first, try and keep it, then work out how to make her follow a hand command. So we spent a lot of our days learning the recall and once she got that I could always call her back if she was getting too far ahead of me. Of course that would only work when she was facing me and if she saw something move on the other side of the paddock she would be over there in no time checking it out and there was nothing I was ever going to be able to do to stop that. She got to many a dead bird or rabbit before I did and I hated the fact that she'd already sniffed it by the time I caught up to her. I don't like the pugs sniffing dead things in case they catch something, but that's just how life is on a farm. And nothing short of putting her on a lead was going to change it and I wasn't about to put Steffy on a lead. She deserved to run freely around the farm enjoying herself at all times. So I'd pay special attention to what I saw ahead of us in the paddocks and if I saw something that looked suspicious I'd just change directions and go retrieve the dead animal once the pugs were all safely inside the house. I'd more or less been doing that here from day one anyway so just paid extra attention once Steffy came, and it wasn't like there were dead animals out in the paddocks all the time, maybe you'll find one or two a year, mainly in springtime when a baby has fallen out of a nest, so we'd just avoid the trees during spring and everybody was happy. Well everybody except the dead baby bird that is but there was nothing I could do about those, you interfere with a nest or a tree trying to make things safer for them and it just makes the bird family nervous or not want to use your trees as their home and I didn't want that, I like having them here. Like that our trees offered a sanctuary for them all. They like to think they are well hidden and most of the time they are, I don't even know there's a nest in the tree until somebody falls out of them and that's a good thing because if I can't see them neither can a predator. I've had years where more than a few babies have fallen out and died and I've felt really sad about that. I did even talk to David about maybe putting a pile of nets around the trees so the birds could be saved but he said they would more than likely get their legs caught in the nets, panic and die anyway, and that the parents would also get their legs and claws caught in the nets when trying to feed the fallen baby bird and if that happened then there would be nobody to feed the rest of the babies, so you'd end up killing an entire family trying to save one. So I let the net idea go but I still feel sad whenever I come across a fallen baby bird and still try and think of ways to save them, so far I've not come up with anything that would work out perfectly for everyone.

When Steffy was seven years old her eye ulcerated. We weren't sure if it got scratched around the farm or if one of the cluster of pugs she sometimes slept with had innocently stretched out their little old legs in the middle of the night accidently catching Steffy's eye. Either way it was a nasty scratch that quickly ulcerated and my heart went out to her it really did. She was so good at looking after everybody else and now this had happened to her and being already deaf I didn't want her to be blind in one eye as well. Steffy had always been such a healthy pug, never anything wrong with her at all, event free as far as health issues went for as long as she'd been with us. Ok she did almost always have at least one bleeder when her nails got trimmed but that's because she made the job almost impossible to do without some form of casualty happening either to her or to one of us. I'm the holder and David is the trimmer, and when doing Steffy's nails one of us usually ended up bleeding. I got many deep scratches from Steffy while she was getting her nails done and David would see the blood streaming and ask if I wanted to stop and I'd always say no because I figured it'd be worse on Steffy if she had to go through this all over again in a day or two. Once the job was started I wanted to finish it. And besides we always did Steffy's nails when the next door neighbours weren't home. We'd learnt from the chainsaw incident and felt it only fair to wait until we saw their car pulling out the driveway before the nail clippers were sought and Steffy was picked up.

Pug eyes are so very precious, they need special looking after and I'm extremely protective of them. Being that they are protruding I always fear them getting hurt. We always have tubes of ointment in our fridge on stand by and have been able to clear things up on our own a good many times if it's only been a surface scratch but with this eye we realised we were dealing with something more. So off to the vet we went with Steffy sitting hunched over on the back seat like a sad little sack. Her body language told us exactly how she was feeling and it hurt to see her in so much pain. I think anything to do with one's eyes is incredibly painful, I mean you get a speck of dust in your eye and it really hurts, so I knew the level of pain Steffy was feeling and I wanted to take her place, take that pain upon myself and spare her the agony, but all I could do was reach my hand round and stroke her and get her to the vet as fast as we could.

After examining Steffy our vet applied a stronger ointment then partly stitched the eye closed to protect it and help it heal. We brought Steffy home to the farm with the instructions of seeing how the eye went for a few days, see if some healing could take place, more or less just giving the eye some time. Keeping Steffy still was the hardest part of all, she had become a little explorer, having to slow down and take things easy didn't thrill her at all. She did seem happier and in a lot less pain though and while that is definitely a good thing it does make it even harder to keep them still because they are feeling fine and want to do what they always do. So you are battling with them to keep them happy and keep the eye safe as well, but we managed to do that, sure Steffy didn't like us for it but she just had to be ignored for the sake of her eye. We thought things were going well and had high hopes of saving the eye, saving the vision. But the next morning we woke up to Steffy screaming the house down, you think her regular scream is loud well this scream was something else entirely. It sounded like the scream of an animal that was in absolute agony. David and I went from deep sleep to fully awake in seconds, we leapt out of bed at precisely the same time and ran into the lounge room. It wasn't light yet so we switched the light on as we ran in and there was poor little Steffy sitting on the end of the couch, in her happy little sleeping spot, with her eye the size of a golf ball. We knew it wasn't good so David went and sat in the car park waiting for the vet to open. We knew the vet nurses arrived early to tend to the overnight patients so they'd be there earlier than the doors would be opened, when they saw Steffy's eye they rang the vet at home and he came in straight away.

The stiches were removed and she was given a few injections, one for pain and an anti-inflammatory as well, they also gave us some strong antibiotics tablets for Steffy to take over the next two weeks. I wanted the eye removed, it looked so painful, like these photos you see of neglected animals when they first come into rescue. It hurt me seeing her like that, I didn't think there was any chance for that eye and I wanted to remove that which was causing Steffy pain as quickly as possible. Get the eye out, get Steffy home and get her healing was what was going through my mind. Fix, fix and fix was my motto and when she was feeling better I would help her get used to life with only one eye. I really had hoped that eye could have been saved though. It saddened me to the core that this was the outcome, really hurt my heart that she was deaf and now would only be able to see the world from the view of that one little eye. Taste, touch and smell were now her most powerful senses and I didn't like that at all because I thought Steffy deserved so much better. I was feeding the rest of the pugs when David rang me to let me know what was going on. I stood on the veranda with a couple of food bowls in my hands and the phone tucked under my chin as I told him how I felt about the eye coming out. But David said our vet thought it best if the eye was left in because at that point he wasn't sure if she would have some vision once the swelling went down. We had to give the eye a chance to reduce in size, go back to normal then see if Steffy could see anything out of it. Once Dave explained that to me I was alright about it because I knew any vision, even the tiniest amount was better than nothing especially with Steffy being deaf.

Well to cut a long story short Steffy never saw out of that eye again and I cried over that I truly did. Cried buckets for her, I just wanted to pick her up and hug her and tell her how sorry I was, but I couldn't pick her up because she didn't like it. So I would sit on the couch with my arm around her and tell her I was sorry for all she had gone through. I gave her extra treats and looked after her while she healed. But the eye was never the same after that. The swelling went down eventually but the eye looked awful, like it was melting, sliding down her face, it looked like really bad makeup in an old black and white horror movie. The rim was out of shape, due to the size of the swelling it had been stretched beyond repair. It hung there all droopy, and the eye itself actually shrunk and sunk, became smaller than her other eye. I felt so sorry for her due to the way she looked. And I did once again think of having the eye removed because I thought once the stiches came out she would be left with a nice neat line, a lovely smoothed over area and be like every other pug out there who was missing an eye. But David and I talked about it and we decided we didn't want to put her through the operation. I felt I would have been only doing it for my sake not Steffy's and I would never put a pug through an operation solely for me. If her shrunken eye was causing her pain or was going to be an issue for her in any other way then I would have done it. But Steffy wasn't in any pain or discomfort, she was happy, once it was all behind her she was back to her old self again, well a little bit chubbier because I felt so sorry for her that I'd gone overboard with the treats but I knew once she was out and about walking around the farm again that the weight would quickly drop off and it did. But if there was any vision left in that eye at all it wasn't very much. I could tell that by the way Steffy moved, to me it seemed like there was no vision there in the slightest, but to her credit Steffy handled her new situation very well.

And as far as looks went well Steffy didn't care what she looked like, once the pain was taken away from her eye she was fine because that's all she cared about. Dogs aren't nearly as vain as we are and it wasn't like the other pugs were treating her differently either, everything and everyone was back to normal so I took my lead from them and tried not to be upset when looking at Steffy's deformed eye. Still I did think she looked even worse when she was going out in sympathy for another pug. She always looked like such a pitiful little soul sitting there next to the pug in need and now she looked even more pitiful. But what did it matter what she looked like really because looks aren't everything, and that is never truer than on this farm. All that mattered was that Steffy was the same pug on the inside, she was still full of love and empathy, she still cared about others more than she did herself. She, with that one little view she had of the world was still able to let me know when one of her siblings wasn't well. The only thing that had changed here was that Steffy now had a shrunken sightless eye. And it wasn't affecting her so I no longer let it affect me, well not as much as I could have let it anyway. My heart still went out to her whenever I looked into her eyes. I mean how could it not do. It seemed so unfair to me that this little pug had all this dumped on her, the being born deaf and now the eye situation, I didn't think she deserved any of it and I still don't.

Steffy didn't let her lack of vison affect her though, she just took everything that happened in her stride, and moved on from it. I love how dogs do this, and wish that I too could be half as strong as they are. I can dwell, I focus far too much sometimes, they accept, they carry on. And I know I do that too eventually but only after letting things affect me for too long and I believe life is far too short for that. I have always thought that their bumps in the road are exactly the same as ours are, they just choose to look at them differently. I think dogs are optimists, just true brave awesome little optimists. And I really admire them for that.

Once Steffy's vision became less she had trouble seeing me when I wanted to call her back from across the paddocks so I had to just let that one go. She did however still respond to me when I wanted her to quieten down because that was always done with a gentle stroke to the side of her shoulder then running my hand along her body. Occasionally she'd have days where she'd be going completely nuts with the screaming so the first attempt wouldn't be enough to stop her because she was too distracted, she wasn't listening to me or should I say "Feeling me". At those times I would have to get her full attention first, get her to look up at me and concentrate, once she did I'd put out my hand, palm forward and sort of press at the air fast. Like "Tap, Tap", no physical contact with Steffy at all, just a hand signal and she would know that meant "You've already been told once so please stop screaming, be quiet and settle down" And she would, there was never any need for a third signal to be invented. But most times she responded accordingly to the gentle stroke of her shoulder and hand running along her body meant which was great.

I've often thought about my relationship with Steffy, I think it's funny that this dog I had so much trouble accepting at first has become such a brilliant little asset to me. Well not only an asset to me but to her pug brothers and sisters as well. And I think that's just how it is in life sometimes. You've no idea what the next person you are going to meet is going to bring to your life, how they are going to affect it, alter it, enrich it. Sure they may not be anything like what you were expecting but time will reveal to you that they are exactly what you needed.

When Steffy was thirteen years old I noticed she had a little growth on the side of her foot. It was only tiny so I kept my eye on it for a little while because it didn't look like anything serious to me, nothing to worry too much about I thought. It looked just like a lump that Ruben had a few years back, we'd rushed him into the vet and it was a nothing lump, just an old dog thing, he still has it now all these years later and it's never changed in appearance, no bigger, no smaller, same colour as it has always been. I check it weekly but it never alters and I figured this lump of Steffy's was exactly the same as Ruben's was. I thought when we next went to the vet I would take Steffy along with whatever dog was going to see him at the time and she'd have the lump looked at then. But a week later I noticed the growth was altering so off to the vet we went and I'm glad we acted quickly because Steffy's lump turned out to be cancer. And with cancer you don't muck around, surgery was scheduled for the following Wednesday. David dropped Steffy off in the morning and picked her up after work. I wrote a note explaining how Steffy didn't like being handled, that she was deaf and only limited vison in her good eye and that being in a strange place would more than likely upset and confuse her. I felt she would be ok with the operation because she was a "Good thirteen" and by that I mean she was good for her age, perfect weight-a little under if anything which is unusual for a pug, good general health, good fitness level, good in herself all round really, yes an old dog but I felt she would come through the operation with no trouble at all. But if they were handling her a lot then that would certainly upset her. I figured if I explained this they would maybe just have one person handling her and that would lessen the stress for her. I did not however tell them about the screaming, never mentioned it at all and the reason I didn't was because I felt if I'd informed them she was a screamer and she started screaming then she may have been ignored because I'd told them that was just how Steffy was. I didn't want her being in pain or having something wrong and trying to alert them to the fact only to have them think Steffy was just being Steffy. I thought I'd rather have her scream the entire place down and they be double checking her, maybe even triple checking her for no reason than to have it the other way round so I left that part out but she mustn't have screamed too much though because nobody mentioned anything when David picked her up.

David said Steffy was so happy when they handed her over to him. He said she looked up, searched for and found his face, sniffed it, knew the familiar scent, knew it was Daddy and just clung onto his neck for a very long time before loosening her grip. Dug her front paws deep into him to the point of hurting but she wasn't for letting go and he wasn't for making her. He just rubbed her little old back and let her know everything was going to be alright now. I wish I'd been there to witness that hug because it was an unusual thing for Steffy to do, she was normally trying to get away from being held, but this time she didn't want to go anywhere she wanted to stay in her Dad's arms where she felt safe, secure and happy. She must have been so relieved to have him there, I bet she didn't know what was going on, it was a long day for us being away from her but it would have been so much worse for Steffy. I envied David that hug, told him how blessed he was to have received it but he already knew that. David said the vet nurse carried Steffy out and she was still pretty groggy from the effects of the anesthetic, she couldn't see where she was going but as she neared him she must have been able to pick up on the familiar aftershave and started screaming loudly, deafening the vet nurse in the process, until she reached him and when she did she found his face, sniffed hard double checking it was him, not just some guy wearing the same aftershave. David was lucky he got to experience Steffy's bliss. He said he thought she was never going to let go, but once she'd had her fill, gotten over the missing him and the gladness of finally being with one of her parents again she finally let go of his neck and it was like "I'm ok now Dad I want to go home".

David paid the bill and carried Steffy out to the car, she slept on the seat beside him all the way home. She was snoring even before he'd pulled out of the parking lot. I think she must have been too unsettled to sleep while she was there, she must have come out of the anesthetic slumber then been fighting to stay awake due to being in unfamiliar surroundings. Once David had her, Steffy finally let go, yielded to the after effects of surgery and slept like a log. She slept well that night too and all into the next day. After that she was back to normal and it was hard to keep her off that foot. She wanted to be outside walking with her siblings, David carried her on the walks for the first few days she was home. She didn't understand why she couldn't come with us and we didn't want her upset, she'd already been through a lot. We walked out the door the first day and heard her screaming so David ran back and got her and walked round the farm with her tucked under his arm. She didn't really want to be carried but was more alright with it then she had ever been because that foot was sore. I think she appreciated the help. She squirmed around a bit in David's arms but we didn't put her down because we didn't want her bursting those stitches open and having to go back to the vet. I knew she would have disliked that even more than being carried. She went down for a wee then came back up again and by the time she'd done what she needed to do she was looking round for David to come and pick her up.

Tending to that foot was a different matter though. For a dog who was a natural nurse to her ill siblings she wasn't exactly the best patient herself. She fought me like crazy whenever I was trying to put a sock on so her bandage didn't get wet. Her operation took place at the start of winter, not exactly the best time for somebody who lives on a farm to have their foot healing. My friend Janie had sent the pugs some lovely little grippy socks earlier in the year so I got those out and used them to keep the bandage dry. I'd put a piece of cling wrap around the bandage first then put the sock over that to keep the cling wrap in place. We went through so many pairs of socks in a day and they'd make me smile when seeing them out there so tiny hanging on the washing line. But I wasn't smiling when I was putting the socks on. I used to put Steffy in Lumen's cot so I could get a better hold of her. I'd have the piece of cling wrap laying flat on the table next to me and the sock beside that. I don't know who was fighting me worse Steffy or the cling wrap. You have no idea how hard it is to make a piece of cling wrap do what you want it to do while struggling with a pug. I'd have Steffy held in place with one arm and be reaching for the cling wrap with the other and that cling wrap wanted to stick to every single surface it came into contact with, well everything besides Steffy's little bandaged foot.

She'd be screaming in my ear and fighting hard to get away and I'd be trying to get the job done as quickly as possible because I didn't want to stress Steffy out, didn't want to hold her longer than I had to because of how she was. Sometimes I was lucky and got the cling wrap on first shot but then as I reached for the sock Steffy would shift position, only slightly mind you but that was all it took for things to unfold and I'd glance down and there beside the bandage would be a bit of cling wrap perfectly formed in the shape of Steffy's foot. And of course there was no way I was ever going to be able to straighten that out and use it again so more cling wrap had to be gotten. All done one handed, well with one hand pulling the cling wrap out while using my neck to hold the dispenser in place, it was all a bit of a disaster really, and a very long two weeks for both me and Steffy. I think it was a long two weeks for the other pugs as well because they were always there at my feet waiting for the sock performances to finish so they could go for a walk.

Steffy had to be taken to the vet to have the dressing changed a few times. When we'd first brought her home they said it should last until the stiches came out but being on a farm it didn't and I was glad because it meant the vet nurses could have a look at the foot and see how it was healing. The growth was actually on the side of her paw and quite a bit of the paw had been cut away, but all the cancer was gotten and that's what matters most. I thought Steffy may have had trouble walking even when it healed because her foot was now uneven but she seemed to manage ok. Her back legs were weak too due to old age and she walked a bit slower but none of that had anything to do with the new paw pad she had.

Each day Steffy was the same as far as cooperation went, didn't want the sock on, didn't want the cling wrap on, didn't want to be held, didn't want to be in the cot. She just wanted to be left alone and of course I couldn't do that, I had to protect that paw while it healed. Day after day I was defeated by a little pug, an even littler sock and a piece of cling wrap that had it in for me even more than Steffy did I'm sure of it. It was like Steffy and the cling wrap had made a pact to drive Mummy insane, and they knew they had only two weeks to accomplish it so were giving it their best shot. Steffy would fly off in one direction and the sock in another and that cling wrap would stick to the knob on the corner of the cot more often than not, stuck to it like a coat of paint and I couldn't peel it off. Honestly you'd have thought I was trying to kill Steffy not help her the way that she was behaving. It was like trying to put a sock on a Tasmanian devil. At the end of it I'd feel like I'd just gone three rounds in a boxing ring with Steffy winning each one. I called David at work and was telling him about it one day and he just laughed and said "It is the little things in life that outwit us". And I'd think to myself its ok for you to say you've not just had to deal with Steffy. Certainly things were a lot easier when David was home holding Steffy while I dealt with her foot and he'd look at me as if he was wondering what all the fuss was about. And I'd ask him if he wanted to try doing it by himself and he'd shake his head and say "Hell no"

In between the morning and afternoon walks I'd carry Steffy out to the shed so she could go to the toilet in there, the bandage stayed dry and didn't get too dirty so that worked out pretty well, I didn't need to put cling wrap on at those times, just the sock would do. Then in the afternoon when we'd go for our usual walk around the farm I'd have to go through the whole routine again and I'd say to myself "Ok Andrea you are going to win this one". So I'd march towards the cot with a determined look in my eye and a little pink sock in my hand. I'd lift Lumen out so I could manage things better. I didn't want her getting caught up in it all, couldn't have that precious little old darling getting hurt by Steffy's thrashing about so she sat on the floor beside her cot looking at us like "What the hell is going on up there". Lumen was protective of her cot, knew it was her domain, was quite territorial at times, she didn't like anybody else invading it. And I was well aware of that and felt a bit bad because when I took her out it was almost like evicting a snail from its shell. Well that's what it felt like I'd just done the way Lumen would be looking at me. But I had other things on my mind so I pressed on, couldn't let the shell-less snail affect me. But Lumen did get a treat when she was put back in her cot, it was like payment for her services, and she really looked forward to that treat and being back in her cot. One day due to Steffy's madness I forgot to give Lumen a treat, just lifted her back in her cot and marched out the door with the pugs, didn't realise what I'd done until I was halfway down the driveway and heard Lumen's unimpressed woofing.

The thing was Steffy made such a fuss over having her bandage covered but once it was dealt with she settled down fast and would walk over the grass with that little pink, aqua, yellow or purple sock on like she wasn't even aware of the drama that had just taken place. She'd have a bit of a sniff and a wee and come walking back to me like nothing had ever happened, I was still remembering it but she never did. I'd make a joke of it, started counting the scores to see who would be that day's winner. In the first week Steffy was the reining champ, but by the second week the tally was normally Steffy one, Mummy one and Lumen, treat eaten and back in her cot sleeping peacefully as the rain fell heavily on our roof. If the operation had been done in the middle of summer things would have been a lot easier, but you just get the cancer removed, play the cards you've been dealt and deal with things as best you can.

But I lost count of the number of times Steffy outsmarted me. Limited vison or not she knew when I was about to lift her into the cot, she must have been able to sense it so she'd run and hide under the kitchen table and you'd almost get her and she'd shoot off and go hide underneath the bed, table to bed, bed to table, over and over again. It was like playing a game with a puppy only Steffy knew exactly what she was doing. I couldn't close the door off either and trap her in the bedroom to make things easier because the blind pugs were used to that door being open and I didn't want them walking into the hard surface and hurting themselves. When they are used to there being a gap there they start walking pretty fast and I didn't want to be on the floor trying to grab Steffy hearing thud after thud after thud. So the door stayed open and all the other pugs followed me into the bedroom. And it'd take a while to get up from being on the floor because once I got down the pugs thought it was fun time and I'd have to tickle everybody's tummy before getting up again. And of course by this time Steffy was in the other room again hiding. Good that she always chose the same spots to hide in, made it easier for me. I was so hot and bothered on one particular day that I needed a cup of strong tea before I came good. But that bandage never did get wet which was great because I didn't want her foot wet while trying to heal. When the stiches finally came out it was wonderful to see the paw had healed perfectly, you see that nice clean cut and all the cancer gone, it made the daily battles worth it. To date that cancer has never come back, they got it with clean margins which, when it comes to cancer, is what you always want to hear.

As of the writing of this book Steffy is still here with us at Grace Farm, she is fourteen years old. Steffy is largely blind now, with little vision in her good eye but she does very well getting around the place and still takes it upon herself to care for her siblings. It's just a different set of siblings she's looking after now. And her back legs are stiff due to age and due to the back leg weakness she's become a little incontinent too. I did think at one time that nappies and a cart could be in her future and that may still be the case but for now the tablets she's recently been put on seem to be helping. And yes in case you are wondering Steffy still screams from time to time, but she doesn't scream as loud as she once did. She has mellowed and quietened down with age as all of us tend to do. Most of her screaming is done underneath the dinner table these days. I always leave a bit of whatever I'm eating on the side of my plate for the pugs, well if what I am eating is dog friendly I do anyway. And Steffy normally just screams for that and if she starts screaming as soon as we sit down I have to pat her shoulder gently to let her know the meal isn't over yet and that she'll just have to wait until we've finished eating. But she knows, as all the pugs know that a little bite sized piece will always be saved for them. Even when I go out to dinner I take a plastic container with me and before I start eating I'll cut portions up to take home for the pugs so I always have a little treat to present to them when I get home. I used to get strange looks but the people we go out to dinner with are used to me doing this now and some even offer me some of their meal to put in my plastic container.

Steffy is beside me as I finish her chapter, she's curled in a ball fast asleep with her precious siblings around her and is totally unaware that there's thunder in the distance. Then again she's not the only one who isn't aware of the approaching storm, once all the pugs are asleep and snoring it's pretty hard to hear any other noise really. I'm only aware of it because I know once it's overhead I'll have to shut the computer down and that'll be it for me as far as writing goes today. So I guess it's a good thing I've just finished this book. It's early autumn here but we don't seem to get the weather we used to do. I don't think we get seasons anymore, well not the seasons we used to have anyway and that affects everything doesn't it. It's like the trees don't know when to drop their leaves. Last week we were in the high thirties, boiling hot with the air conditioner running day and night. Today it's only eighteen degree's and it's been raining all day long, heard it start hitting the roof at three o'clock this morning and it's now four in the afternoon and it's not stopped. The pugs haven't been able to go for their regular walks so they are getting a bit edgy, they love their walks, they love their little daily routine and when it's interrupted nobody is happy. But it's nice for me writing with the sound of rain falling on our tin roof. That can be a beautiful and relaxing thing to hear while I'm typing away. The pugs always sleep beside me when I write because being together makes us all happy. Every now and then I will pause, look around at my little old blessings, maybe watch them sleeping for a few seconds before I start typing again. The sight of them all has always made me feel incredibly lucky and very well blessed. Of late Steffy has been the first one to wake up from the afternoon naps, I think it's due to her bladder not being able to hold on anymore. So she'll wake and she'll come over to me so I can lift her down and over the last year or so she has not been too bad of a hugger either. She'll let me snuggle her for a lot longer than she ever used to do. She kisses the side of my face as we embrace, and she sits in my arms quite happily for a little while, she's both comfortable but not comfortable if you know what I mean. And we'll snuggle until she lets me know when she's had enough, and she does that by wriggling around like crazy, so I'll kiss her little old boney head one last time, lower her to the ground and watch as she staggers off towards the door. And that is a beautiful sight for me to see, yes her back legs are indeed bandy but I've been taking care of her and that little body of hers for many years now. Every part of that little old body is dear to me, so I'll watch her until she's out of sight then I begin lifting her siblings down.

ABOUT THE AUTHOR

Andrea Comer was born in the United Kingdom and migrated to Australia with her family when she was six years old. From a very young age Andrea became aware of the way animals were treated in this world and vowed that one day she would create a place where elderly animals could live out their natural lifespan without knowing fear, feeling pain or enduring suffering. Grace Farm Senior Pug Sanctuary was a dream she carried in her heart for a very long time before it became a reality. Andrea lives on a farm with her husband and a cloud of elderly pugs, sheep and horses. Her days are spent taking care of her large four legged family, but sometimes in the late afternoon when the pugs are sleeping she has time to write.

Books by this author

The Joy of Horton   ISBN 978-0-9953904-0-9
Grace Farm Senior Pug Sanctuary ISBN 978-0-9953904-1-6